'Hamilton is rema[rkable in his] range, and now he [has written a] vulnerable book of philosophical abstraction and application . . . I want people to read this book.'—*Pete Haye, The Monthly*

'Few people who survived Auschwitz continued to believe in the all-powerful all-good heavenly Father or the scriptures. Clive Hamilton seems to pick up this challenge, ignore the illusions of secular prosperity and lead us to something different. I think the environmental urgency he responds to forces us to new thinking about the mysteries of existence.'—*Former NSW Premier Bob Carr, in The Australian*

'Path-breaking'—*Justice Michael Kirby*

'This remarkable book is without parallel in Australian philosophical literature . . . what is unique about this book is Hamilton's brilliantly challenging, and critically independent, use of the philosophical work of the great German thinkers Immanuel Kant and Arthur Schopenhauer.'—*Rev Colin Goodwin, The Melbourne Anglican*

'. . . an audacious attempt to build a metaphysics of morals . . . it is one of Hamilton's gifts that he writes as if he genuinely seeks to engage the reader in conversation.'—*Canberra Times*

'A careful and satisfying construction of the connectedness of history, and the basis of morality, religion and philosophy.'—*Megan Yarrow, media-culture.org*

'Clive Hamilton seeks to engage his readers in a conversation as well as self-reflection. . . . a must-read for those interested in metaphysics, sociology, psychology or even the culture of business.'—*Varsity, New Zealand*

Clive Hamilton is one of Australia's leading public intellectuals. He is Professor of Public Ethics at the Centre for Applied Philosophy and Public Ethics, a joint centre of the Australian National University, Charles Sturt University and the University of Melbourne.

Formerly Executive Director of The Australia Institute, he is author of a number of bestselling books, including *Growth Fetish* (2003), *Affluenza* (with Richard Denniss, 2005), *What's Left: The death of social democracy* (2006), *Silencing Dissent* (edited with Sarah Maddison, 2007), *Scorcher: The dirty politics of climate change* (2007), and *Requiem for a Species: Why we resist the truth about climate change* (2009).

www.clivehamilton.net.au

The Freedom Paradox

Towards a post-secular ethics

Clive Hamilton

ALLEN&UNWIN

First published in 2008
This edition published in 2011
Copyright © Clive Hamilton 2008

All rights reserved. No part of this book may be reproduced or transmitted in any form or by any means, electronic or mechanical, including photocopying, recording or by any information storage and retrieval system, without prior permission in writing from the publisher. The Australian *Copyright Act 1968* (the Act) allows a maximum of one chapter or 10 per cent of this book, whichever is the greater, to be photocopied by any educational institution for its educational purposes provided that the educational institution (or body that administers it) has given a remuneration notice to Copyright Agency Limited (CAL) under the Act.

Allen & Unwin
83 Alexander Street
Crows Nest NSW 2065
Australia
Phone: (61 2) 8425 0100
Fax: (61 2) 9906 2218
Email: info@allenandunwin.com
Web: www.allenandunwin.com

Cataloguing-in-publication details are available from the
National Library of Australia
www.trove.nla.gov.au

ISBN 978 1 74237 578 6

Set in 11/14 pt Bembo by Midland Typesetters, Australia
Printed and bound in Australia by McPherson's Printing Group
10 9 8 7 6 5 4 3 2 1

The paper in this book is FSC certified.
FSC promotes environmentally responsible,
socially beneficial and economically viable
management of the world's forests.

Contents

Acknowledgments xi
Preface xiii

PART ONE *Freedom reconsidered*

1	The disappointment of liberalism	3
2	Rationale	7
3	Types of happiness	13
4	Freedom and happiness	20
5	Types of liberty	25
6	Inner freedom	33
7	Do we prefer what we choose?	38
8	Self-deception and akrasia	45
9	A digression on the ethic of consent	55
10	Exercising inner freedom	61
11	Subtle coercion	68
12	The decline of free will	74
13	From political philosophy to metaphysics	80

PART TWO *Philosophical foundations*

14	The need for metaphysics	85
15	Consciousness and the subject	92
16	Phenomenon and noumenon	98
17	The 'legislation for nature'	104
18	Scientific thinking	113
19	Knowing and being	119
20	Instances of non-sensible intuition	124
21	The noumenon and the Self	133
22	A digression on the existence of God	142
23	On death	150

PART THREE *Towards a post-secular ethics*

24	Modern moral anxiety	161
25	Moral relativism	168
26	Reconstructing a moral code	176
27	Rationalist ethics	183
28	Genuine philanthropy	195
29	The moral self	201
30	Emotions as judgments	211
31	Further thoughts	221
32	Avatars of virtue	230
33	Egoism and malice	235
34	Eternal justice	239

PART FOUR *Moral judge or moral adviser?*

35	Becoming good	247
36	The theory in practice	256
37	Suicide	263
38	Sex	270
39	Nature	289

PART FIVE *Freedom rediscovered*

40	The ground of inner freedom	297
41	Finding inner freedom	305
42	The individual and the collective	313
43	Aesthetics	316
44	Happiness reconsidered	327
45	The human condition	334

Notes	340
Index	367

*All liberation depends on the consciousness
of servitude.*
                    Herbert Marcuse

Acknowledgments

I AM GRATEFUL TO Clare Hall and the Department of Land Economy at the University of Cambridge for a four-month visiting fellowship and to Geoff Harcourt, without whose recommendation the fellowship would not have been offered. It was in the university library that the ideas for this book first germinated, where the 1 per cent inspiration occurred. Much of the subsequent perspiration occurred in cabins in serene places in New South Wales—Possum Creek, Gumboot Gully, Guerrilla Bay, the Warrumbungles and Sunrise Beach.

Four academic philosophers with expertise in German idealism read and commented on an earlier draft of this book, and I thank them. Their responses were bracing and stopped me making many blunders; their anonymity saves me from embarrassment should I pass them in the street.

I am also indebted to John Carroll, Paul Collins, Sarah Maddison and David McKnight, all of whom read a later draft and provided detailed comments that helped me improve the book considerably. Each of them disagrees—at times strongly—with various claims in the book, so the customary release from responsibility for what appears in the final version applies with greater than usual force.

Chris Pirie has done a superb job as editor. She must have run out of green ink, and the manuscript was vastly improved for it.

Finally, I would like to express my deep gratitude to Elizabeth Weiss, academic publisher at Allen & Unwin, who understood immediately why I wanted to write this book. In addition to unstinting encouragement and support throughout the writing, she provided a stream of insightful comments on various drafts that enriched and refined my own understanding of the concepts and arguments. An author could not ask for a better publisher.

Preface

WHY IS IT THAT, despite the wealth and the freedom now enjoyed by most citizens of rich countries, we do not appear to be the autonomous, fulfilled individuals we were told our wealth and freedom would bring? This book attempts to answer this question: it does so by focusing on the personal rather than the political. Of course, the individual is always conditioned by powerful social forces, but when those influences are stripped away we are left with just an individual and a conscience.

I begin by arguing that the opportunities created by the great popular movements of the nineteenth and twentieth centuries are now being sacrificed to a new form of coercion, one unleashed by the very forces of social and economic liberalism that promised to set us free. This newly exposed form of 'unfreedom' is unusual because it is not imposed from without: everywhere the citizens of affluent countries collaborate in their own subordination. My first aim is to explain why this is so. If we truly want fulfilled and purposeful lives, why do we settle for a life of consumer conformity marked by the pursuit of substitute gratifications such as wealth, the perfect body, celebrity and status? To find the answer we must consider not just the social and cultural forces that seduce us but also the deeper question of what to do with a life.

Oppressive laws and social structures have been overthrown by movements ranged against entrenched elites, but the forces that deprive us of our 'inner freedom' are harder to identify. In an age of over-consumption, intemperance and moral confusion, the structures that prevent us from flourishing have lodged themselves in our psyches. The source for the kind of transformation that is now needed lies beyond the cultural, political and social philosophies that have formed the bedrock of progressive thought. We need to look to metaphysics—ideas about knowing and being that are beyond the psychological and social structures that condition everyday experience—to discover what unites us all in our humanity.

Part Two of the book sets out a metaphysical argument that provides the basis for understanding the cause of this new form of unfreedom. It also explores some of the big questions of meaning that challenge modern humankind: What should we make of a life? How should we think about death? Has rationality become an obstacle to further progress? Does the death of God consign us to a life of superficiality?

In rethinking my own position while writing this book, I found I had to discard many of my old beliefs and embrace some I could not have expected. Readers might be asked to make a similar, possibly uncomfortable, journey. I hope to show by the end that, in contrast with the prevailing view that being free means being able to do what we please, we cannot be truly free without committing ourselves to a moral life.

This might seem a paradox, but in fact being free and being moral are inseparable. Being free entails imposing constraints on ourselves; in turn, those constraints provide us with our sense of self. The philosopher Harry Frankfurt argues that we identify with what we care about. Our values and the things we love impose obligations on us. And if we fail to live up to our values we betray ourselves. A moral free-for-all, therefore, cannot allow us to express who we are; it is the constraints we impose on our choices that solidify our sense of self. Greater choice, coupled with a lack of self-control, lead to a disintegration of identity. People who have difficulty locating, articulating and adhering to their values thus have a weaker sense of who they are. This is why questions of meaning and morality cannot be divorced.

The metaphysical and ethical arguments I put forward in this book owe most to the work of German philosopher Arthur Schopenhauer, who saw himself building on and correcting the revolutionary system of 'transcendental idealism' developed by Immanuel Kant. It was Kant who had the blinding insight that a free will and a will under moral law are one and the same, although he was anticipated by a French philosopher, Jean-Jacques Rousseau, who wrote that 'the mere impulse of appetite is slavery, while obedience to a law which we prescribe to ourselves is liberty'.

In Parts Three and Four I develop and apply a moral philosophy based on the metaphysics of Part Two. Our world is one of moral relativism, and the idea of a moral philosophy and the ethical injunctions that flow from it make many people feel nervous. They fear that by stating their own moral standpoint too strongly they will be devaluing the standpoint of others. This is the laudable sentiment behind post-modern ethical thinking, but it has reduced morality to 'just what I think'. To be persuasive, and to avoid the trap of moral chauvinism, a moral philosophy must grow from something that is common to humanity rather than distinctive to particular communities or cultures. For this reason it must be based on metaphysics—an understanding that goes beneath or beyond the particularities of social and personal experience.

The ancient Greek mathematician Archimedes wrote, 'Give me one fixed point and I will move the Earth'. If we can find a fixed point, it will allow a moral philosophy to be nailed down, and moral relativism vanishes. I argue that there is such a locus, a metaphysical absolute that is the basis for all important moral judgments. After consideration of the alternatives, I adopted the term 'noumenon' (usually pronounced '*noo*menon') to describe its source. Kant uses this word for his concept of the 'thing-in-itself', which can be thought of as the world as it is, in its pure existence, before we bring our forms of understanding to it. The noumenon is always discussed as a partner of the concept of the 'phenomenon', the world of everyday appearances. As this suggests, the distinction is really about how we experience and understand the world.

Although fundamental to the work of Kant and Schopenhauer, the distinction between noumenon and phenomenon is more a characteristic of Eastern philosophies, in which the idea of the noumenon is captured in terms such as 'universal essence' and 'subtle essence'. Throughout the book I note some parallels between my argument and those from Eastern traditions, where it has long been understood that the noumenon can be known (if at all) only by transcending the everyday forms of understanding.

Although the noumenon is usually thought of as a characteristic of the world 'out there', I take up Schopenhauer's most original insight (which he subsequently recognised in the

Preface

classics of Hinduism) that the noumenon must also be found within us. In developing my moral philosophy, I call this fixed point within us 'the moral self'. Establishing a fixed moral point allows me to develop an ethical position that repudiates moral relativism but avoids all theology—in other words, a post-secular ethics. In Part Five I conclude by arguing that the modern problem of freedom can be resolved only if we recognise and live according to our moral self. Despite being personal in its orientation, my book takes freedom and morality as its themes and is thus political in its implications, although these implications are not spelt out here.

I hope this brief overview makes it clear to the reader that, byways and digressions aside, a coherent argument runs through the book. The entire thesis hangs on a single insight, the simple but profound realisation, common to so much philosophy and religious thought, that each of us is united with all things, an idea expressed most purely in the words of the Hindu classics—thou art that.

PART ONE
Freedom reconsidered

There is only one inborn error: and that is the notion that we exist in order to be happy.
Arthur Schopenhauer

ONE

The disappointment of liberalism

AT THE BEGINNING OF the twenty-first century, citizens of rich countries confront a perplexing fact: despite decades of sustained economic growth, which have seen the real incomes of most people rise to three or four times the levels enjoyed by their parents and grandparents in the 1950s, people are no happier.[1] Indeed, the proliferation of the maladies of affluence—such as drug dependence, obesity, loneliness, and psychological disorders ranging from depression, anxiety and compulsive behaviours to a widespread but ill-defined anomie—suggests that the psychological well-being of citizens in rich countries is in decline. Perhaps the most telling evidence is the prevalence of depression. In the five decades that followed the Second World War—which are regarded as the golden age of economic growth—the incidence of depression in the United States increased tenfold.[2] Major depression, already the greatest cause of disability, is expected to become the world's second most burdensome disease by 2020.[3] The market has turned its attention to ways of capitalising on the sicknesses of affluence; pharmaceutical corporations are leading the way, antidepressant drugs free of side-effects now being their Holy Grail.

This leads to questions that go to the heart of the modern world. If affluence—the object of so much determined effort—has failed to improve our wellbeing, why have we tried so hard to become rich? Has our pursuit of riches led us to sacrifice some things that contribute to more satisfying lives, including the strength of our relationships, a surer sense of self, and the quality of the natural environment? In short, has the whole growth project failed?

And there is another troubling question that must be asked. Has the struggle for freedom delivered on its promise? The gains in themselves cannot be decried, but we need to ask whether the personal and political freedoms won by social movements during the nineteenth and twentieth centuries have succeeded in ushering in societies peopled by autonomous, creative, contented individuals living harmoniously in their communities. The answer must be 'no'. The liberation movements of the 1960s and 1970s targeted other sources of oppression—sexual conservatism, subjugation of women, homophobia, and racism in its many guises. It now appears that, by removing sources of oppression based on gender, sexuality and race, these social revolutions have left us free to be miserable in new, more insidious ways.

If the barriers to the flourishing of our potential have been removed but we fail to flourish, depression would seem a natural response. Moreover, the liberation movements have ceded to us unprecedented moral confusion. The 'ethic of consent' that replaced the strictures of conservative morality has led to forms of behaviour raising deeper questions about personal responsibility that we have scarcely begun to understand.

The disappointment of liberalism

These disappointments of affluence and freedom must be seen as a challenge to liberalism—and especially to its more dogmatic child, libertarianism, the anti-collectivist political philosophy that has given us modern conservatism.* For decades libertarianism has been implicitly promising that the way to a good society is through economic growth and higher incomes. Writing in 1944, the high priest of libertarianism, Friedrich von Hayek, observed that the success of the expansion of individualism and commerce had 'surpassed man's wildest dreams':

> ... by the beginning of the twentieth century the working man in the Western world has reached a degree of comfort, security, and personal independence which a hundred years before had seemed scarcely possible.
>
> What in the future will probably appear the most significant and far-reaching effect of this success is the new sense of power over their own fate, the belief in the unbounded possibilities of improving their own lot, which the success already achieved created among men.[4]

I do not disparage the daily freedoms this abundance has bestowed on ordinary people; I simply say that people's sense of power over their own fate is almost as distant as ever. Hayek's grand vision has come to nothing.

As if in recognition of the disappointment of liberalism, in rich countries today there are signs that continual striving for personal freedom and economic security has been superseded

---

* Although the terms 'neoliberalism' and 'libertarianism' are in some contexts interchangeable, I use 'neoliberalism' when referring particularly to economic considerations—and especially the policy lessons drawn from neoclassical economics—and 'libertarianism' to refer to the broader anti-collectivist political philosophy underpinning it.

by a new endeavour. Earlier generations' political demand for democracy and liberation has become a personal demand for freedom to find one's own path.[5] Now that the constraints of socially imposed roles have weakened in rich countries, oppression based on gender, class and race is disappearing. The daily struggle for survival has for most people been banished. We have entered an era characterised by 'individualisation', where for the first time in history we have the opportunity to 'write our own biographies', rather than have the chapters foretold by the circumstances of our birth. For the first time the ordinary individual in the West has the opportunity to make a true choice.[6]

In place of the class struggle and demands for liberation, the citizens of affluent societies have a new quest—the search for authentic identity, for self-actualisation, for the achievement of true individuality. Some have found promising paths in spiritual traditions or psychological 'work', but most have ended up seeking a proxy identity in the form of commodity consumption. People continue to pursue greater wealth and consume at ever higher levels because they do not know how better to answer the question 'How should I live?' This is widely understood. *The Times* of London observed:

> It is the paradox of our lives. We've never had more freedom to shape ourselves in the way we want but we've also never been subject to so many pressures telling us what is desirable. While we stand in front of a supermarket display confronted with more bewildering choices than ever before, the voices telling us what to reach for are more insistent, and insidious, than ever.[7]

TWO
Rationale

IT IS NECESSARY TO place this critique of the modern affliction in a more considered philosophical framework, and John Stuart Mill's famous essay 'On liberty', first published in 1859, is a good place to start. Mill set out a world of personal and political freedom he and his followers imagined would bring about a society of free and contented individuals:

> A person whose desires and impulses are his own—are the expression of his own nature, as it has been developed and modified by his own culture—is said to have character. One whose desires and impulses are not his own has no character, no more than a steam-engine has character.[1]

Mill's thoughts about liberty are at the core of how we in the West understand ourselves as democratic societies. Yet, after reading 'On liberty' today, one feels a niggling sense that Mill's optimistic vision has turned out to be a disappointment. Oddly perhaps, the germ of a new understanding of freedom can be found in Hayek's *The Constitution of Liberty*, which might be considered the seminal text for the libertarian philosophy that from the 1970s has had such an influence on the modern world.[2]

It is apparent from reading Mill and Hayek that both these political philosophers began with the world as they found it (and this is why I begin with a brief statement of where we find ourselves in the world). Mill was absorbed by the great political debates of his time, a time when representative democracy was still emerging in Europe and legal protections for the individual were only half-realised in some countries and still under threat. Mill's radical successors in the second half of the twentieth century, libertarians such as Milton Friedman (the Nobel Prize-winning economist who, like all modern libertarians, was inspired by Hayek), were reacting to what they saw as the greatest threat to freedom at the time—socialism in all its forms, with the danger it posed for economic freedom.

In this context I see it as self-evident that the advancement of human wellbeing is in itself a desirable goal and, along with freedom, should form the primary objective of any society. There are, however, two modern perspectives that take a different view. First, environmentalism usually argues that the ecological integrity of the Earth should be the principal objective of human action, individually and collectively, and that the wellbeing of humans is a desirable aspect or by-product of this objective. A decline in environmental health inevitably impinges on the wellbeing of humans, although maintenance of human populations should not always take precedence. Some environmental thinkers have maintained that sharp reductions in human populations, achieved through birth control, are necessary to meet the principal objective. Others argue that 'sustainability' must encompass social as well as ecological sustainability—that is, the long-term viability of communities that cultivate the factors which contribute to human happiness, consistent with the ecological goals.

Second, and more importantly for my purpose, the dominant political philosophy of our age, libertarianism, rejects the view that promotion of human wellbeing is self-evidently good and should be the principal objective of any society. Instead, it holds that the objective of society and of government should be not to set or endorse goals but to promote as much individual freedom as is feasible and to allow individuals to determine their own goals. Hayek was unabashed about this: 'Above all . . . we must recognise that we may be free and yet miserable. Liberty does not mean all good things or the absence of all evils.'[3] In his feted defence of liberal democracy as the political and economic system that is both inevitable and best, Francis Fukuyama argued that some states or conditions are natural or inevitable even though people might be happier in other states.[4] For Hayek, Friedman, Fukuyama and other champions of the free market, liberty—not happiness—is the ultimate or inevitable goal.

In my view, if social conditions and the political and economic structure are making people miserable (even if they are free to pursue misery in their own ways), this is a matter of public concern. And, just as Hayek defends liberty against the tyranny that might be imposed by majorities, so the very freedoms he wants to protect might be jeopardised if the masses are told they are ungrateful when they question the value of the freedoms assigned to them. This is not to support the proposition that it is better to be happy in chains than to be unhappily free; rather, it is a call to look more closely at the nature of the liberties that Hayek and his followers have so successfully advanced and the social circumstances in which those liberties have taken root.[5]

FREEDOM RECONSIDERED

There is a need—more pressing by the day—to question the value of the economic, political and personal liberties that have been won. For one can reasonably say that free-market capitalism in the West is, to use a much-abused term, in crisis. It is not just under attack from various forms of fundamentalism (Islamic from without and Christian from within): it is suffering from a process of internal decay characterised by widespread alienation and a deep, but mostly private, questioning of the value of modern life. Of course, the fundamentalist assault and entrenched alienation are not unrelated. At the heart of the matter is one question: If the freedoms won, combined with abundance, are so good for us, why are we so discontented?

—▸—

The political history of the modern world has been dominated by struggles to wrest political liberty and personal freedoms from the forces of autocracy and plutocracy. In the twentieth century, liberty was imperilled by fascism and communism. Political freedoms have at times come into conflict with personal liberty: Hitler was, after all, elected. Libertarianism succeeded in extending personal liberty through limiting the role of government in economic activity—although many would argue that the collective interests were thereby damaged—and the liberation movements of the 1960s and 1970s advanced personal freedoms in social and moral life. But, if our objective has been to allow humans to lead fulfilling lives, then, without in any way maligning the liberties won, we must ask whether these freedoms are enough and whether other forces that commit us to a new and more deeply rooted form of servitude have been unleashed.

I argue that extension of the freedoms of the market and the personal freedoms won by the liberation movements have actively worked against our freedom to choose to lead more fulfilling lives. The consequence is that people today find it more difficult to know who they are and so understand how to advance their interests. I argue, too, that the dominating political concern in rich countries today is the conflict between economic and political liberties on one hand and 'inner freedom' on the other and that only in a society that nurtures inner freedom is it possible to live according to our true human purpose.

Some, especially social democrats, might interpret my argument as an unduly individualistic political philosophy—one that pays too little attention to our social natures and the imperative of cooperation in the pursuit of our own wellbeing. Mrs Thatcher's epoch-marking assertion that 'there is no such thing as society, only individuals' was shocking because it seemed to deny that each of us is a product of our society and is in constant interaction with it. It would be more accurate to say 'there is no such thing as an individual'—certainly in the form of the self-interested, rational maximiser imagined by neoclassical economists. But it must be conceded that we have made the transition to an individualised society and that the 'social' as traditionally conceived by social democrats is in decline; that is, the social groupings that previously defined us in practice and provided the categories for sociological and political analysis are no longer relevant (or are at least of greatly diminished relevance). So, in this sense, we are individuals for the first time.

This discussion is thus a prelude to answering the question of how we can reconstruct the social in a newly individualised world. In a world where we are no longer bound together by our class, gender or race, why should we live cooperatively? There are, as neoliberalism concedes, utilitarian reasons—reduced transaction costs, economies of scale, savings arising from the collective provision of certain goods, and so on. These forms of cooperation are generally justified on the ground that they are more 'efficient'. But that is not enough; indeed, such an argument reinforces a neoliberal conception of the individual that is fundamentally hostile to the social. We must reconstruct the idea of solidarity. And if we are to reconstruct the idea of solidarity we must first reconstruct the individual. Who is it that joins with others in pursuit of common goals? On the way to answering this question we must rescue the idea of autonomy from the 'free choice' of neoliberalism and, indeed, from the idea of liberation inherited from the 1960s and 1970s.

THREE

Types of happiness

> *The liberty of the individual must be thus far limited; he must not make himself a nuisance to other people.*
>
> John Stuart Mill

JOHN STUART MILL'S FAMOUS dictum on the extent of liberty provided the intellectual foundation for modern liberal democracy. Polities in the West, especially during the last three decades, have generally adopted the moral position that people should be able to do whatever they like as long as it does not interfere with the rights or wellbeing of others. How the principle should be applied in particular circumstances is the subject of impassioned political contest. Debates about abortion, gun ownership and gay marriage come to mind. The debate might be advanced by people who feel their individual rights are being restricted by moral positions they do not adhere to. Often there are also third parties whose interests are contested, although moral disapproval can be veiled by an argument that the activity in question is a nuisance to others.

Mill's principle was upheld with particular energy by those at the forefront of the liberation movements of the 1960s and 1970s. The restrictions law and custom imposed on sexual expression, women's rights and the rights of minorities could not be sustained in the face of the simple demand that people should not be restricted merely by outdated convention or prejudice. The radicals of the right have been as quick to appeal to the principle as the radicals of the left. Advocates of economic liberalism have insisted that governments restrict the market behaviour of consumers and producers only to the extent necessary to prevent exploitation.

Like some of his libertarian successors, Mill made it clear that the value of liberty lay in the promotion of individuality and that individuality is 'one of the leading essentials of well-being'.[1] But for Mill it was not only the forces of the state that posed a threat to personal happiness by restricting the opportunities for free expression of one's true self. He foreshadowed one of his neglected arguments a few paragraphs after his famous dictum:

> Where, not the person's own character, but the traditions and customs of other people are the rule of conduct, there is wanting one of the principal ingredients of human happiness, and quite the chief ingredient of individual and social progress.[2]

In 'Of individuality, as one of the elements of well-being', a section of an essay entitled 'On liberty', Mill dwelt on convention's debilitating effect on the creativity of individuals and nations: 'He who lets the world, or his own portion of it, choose his plan of life for him, has no need for any other faculty than the ape-like one of imitation'. Further:

> The despotism of custom is everywhere the standing hindrance to human advancement, being in unceasing antagonism to that disposition to aim at something better than customary, which is called, according to circumstances, the spirit of liberty, or that of progress or improvement.[3]

Perhaps it was this Alain de Botton had in mind when he suggested that one of the proven methods of escaping the debilitating effects of status seeking is to lead a bohemian life, in wilful revolt against the despotism of custom.[4] The connection between liberty and the assertion of individuality was taken up by both Hayek and Friedman, although they felt no compulsion to associate greater liberty with greater happiness. Freedom was the goal—an end in itself. Latter-day libertarians were motivated by what they saw as the threat to innovation and entrepreneurship posed by *dirigisme*, or state control. The constraints imposed by custom on the expression of individuality were precisely the targets of the radical liberation movements of the 1960s and 1970s; these movements were pleas for the right to self-determination, and there was no doubt in the exponents' minds that the freedom demanded would usher in an era of greater personal contentment than ever before seen.

It is worthwhile trying to gain a better understanding of the relationship between liberty, individualism and happiness, and an exposition of the nature of happiness is a good place to begin. Martin Seligman, the doyen of American psychology, has distilled the results of a large number of empirical studies and qualitative discussions dating from the time of Aristotle to distinguish between three approaches to wellbeing—the pleasant life, the good life and the meaningful life.[5]

The pleasant life, or life of pleasure, is one motivated by hedonism—the desire to maximise the number of emotional and physical 'highs' that is the signature of modern consumer capitalism. It is possible to learn the skills necessary to foster the pleasant life, including skills in amassing income that can give greater access to hedonistic pursuits. For people committed to the pleasant life the focus of activity is always outwards—looking to the external world to provide sources of satisfaction. Status seeking through career success, for example, can be counted as a feature of the pleasant life because of its emphasis on external reward, although career success as an outgrowth of the desire to augment one's capacities might be regarded as a characteristic of the next approach, the good life.

The hedonic conception of happiness is the one assumed by the utilitarian approach of neoliberal or free-market economics. Nineteenth-century German philosopher Arthur Schopenhauer made an acute observation:

> ... human life, like all inferior goods, is covered on the outside with a false glitter; what suffers always conceals itself ... the more he is wanting in inner contentment, the more he desires to stand out as a lucky and fortunate person in the opinion of others.[6]

The good life is similar to the Aristotelian idea of eudaemonism. It can be thought of as a life devoted to developing and refining one's capabilities and thereby fulfilling one's potential. Aristotle argued that each of us has a *daemon*, or spirit, and that the purpose of life is to discover and honour it.[7] When we have developed our capabilities and are expressing them through our actions, we are capable of having 'flow' experiences—a state of absorption in which normal emotion is absent. This can include deep contemplation.

The contrast between the pleasant (hedonic) life and the good (eudaemonic) life reflects the ancient dispute between the Epicureans and the Stoics, and there is now a body of psychological research supporting the distinction.[8] The former is an intensely subjective idea of wellbeing explored through notions of positive affect (or emotion) and measures of life satisfaction. It is easily, but not very reliably, measured by surveys of subjective wellbeing. By contrast, psychologist Carol Ryff includes among the characteristics of eudaemonic wellbeing purposeful engagement, positive self-regard, high-quality relationships, environmental mastery and continued personal growth. This is similar to the idea of human 'flourishing' emphasised by Martha Nussbaum, who, along with Amartya Sen, favours a 'capabilities' approach to human wellbeing.[9] The focus of activity is inwards, but success manifests itself in the outside world, a fact that turns out to be crucial. Suffice to say here there is nothing inherently virtuous about the good life—except insofar as one believes that cultivating our talents is intrinsically worthwhile.

The meaningful life, the third approach to living, is similar to the good life in that it requires the development of one's 'signature strengths'. But whereas the pursuit of the good life can be self-centred—the athlete or musician perfecting their skills through years of training and having flow experiences 'in the zone'—the meaningful life entails a commitment to something greater than oneself, a higher cause. This arises from a notion of the self that differs radically from that of the inherent skills or capabilities defining the good life. Indeed, the notion of the self in the good life is a humanistic one that is, basically, not unlike the notion underpinning the pleasant life. In the conception underlying the meaningful life, however, the boundary between the self and the other is permeable. The meaningful life corresponds to what the philosophers of the past understood to be the pursuit of virtue, or selfless moral principles. This idea is consistent with a religious interpretation of human life, but it can also be founded in a metaphysics of self, an idea I turn to in Part Two.

There is a considerable amount of research comparing levels of happiness (measured, imperfectly, by reported life satisfaction) among people who set themselves external goals such as wealth, fame and sexual conquest and people who set themselves intrinsic goals such as strong relationships, self-development and contributing to the community.[10] The research results consistently show those with an internal orientation reporting higher levels of happiness than those who pursue external rewards. There is a correspondence between the pleasant life and external rewards on one hand and the meaningful life and intrinsic rewards on the other. The good life lies somewhere in between. Consistent with this, Seligman reviews evidence showing that pursuit of the pleasant life does not improve life satisfaction but that pursuit of the good life or the meaningful life is strongly associated with higher reported life satisfaction. This does, however, raise the questions of what we mean by 'life satisfaction' and whether people pursuing a pleasurable life have a different view of happiness. Raising children, for example, is stressful and at times makes us unhappy to the point of dissatisfaction with our lives, yet most humans who are able to have children choose to do so because it brings purpose and meaning to their life.[11]

These themes, including eudaemonism, are considered later, but several comments are pertinent here. Modern consumer society is able to reproduce itself every day because it persuades us that the pleasant life is a worthwhile pursuit. Consumerism has so infected the culture and organisation of our lives that the market can no longer be seen as a mechanism through which people satisfy their various needs: it is the primary means of generating our needs and then satisfying them. For many, satisfying these manufactured needs becomes the purpose of life. Areas of personal and social life that a few decades ago were well beyond the purview of the market have become infused with the market's values, transforming how we think about them. Choosing a mate, education and entertainment, for example, have become increasingly commodified and are thus considered in terms of their capacity to deliver pleasure. The market now even offers us our identity—both our self-definition and the persona presented to the outside world—something previously determined by our place in the community. In this way it defines a particular form of individualism, a means of thinking about oneself in relation to the rest of the world, as well as a new form of the social.

Seligman's distinction between the pleasant life, the good life and the meaningful life is useful but does leave us wondering about the basis for a meaningful life. Why do some people pursue a meaningful life, and what is its psychological and metaphysical foundation? What is the moral value of a pleasant life as compared to a meaningful life? Later I suggest that the meaningful life can be considered equivalent to the idea of living 'close to one's nature', but there is an expanse of ground to cover before reaching that point.

FOUR
Freedom and happiness

IN SOME RESPECTS THE distinction between the pleasant life, the good life and the meaningful life presupposes high levels of personal and political freedom as well as conditions of abundance. The poor usually do not have a chance to pursue the good life by way of education and training because they are daily constrained to meet their basic needs, although history is full of examples of indigent individuals who have risen to high positions through determination and spirit. In any case, psychological studies of the kind I refer to mostly apply to rich democratic nations.

Unlike their libertarian successors, classical liberals were in no doubt that the objective of political philosophy, as well as political economy, should be to promote social wellbeing and individual welfare. But they did acknowledge, at least in passing, that the relationship between liberty and happiness is not straightforward. Could greater liberty be contrary to our wellbeing? The prevailing and, I argue, superficial view is that, as long as it does not cause a nuisance to others, more freedom must be a good thing because oppression, or 'unfreedom', makes us unhappy. A number of observations can be made immediately. There is a common belief, supported by much evidence[1], that having more control over one's life contributes greatly to individual wellbeing and that open societies, in which people are generally able to make their own decisions about their vocation, place of work, place of living and relationships, enjoy a higher degree of wellbeing than societies in which people are restricted in these choices. Dictatorships are rarely happy places to live in, and oppressed groups in otherwise free societies generally suffer from their oppression.

On reflection, though, it must be conceded that the relationship between control over one's life—that is, free choice—and improvements in wellbeing is beset by ambiguity. There is perhaps least contention about the idea that lack of control over the means of daily living is a severe disadvantage, although it has been noted that the wealthy appear to fret more about money than others. Freedom in political life is associated with greater social wellbeing, yet it is remarkable how many citizens of democracies fail to exercise their political freedoms: half of all US citizens do not exercise their right to vote. It is also accepted that in some circumstances restrictions on civil and political rights contribute to the common good, although this principle can be flouted by those who want to assert control. There are, however, some situations that deserve deeper consideration.

In the 1980s and 1990s women who were liberated from patriarchal constraints often felt they had failed if they did not succeed in the world of careers and economic independence that had opened up for them. This suggests that freedom often comes with obligations or expectations and that it is not enough simply to 'enjoy' it as a potentiality: it must be practised. As this implies, social context is everything. The children of immigrants who move from more traditional societies to more open ones—such as Pakistanis living in England or Latinos in the United States—frequently feel the restrictions of custom and family obligation far more keenly than they would have if they had been brought up in their home country. The freedoms offered by liberal society can be a source of painful familial conflict and personal anguish; in the most indefensible cases they can end in honour killings. In some circumstances, a good case can be made for arranged marriages, and we should be careful about imposing, in the name of freedom, current Western beliefs about romantic love on cultures for which it is foreign—especially since such a high proportion of marriages based on romantic love now end in divorce.

Individuals who have for years been willingly or otherwise confined to institutions are sometimes reluctant to leave them when given the opportunity or asked to. Prisoners who reoffend in order to be returned to jail are the most obvious example. Religious devotees, such as nuns from closed orders, sometimes find it impossible to cope with the ordinary freedoms enjoyed by people on the outside. Moreover, sometimes incarceration and deprivation cultivate a flowering of human virtues, of love, devotion and compassion. Of course, it is absurd to suggest that anyone can be happy in a concentration camp, where starvation and brutality are the norm. But the experience of a few—on the Thai–Burma railway, for instance—suggests that it is possible to mine the depths of human love, sacrifice and resilience in an environment of extreme adversity and that this experience can induce a state of 'grace' that transcends everyday happiness.

As a general rule, greater freedom in economic activity is another contributor to individual and social wellbeing. It is a generalisation that affords exceptions, even in the arena where it appears least vulnerable—the promise of consumer choice. Here, as everywhere, the benefits are best enjoyed when taken in moderation. Increasingly we hear complaints about too much choice. Has deregulation of the telephone information service in Britain—leading to a proliferation of companies offering slightly different services at widely differing prices and making it impossible for any but the most obsessive and time-rich consumer to work out the 'best' price—increased anyone's welfare?

There is, however, a deeper question that must be asked about the relationship between freedom and human happiness. Consider the 'capabilities approach' developed by Amartya Sen. Like Maslow's hierarchy of needs, Sen's checklist method defines a series of capabilities that in an ideal world all citizens would be able to develop. Nussbaum codifies the approach by listing ten capabilities and argues that, in the absence of obstacles to these capabilities, people will be able to flourish. Among the capabilities are good health, development of one's intellectual capacity, loving and being loved, the ability to socialise and empathise, and enjoyment of political and personal freedoms.[2] But here is the conundrum. For a large majority of the citizens of wealthy democratic nations there are no significant external obstacles to fulfilling all ten of the capabilities. So, although people might be *able* to flourish, the question is will they *choose* to? In an era of television catatonia and retail therapy, will free citizens choose 'to imagine, think and reason in a "truly human" way', as Nussbaum puts it, or are they conditioned or predisposed to pursue a stream of pleasurable episodes and never fulfil their capabilities and thus realise their potential as humans?

FREEDOM RECONSIDERED

Social context matters, and this is why some of the thinkers and activists who were at the forefront of the women's movement feel so disappointed. Germaine Greer has argued that women sought liberation but settled for equality, an equality that allows them to feel alienated and exploited in the same ways men do: 'Equality is cruel to women because it requires them to duplicate behaviours that they find profoundly alien and disturbing'.[3] In a peculiar way Hayek put forward the same argument. Writing in an era when democratic socialism dominated or was about to dominate much of Europe, he quoted Lord Acton: 'The finest opportunity ever given to the world was thrown away because the passion for equality made vain the hope for freedom'.[4]

This suggests that a certain level of social and psychological maturity is needed if we are to make proper use of the liberties that have been won—an obvious point when we remember we do not hesitate to restrict, by law and parenting, the liberties children can enjoy. Yet we imagine that the forces of the id that are so alarming in children somehow become legitimate when the child graduates to adulthood at age 18 or, in some countries, 21. Perhaps we are not sufficiently in command of our ids until we are 40 years old, or 60; perhaps some people never learn to control their most basic urges. Culture and social structures themselves have a defining influence on the level of maturity. If it is true that people in Western societies are becoming more self-centred—so that we are placing short-term gratification before longer term development goals and are entering relationships to extract maximum pleasure—then we are becoming less mature. And if that is the case, are we less able than we were to cope with the liberties so hard won by previous generations? These questions call on us to consider more closely the nature of liberty and happiness.

FIVE
Types of liberty

WE HAVE REACHED A time in history that demands a reconsideration of the nature of liberty. We have come to this point partly because of the success of neoliberalism, especially in the 1980s. Libertarian ideas now dominate the polities of rich countries, and much of the rest of the world, in a way few could have imagined. As noted, the most important figure in the libertarian revolution was undoubtedly the Austrian philosopher and economist Friedrich von Hayek, and it turns out that his seminal tome *The Constitution of Liberty*, first published in 1960, is a useful place to begin a reformulation of the idea of liberty.[*]

---

[*] It is ironic that the neoliberal revolution of the 1980s and 1990s—the express purpose of which was to extend and reinvigorate personal freedoms and individual liberty—was effected by a coterie of intellectuals and political activists who succeeded in their objective in the face of clear but ineffectual opposition from the mass of ordinary citizens in whose name they purported to act. Nowhere did the main changes brought by 'reforming' governments under the influence of neoliberal philosophers, economists, policy advisers and commentators enjoy majority support. Whether the policy was privatisation of public assets, deregulation of particular industries, financial liberalisation, the

FREEDOM RECONSIDERED

Hayek distinguishes between individual and political liberty. Individual liberty (or personal freedom) is defined as the possibility of a person acting according to their own decisions:

> Whether he is free or not does not depend on the range of choice but on whether he can expect to shape his course of action in accordance with his present intention, or whether somebody else has power so to manipulate the conditions as to make him act according to that person's will rather than his own.[1]

Political liberty refers to the free participation of men and women in the processes of democracy, including choosing their government. Thus individual liberty refers to the freedom to make private choices and political liberty refers to the freedom to participate in the making of public decisions.

In his essay 'Two concepts of liberty', Isaiah Berlin draws the familiar distinction between negative and positive freedom and explores the contradictions and dangers in the way the idea of negative freedom has been used.[2] (Negative

---

* *Footnote continued from page 25*

imposition of user-pays, free trade, or a preference for inflation control over reductions in unemployment, the majority of citizens always preferred the alternative. About the only policy that enjoyed majority support was lower taxes, but even this lost its shine when the public realised that lower taxes must be accompanied by reduced public services. In the 1990s numerous surveys revealed majority support for higher taxes, as long as the resultant revenue would be committed to a socially useful purpose, such as improved health systems. But Hayek and his neoliberal acolytes would lose little sleep over the erosion of democracy in the interest of freedom. Democracy, defined as majority rule, is only a means to an end, the end being liberalism—that is, a social order in which the coercive power of government is limited as far as possible. This raises the question of the means by which it is legitimate to limit the powers of a democratically elected government. Hayek had an answer:

freedom is 'freedom from'; positive freedom is 'freedom to'.) He quotes Mill to the effect that 'there ought to exist a certain minimum area of personal freedom which must on no account be violated',[3] and says that this requires a 'frontier' between the areas of private life and public authority. Philosophers of liberalism agreed 'that some portion of human existence must remain independent of the sphere of social control' and that to invade that sphere is a form of despotism. One such liberal, Benjamin Constant, proposed that at a minimum this sphere must protect freedom of religion, opinion and expression, and property.[4]

Berlin argues that Mill attributed to liberty too much power for the good and did so by confusing two notions. Mill maintained that all coercion is inherently bad, even though some coercion might be necessary in the interest of the greater good, including to protect others' freedom. The second idea, which shines through in 'On liberty' and is later taken up by libertarians such as Hayek, is that the best society is one in

---

* *Footnote continued from page 25*

> Liberalism regards it as desirable that only what the majority accepts should in fact be law, but it does not believe that this is therefore necessarily good law. Its aim, indeed, is to persuade the majority to observe certain principles. It accepts majority rule as a method of deciding, but not as an authority for what the decision ought to be (*The Constitution of Liberty,* pp. 103–4).

Hayek and his fellow conservatives always put their form of freedom before democracy—perhaps understandably for those who had witnessed the election of Hitler—for it has to be conceded that democracy will not always act to safeguard the liberty of the individual. It must be said, though, that democracy encompasses certain freedoms: if a clear majority of citizens asks the government to set taxes at a high level, there are no individual liberties that can be asserted to overrule this collective act of free will.

which citizens pursue or express 'a certain type of character of which Mill approves—critical, original, imaginative, independent, non-conforming to the point of eccentricity, and so on— and that truth can be found, and such character bred, only in conditions of freedom'.[5] But, suggests Berlin, history shows that 'integrity, love of truth and fiery individualism grow at least as often in severely disciplined communities' such as strict religious societies and military dictatorships. In this way, liberty, in the sense of 'freedom from', is conceivable in some forms of autocracy, albeit relatively benign ones that permit a good deal of personal freedom. Positive freedom, on the other hand, requires political participation and democratic rule.

Although Berlin might be right in his claim that forms of imaginative and independent individualism are not inconsistent with authoritarian political systems, a more telling observation would have been that attainment of high levels of personal and political freedom in the West has not, in general, given rise to societies peopled by free spirits giving expression to their creativity and imagination. Quite the reverse. Western society is characterised by an ever-devouring conformity flimsily camouflaged by a veneer of confected individuality in which true independence of thought, expression and identity is almost nowhere to be found in the general population and lives on only in isolated and increasingly irrelevant pockets of academic and artistic free thinking. Such independence is certainly only rarely evident in general political discourse and media commentary, which are marked by a dull predictability that is all the more apparent for the attempts to conceal it by way of spin. Entrenchment of personal and political freedoms in Western societies has been responsible for the atrophy of true individuality, especially under the impact of consumer capitalism and neoliberal politics since the early 1980s.

Types of liberty

Modern consumer capitalism encourages conformity, one-dimensionality, and an intolerance of those who seek to break away from the expressions of individuality manufactured by the market.

In this context, much is revealed by the emergence of the class of citizens known as 'downshifters'—people who have voluntarily decided to reduce their incomes and consumption in order to free up time and energy for other pursuits. They represent a surprisingly large proportion of the populations of rich countries.[6] Yet, having exercised their freedom by choosing to assign to market considerations a lower place in the order of life's priorities, these people report that they face suspicion, accusations of 'madness', and loss of status.[7] The obstacles put in the way of those who want to partially withdraw from the market are formidable and include being told they will no longer be able to participate in normal social discourse and they will be impoverished in retirement.

It is astounding, therefore, that perhaps as much as a fifth of the population of Anglophone nations have opted for this life change in the last decade or so. The phenomenon is a sign that, in the face of unprecedented freedoms and abundance, the pressure to conform to a market model of happiness has for many become unbearable. Libertarians do not know how to respond to this incipient revolt: although they must applaud people who exercise their free will, they are baffled and distressed when these people exercise that freedom by rejecting the values of the market. If one believes that the world is populated by *Homo economicus*, rational economic man, what happens to that world when rational economic man freely chooses to transcend himself?

Contrary to the imaginings of both Mill and Hayek, the source of the creative, imaginative and independent spirit we so admire must be elsewhere than in the granting of personal and political freedoms in a liberal capitalist order. Hayek himself gives a clue to what this source might be. In a brief but pregnant passage the arch-libertarian defines a third form of freedom—'inner freedom', or 'metaphysical liberty'—which he contrasts with both individual and political liberty:

> It refers to the extent to which a person is guided in his actions by his own considered will, by his reason or lasting conviction, rather than by momentary impulse or circumstance. But the opposite of 'inner freedom' is not coercion by others but the influence of temporary emotions, or moral or intellectual weakness. If a person does not succeed in doing what, after sober reflection, he decides to do, if his intentions or strength desert him at the decisive moment and he fails to do what he somehow wishes to do, we may say that he is 'unfree', the 'slave of his passions'.[8]

Throughout the rest of his sizeable volume Hayek does not return to this third form of freedom; one suspects he mentioned it only because it helped him untangle the idea of 'freedom of the will'. In introducing the concept, Hayek defines inner freedom as the extent to which a person is 'guided' in his actions by his own considered will or lasting conviction. This implies there is a force that might, in defined circumstances, guide decision making, so the question of who or what that force is then arises. The introduction to this discussion suggests the answer. Is not the absence of inner freedom, precisely as Hayek defines it, the dominant characteristic of modern consumer capitalism—a social system that cultivates behaviour prompted by momentary impulse, temporary emotions, and moral and intellectual weakness?

Is it not the purpose of the marketing society to make us the slaves of our passions? Has not happiness itself, and thus perhaps the goal of life, been redefined so that today the popular belief that motivates most of our behaviour is the notion that happiness can be no more than the gratification of our whims?

The distinction between political and individual liberty on one hand and inner freedom, or metaphysical liberty, on the other is the key to a different—one might even say new—approach to political philosophy, one that resonates with both the material circumstances and the *Zeitgeist* of advanced consumer capitalism. It accords with the real conditions in which citizens of rich countries find themselves living. For if one does not possess inner freedom but is instead continually responding to impulses, expectations and outside pressures, or if one is driven by fantasies, chemical or psychological addictions or felt inadequacies, or if one is in thrall to a consuming belief—all of which induce behaviour that in moments of clarity and reflection one knows to be contrary to one's interests—then all the abundance that surrounds us and the political and personal freedoms available to us amount to nothing. If such influences are only occasional, or if they are frequent but affect only a small minority, the argument for a social system that gives a privileged place to political and individual liberty, including economic freedom, is plausible since most of us would know most of the time what is in our interests and act accordingly. But if a systematic force—entrenched social custom, religious zealotry, political fanaticism, widespread psychological instability or just some characteristic of being human—conspires to deprive us of inner freedom, we must ask whether the external freedoms are enough.

FREEDOM RECONSIDERED

Furthermore, the absence of inner freedom must entail a distortion of the proper exercise of personal and political freedoms. What does it mean to have personal freedom if one's choices are determined and manipulated by powerful external forces? Do we enjoy political freedom when we are conditioned to believe that the only responsible vote is one for a party that promises to put the interests of the economy before everything else? The challenge to liberalism becomes more awkward if a case can be made that some people's exercise of their external freedoms in the marketplace has, in fact, been a cause of the erosion of our inner freedom, a case put forward later in this discussion.[9]

SIX

Inner freedom

INNER FREEDOM IS THE freedom to act according to one's own considered will, by one's 'reason or lasting conviction' in Hayek's felicitous phrase. It is the ability to use one's reason and sense of what is right to stave off influences that would prevent one behaving or living in keeping with one's considered judgment. At least, this is the definition we can adopt for now. Inner freedom is better understood not as some well-defined realm of the self, divisible into areas of life such as religion and opinion, but as a characteristic of cognitive processing, of thought, of decision making.[1] To the extent that inner freedom is distinguished from individual and political freedom, our inner freedom does not depend on external authority (or at least not directly); instead, it ultimately depends on how we defend ourselves. It is the freedom gained by repelling interference, manipulation, temptation and social pressure. It is the freedom that, although often hard won, is nevertheless there to be won—unlike freedom from the constraints of political authority or government impost, which is granted after collective political struggle.

FREEDOM RECONSIDERED

In the absence of inner freedom we might act in a manner contrary to our own interests, although philosophers have long debated whether it is possible for us to act in such a way. Of course, the neoclassical economists must insist that we cannot: whatever we do in the market is always in our interests, a belief that provided the rationale for the removal of restrictions on 'market freedoms' in recent decades. But few among the general public would doubt that we can, and often do, act, in the market and elsewhere, in a manner contrary to our own interests. Although this might be easy to accept for individual decisions driven by impulses or moral lapses, it is not a big step to maintain that indeed whole lives can be constructed on a 'false' set of beliefs about how best to live a contented life. If a person can be motivated by an impulse to act once against their own interests, the same person might be prompted to act impulsively time and again, even though they acknowledge that acting on those impulses might not be in their interests. Serially impulsive behaviour becomes compulsive behaviour—as if the person is driven by an outside force over which they have little or no control; compulsive drinkers, gamblers, eaters, shoplifters or workers come to mind. Remorse and resolve are often insufficiently powerful antidotes.

Before going further, it is worth commenting on the relationship between inner freedom and the notion of false consciousness, usually attributed to Marx but more accurately attributable to later Marxists. False consciousness describes the beliefs, ideology or ideas that oppressed people hold about themselves and that prevent them from seeing the objective conditions and explanation of their oppression. Initially used to explain why some proletarians appeared to support capitalism, the notion was later applied, in the second wave of feminism, to describe the views of women who argued that (or acted as though) females were not oppressed by the patriarchal system but instead benefited from it. The absence of inner freedom is not the same as false consciousness since inner freedom puts forward the idea that the individual knows at some level, through reflection, what is in their own interests.

Isaiah Berlin warns of the perils of equating our 'true' selves with our freedom—a warning that must be borne in mind when assessing the argument of this book:

> This monstrous impersonation . . . is at the heart of all political theories of self-realisation. It is one thing to say that I may be coerced for my own good . . . It is quite another to say that if it is my good, then I am not being coerced, for I have willed it, whether I know it or not, and am free (or 'truly' free).[2]

It cannot be emphasised too strongly that liberation of the true self, and the exercise of inner freedom, can by its very definition occur only through consent and never through coercion.

In modern consumer society there is a more useful way to think about the problem. It is well established in the psychological and sociological literature that people are capable of operating at two levels of cognition. The first is a short-term impulsiveness based on our immediate feelings and beliefs about ourselves—what might be called 'superficial awareness'. The second is a more considered position based on reflection on our moral values and longer term interests, including perceptions of our part in society—what might be called 'considered awareness'. To put it simply, sometimes we form views and act as self-centred individuals and sometimes we do so as citizens. To illustrate using some research I am familiar with, if people in rich countries are asked whether they can afford to buy everything they really need, most say 'no'.[3] Even though, by any reasonable definition of 'need', they manifestly can afford to buy more than they need, they feel in some way deprived because there are constant pressures on them to acquire more consumer goods and to set higher lifestyle benchmarks. This is the consciousness most people walk around with. It creates a gnawing discontent that seems remediable only by having more, although more never satisfies. Yet if we ask the same people whether their society is too materialistic, placing undue emphasis on money, nearly all agree. When asked to reflect on the state of society or to stand back and examine their own lives, respondents are also asked to express a view about the social interest, which includes their own longer term interests. Posing questions such as these has a 'moralising effect' on people's decision making.[4] Few who are already wealthy are willing to defend their need for more money in a public setting, especially one where there are people with considerably lower incomes. Similarly, many people from wealthy countries who feel deprived at home begin to count their blessings when they visit poor countries.

The distinction between superficial and considered awareness is closely related to the distinction, drawn in discussions about deliberative democracy, between 'instrumental rationality' and 'deliberative rationality'.[5] Citizens' juries and processes of deliberative democracy, in which citizens come together and hear evidence and arguments in a spirit of pursuing the common good, often reach conclusions that are radically different from those resulting from a simple vote of members at the outset.[6] In the latter case people act with superficial consciousness; in the former they act according to a more considered evaluation of what is in their own and society's interests. Compared with instantaneous responses, a consideration of what is 'right' is far more prominent when people are asked to reflect on the question at hand; this is even more likely to be the case if they do it in company with others. Both forms of consciousness reflect the 'real' conditions in which people find themselves and neither can be said to be 'false', but considered awareness, while not infallible, is 'truer' in the sense that it is more likely to express the person's 'real' opinion—that is, the one they themselves would identify as such. In short, decisions made on the basis of considered awareness are less likely to be regretted.

The implication of the distinction between superficial and considered awareness is that when we allow the former to prevail we could be acting rashly. This gives rise to two closely related concepts that are crucial to understanding inner freedom—self-deception and akrasia. Before turning to these, though, let us look from another angle at the question of whether we always choose what is in our best interests.

SEVEN
Do we prefer what we choose?

HUMANS ARE UNIQUE IN possessing first- and second-order preferences. First-order preferences are the ones modern economics recognises, the ones revealed by our behaviour in the marketplace. Second-order preferences are the preferences we have about our own preferences.[1] The subject has been explored by US economist David George, who provides the example of his consumption of fast food. As he sits eating a greasy hamburger he is wishing he were eating something healthier. His second-order preference is a preference for his food preferences. It is not just another preference; it is a deeper order of preference. One reason for his first-order preference prevailing is the circumstances in which we make decisions. Snap decisions are more likely to follow first-order preferences, while more considered judgments are more likely to see us following our second-order preferences. Acting on first-order preferences is the defining feature of people who pursue the pleasant life; acting on second-order preferences defines those who pursue the good life.

In an affluent society, producers of consumer goods have a strong influence on our preferences, especially our first-order preferences. They often set out to tempt us to allow our first-order preferences to overrule our deeper preferences, and they provide opportunities for instant gratification by appealing to our weaknesses. The modern obesity epidemic can be understood in these terms. Most obese people would prefer to be thinner; they prefer to prefer less food. Some go to extreme lengths to ensure that their second-order preference prevails—for example, by checking themselves into sanatoriums, where their craving for junk food cannot be satisfied. Yet it is the objective of suppliers of junk food to persuade us to allow our first-order preferences to prevail, and this raises the question of how the market shapes the circumstances in which we express our preferences.

Following the philosopher Harry Frankfurt, David George points out that only animals consistently act on the basis of their first-order preferences.[2] A sheep wants to eat: it eats. Humans are unique in having the capacity to reflect on the desirability or otherwise of their preferences—in other words, to prefer to have one set of preferences over another. We are capable of reflecting on the sort of person we want to be, the sorts of likes and dislikes we think will be in our interests. We can desire to be different, even a different sort of person. We go to wine appreciation classes not necessarily because we desire wine but because we desire to desire wine. We might want to become a sophisticated person and so set about cultivating or creating the tastes and lifestyle of that sort of person. In doing this, we use our willpower to resist some urges and cultivate others.

Yet conventional economics would have humans, in essence, no different from animals. This is not contradicted by humans' capacity to experience altruistic motives. Economics can easily incorporate altruism in a preference set. But it then becomes just another first-order preference to be traded off with others. Most non-economists see this as a cheapening or distortion of the altruistic motive: after all, a dog might stay by its dying owner and starve to death. For a Kantian, for whom rationality distinguishes humans from other creatures, the existence of second-order preferences makes us human because it is those preferences, not our immediate urges, that prove we have free will. Thus the promotion of choice in itself—the prime aspiration of mainstream economics and neoliberal policy—tells us nothing about freedom. A cat might be able to choose from among six different cat foods, but that does not make it free; it simply means it has a choice. I am free only if I have the self-control, the will and the intellectual capacity to choose my preferences.

Why should the market create or intensify the conflict between first- and second-order preferences? The idea of consumer sovereignty assumes that first-order preferences are a given, that they are exogenous to the system. In modern consumer capitalism, however, this assumption is no longer tenable: the marketing industry exists to create and manipulate our tastes. In fact, a large part of people's growing incomes in the coming decade will be spent on goods for which the marketers have not yet created a craving. Second-order preferences, although not immune to outside influences, have a much greater claim to be exogenous, or taken as given.

One reason for this is the role of moral considerations. It is reasonable to assume that first-order preferences are more likely to be based on personal benefit—the sort of motive customarily assumed in economics texts—while second-order preferences are more likely to be influenced by moral considerations. It can also be argued that the market usually encourages us to favour self-interested behaviour instead of morally motivated behaviour. A childcare centre decided that the best way to deter parents from picking up their children late would be to impose a fine, a financial disincentive. A cost-free activity (getting 10 to 15 minutes of free childcare) suddenly came at a price. To their astonishment, the childcare workers found that parents began picking up their children even later. Why? What was previously a decision made with a strong element of moral suasion ('It's unfair to freeload and to exploit childcare workers who want to go home on time') had become an economic transaction ('How much extra time am I willing to pay for?'). Putting a price on lateness made parents consume more of it.

Economists often try to explain 'moral' behaviour by referring to a personal benefit, such as the good feeling we experience when we act ethically. In other words, there is compensation for giving up something. Much giving behaviour can undoubtedly be understood in this way, as people who have had contact with the philanthropic community will know. But to characterise moral behaviour as conferring some form of personal benefit is a perverse way of seeing it, an interpretation confined largely to free-market economists. Any number of philosophers have understood moral acts as acts carried out for their own sake and not because the actor expects any benefit, psychic or otherwise. As Lanse Minkler writes, 'The moral principles must become one's own for the person of integrity . . . To violate one's own moral principle would be to confuse one's identity'.[3]

Another reason, considered by David George, to expect the market to bring our first- and second-order preferences into conflict is that the market allows us to satisfy our desires more

FREEDOM RECONSIDERED

quickly than we might otherwise be able to. Indeed, much marketing effort is directed at persuading us to act immediately, to buy impulsively, and have the salesperson 'close the deal'. The dangers of impulsiveness are reflected in laws that require cooling-off periods for transactions involving real estate or items bought at the front door or by phone. Legislators know we are prone, especially when under pressure, to act on our first-order preferences—our unpreferred preferences—when, had we more time, we would make a different decision.

It could be argued that the rapid increase in the availability of consumer credit during the last two decades has been aimed at encouraging most of us to buy more by shopping impulsively, even compulsively. If we did not have credit cards we would almost certainly buy less because the time lapse between the generation of desire and the acting on it would, for many items, be much longer. The contrast with the model of the neoclassical economist could not be starker. Consumers are imagined to go to the market to buy a particular good that will satisfy a need arising out of their pre-determined preferences. This process of 'choice' is the quintessential justification of free-market economics. In fact, it is probably more accurate to say that the modern consumer goes to the market a needy mass of confused and neurotic urges looking for a salve. This is what the marketers assume, and it is the basis on which they work. They are masterful at creating our 'preference' for their products but are the first to appeal to the sovereignty of 'consumer choice' the moment anyone suggests any restriction.

This also helps explain why we watch so much rubbish on television. It is the result of channel surfing and instant decision making, and it often leads us to ask ourselves, 'Why am I watching this crap?' The answer is that we are acting according to first-order preferences, ones that we would prefer not to have. If we had to nominate the programs we wanted to watch at the beginning of the week and then have them locked in, it is a fair bet the quality of the television we watched would be higher and we would be more contented at the end of the week.[4]

Unlike the political defenders of the market and so-called free choice by consumers, the advertisers and marketers are much more sanguine about the way they persuade consumers to do things they do not want to do. Thus the head of planning at a global advertising agency has said, 'Most people don't have a sense of self-worth. Buying luxury goods makes us feel special and successful. They make us feel valuable in a world that often tests our sense of self-worth'.[5] It is for these kinds of reasons that the market is more likely to influence first-order preferences in a way that conflicts with our deeper, second-order, preferences. Second-order preferences have greater authority in that they are more likely to represent our best interests because they are the result of rational deliberation. The social problem that arises from this analysis is not that the market, through advertising, changes our tastes: it is that the market has a tendency to create conflict between our first- and second-order preferences, an 'inefficient' outcome. If this is so, the presupposition of free-market economics—that we go to the market to express our preferences and thereby advance our welfare—is turned on its head. Increasingly, it is only by turning our backs on the market that we can give expression to our true preferences.

All this is to say that I place greater value on people exercising their second-order preferences than their first-order ones, and that the good life is preferable to the pleasant life. This is not because second-order preferences are intrinsically more virtuous—unless the exercise of rationality is itself considered a virtue, a position taken by Kantians but not by me, as becomes apparent in Part Two of this book. Life is punctuated by conflict between our immediate urges and our preference to defer some gratifications, between self-interested decisions and moral ones. The danger for people who are unable to control their immediate urges is that they become subject to manipulation and exploitation, and it is this that confers greater value on the good life.

EIGHT

Self-deception and akrasia

EXERCISING INNER FREEDOM IN the way Hayek defined the term means acting according to our considered will and lasting conviction. To do this, we must reflect on what is in our interests and then have the conviction to act on that judgment. Self-deception is the enemy of considered judgment, and akrasia, or weakness of will, is the enemy of our determination to act as we think we should. Self-deception and akrasia are ever-present in our lives. Moreover, modern marketing society acts constantly to exploit these foes of inner freedom.

SELF-DECEPTION

There is a considerable amount of philosophical literature on the idea of self-deception.[1] Some have argued that self-deception is impossible because it involves forming the intention to deceive oneself. Others have posited various ways of partitioning the mind and operating as if there are two people inhabiting it. In this case, knowledge of the plans, intentions and motives of one is, one way or another, denied the other; we can imagine a deceiver and a deceived. A less radical construction is to suppose that, instead of two contradictory beliefs being held, the true belief can be held unconsciously while we act on a consciously held but false belief. These ideas are familiar to psychoanalysis. Anna Freud developed the concept of defence mechanisms that enable us to conceal uncomfortable truths from ourselves. As Alfred Mele says, 'Using these strategies, the ego (the coping part of the mind) defends itself against onslaughts from the id (unconscious sexual and aggressive desires), the superego (socially instilled values) and external reality'.[2]

The main defence mechanisms are repression, in which we exclude from awareness certain memories, feelings or associations that would be upsetting if consciously acknowledged; denial, in which we act as if we are unaware of some fact that is apparent to others; projection, whereby we unconsciously attribute to others our own negative qualities or feelings; regression, in which we revert to an earlier stage of emotional development so as to avoid responsibility for an action; sublimation, in which we divert unacceptable behaviours and thoughts into more acceptable forms; and reaction formation, in which we adopt behaviour that is the opposite of our true feelings or thoughts. Use of these mechanisms is never deliberate: if it were they would have no effect. We deploy them unconsciously and are thus deceived. Obviously, the tension between the conscious attitude and the real thought, emotion or action will manifest itself somehow, if only through a vague feeling that something is not right, leading ultimately to the need to face up to the truth whatever the apparent cost. For our purposes, repression is the most important defence mechanism because it can be used as a generalised defence against examining the direction and meaning in our lives.

Not only does self-deception take the classical psychological routes involving unconscious processes, it also involves techniques we use to manage our attention in ways that exclude from our decision making uncomfortable facts and feelings. Looking at daily patterns of self-deception from this angle, Mele notes:

> Tactics of self-deception include quick oscillations of attention towards pleasing aspects of our lives and away from anxiety-producing ones . . . The fundamental strategy . . . in self-deception is to distort the standards of rationality for belief by exaggerating favourable evidence for what we want to believe, disregarding contrary evidence, and resting content with minimal evidence for pleasing beliefs.[3]

Mele uses the example of a woman who, despite strong evidence to the contrary, refuses to believe her husband is having an affair. Admitting the truth has intrinsic benefits, but believing a lie is less painful, at least for a time. In this case our emotional preference overrules our reason. In other words, our preference for the world to be a certain way can lead us to believe it is so. Everyone knows they have at times been 'in denial'.

Although ubiquitous in daily life, self-deception is inconsistent with the exercise of inner freedom. Some philosophers and economists have tried to resolve the contradiction between the theoretical impossibility of self-deception and its daily manifestation by declaring that the facts cannot be true, which serves only to make conspicuous the irrational obsession they have with rational behaviour.[4]

Another commentator, Herbert Fingarette, also focuses on the way we use our attention to deceive ourselves. The difficulties with the idea of self-deception evaporate when we accept that not everything we are taking into account and to which we are responding intelligently is within our field of attention: 'If focusing attention on some fact is apprehended as promising intense distress, that is a very strong reason for avoiding doing so'.[5] If I have done something shameful that, if admitted, erodes my sense of myself as a good person, to avoid this unpleasant sensation I can refuse to pay attention to my feelings. My recall of the event might become less reliable, I can reinterpret my own and others' actions and motives, and I can explain away uncomfortable aspects of the incident. It might be better in the long run to face up to the shame, admit to myself and others that I was wrong and hope to move on, but that involves a degree of short-term pain and societal disapproval that I might be unwilling to endure.

At some stage in their life many people realise they have systematically deceived themselves for years in a way that has denied them a life lived with authentic purpose or a deeper moral sense. They feel that, in response to family or social pressures, they adopted a career or life path in pursuit of goals that proved illusory. In other words, they spent years or decades deceiving themselves about what would make them happy.

Why do we deceive ourselves? The decision to adopt life goals other than those that are socially sanctioned entails risks and takes courage. It is easier to live a series of short episodes in which the urge for a more authentic life—in which we behave according to our deeper understanding of what is in our interests—is suppressed. We can do so in several ways: we might simply repress the urge to change because change seems unattainable; we might sublimate the urge by converting it into something else, such as the acquisition of things; we might live our dream vicariously through hero worship or reading of certain types of books; or we might persuade ourselves that the goal of an authentic life is a mirage and we should just 'get on with it'. The ego uses these mechanisms to defend itself against the upwellings of meaninglessness we all sense at times. Perhaps one might see them as legitimate coping strategies in a world that appears to admit no alternative.

It is easy to deceive ourselves when money is at stake. I once participated in a studio debate on the topic of greed.[6] Three members of the audience had made money by participating in a scheme known as 'Heart'. A person puts in £3000 and if they sign up two more people to the scheme (who in turn sign up others) they 'win' £24 000. It is a classic pyramid scheme, a zero-sum game in which nothing is created and wealth is merely redistributed. To the extent that someone wins, others must lose. The only way for everyone to keep winning is for the scheme to go on forever, which will not happen. (It is similar to a game I used to play at school. Several students would join hands. The boy at one end held a dynamo that, when the handle was turned vigorously, would generate an electric current that passed along the line harmlessly until the chain was broken and the last person received a shock. If you found yourself on the end, your objective was to race around the schoolyard and grab someone else before the shock arrived. Everyone had fun except the person at the end.) The pyramid scheme must come to an end, and when it does those who have contributed £3000 without having received their return will be the losers.

Yet the people who defended the Heart scheme appeared incapable of understanding this simple point and had persuaded themselves that somehow everyone who participated could win. No matter how many different ways the simple insight was explained to them, the light just could not be turned on. These were normal, intelligent people, so they could maintain this position only by self-deception. They argued that no one was forced to participate and there were no hidden traps for the unwary. Their greed, like that of the people who willingly followed them into the scheme, was too powerful for their moral sense but, loath to concede this, they were forced to suppress awareness of the moral dimension of their decision. Their financial interest interfered with their reasoning, since to admit that the people at the end of the line must suffer would mean they had profited from others' loss and that those who had lost were not undeserving but unlucky, vulnerable, or both. This is one way our motivations or preferred outcomes can override the facts to determine our beliefs. It is hard to know in the Heart case whether the people who were deceiving themselves were doing so by means of rationalisation, wilful ignorance or systematic ignoring.[7]

Lying to ourselves can sometimes serve our interests. Suppressing details of a traumatic event can be an effective coping strategy, although the trauma might manifest itself in unexpected ways. Or we might downplay our failures in order to maintain our self-esteem. But in coming to understand inner freedom we are especially interested in how self-deception damages our own interests. Perhaps it is better to say that, as long as we are deceiving ourselves, we are not being true to ourselves and so are not authentic; we have closed ourselves off from the knowledge of what is in our long-term interests.

The existence of self-deception prompts us to ask who is responsible for the deception. An answer is suggested by the distinction between first- and second-order preferences, which correspond to what might be called the superficial self and the considered self. The self of second-order preferences is the truer self, the one whose opinions most people would claim as their real views.

The techniques of modern marketing, and modern culture's general retreat to superficiality, provide ammunition to strengthen the superficial self in its attempts to bamboozle and sideline the considered self.

AKRASIA

We all face moral decisions, often daily. Most of us know, for example, that we could do a great deal more to reduce our contribution to environmental decline. We could drive less, recycle more, and delay replacing goods until they are worn out. Yet we often find the effort too much, even though it might in fact be trifling. Our will fails us. A married man might be so possessed by desire for a woman other than his wife that he embarks on an affair despite knowing it will cause great hurt to those he loves. A lawyer might cheat on her tax return; she knows she cannot be caught, yet she feels, perhaps beneath layers of rationalisation, that it is wrong.

Impulsiveness like this is inconsistent with the exercise of inner freedom. Before exploring this further, though, we should distinguish between impulsiveness and spontaneity, for there is no doubt there are pleasures in spontaneity, and a life ruled by planning would be dull and would probably reflect a degree of neuroticism. (John Stuart Mill's early life, which was planned by his father as an intellectual experiment, comes to mind.) I knew a man who kept a list, regularly revised as further information came to hand, of the items he would

FREEDOM RECONSIDERED

need to take with him to the local hospital should he suddenly fall ill or have an accident. He kept a second list tailored to the conditions of a second local hospital and two similar lists for his wife in case she fell ill or had an accident. Rational yes, but a bit mad. Nevertheless, it is difficult to imagine anyone living a life of inner freedom unless they repeatedly exercise their capacity for rational deliberation and do so in a way that allows them to resist the daily inducements to impulsiveness.

Philosophers have long discussed this phenomenon. The word 'akrasia'—coming from the Greek *a*, without, and *kratos*, power—is usually interpreted as 'lack of self-control', although it is also thought of as weakness of will, the failing that allows us to act without restraint. Akrasia occurs when one acts in a way that is contrary to one's considered judgment. This should not be taken to imply a sharp distinction between reason and passion, since our desires are naturally included when we make considered judgments. Reason therefore encompasses 'calm desires' or 'tranquil passions'.[8] Some of these desires can be moral in character—for example, the desire to act ethically—but akrasia can also be present when we simply submit and allow our passions or desires to overrule our considered judgment.

British Labour MP Dianne Abbott was well known for her condemnation of private schooling. She argued that private schools are elitist, entrench privilege and are especially exclusionary for black citizens, of which she is one. Yet when it came to placing her own child in high school she opted for a private school. She argued that, although it had been a difficult decision and would attract accusations of hypocrisy, she had made the judgment that the education of her child came first and he would be better off in a private school than in the local public school, where most of her constituents sent their children. She decided that her desire to advance her family's interests should prevail over her moral conviction.

We can think of Dianne Abbott's decision in this way. Although sending her child to the public school would be more in conformity with her ideals, sending him to a private school would give him a better chance in life and is therefore in her interest as a parent. Each of these arguments falls into a different arena of consideration—one the arena of moral deliberation, the other of self-centred interests. We all must decide when to allow moral considerations to prevail. Akrasia occurs when we hold particular convictions but, instead of weighing them against our private interests, we allow our personal desires to overwhelm the decision because we are too 'weak' to prevent this. There are times in our lives when we are more prone to this sort of behaviour—when we feel alone, vulnerable, upset or ill-treated. We might feel a need to comfort ourselves as a result of grief over a loss or a rebuff from friends or society. We might feel resentful and want to 'punish' society or our deity by transgressing ethical rules, or we might persuade ourselves that moral rules are all well and good when we can 'afford' them emotionally or financially. Because she carefully weighed up the alternatives and considered the consequences of her choices, the MP cannot be said to have acted akratically. It was just that her moral conviction was not as strong as her public pronouncements suggested.

Although rational deliberation might or might not take account of moral considerations, akrasia implies that such considerations are included in the weighing up of courses of action. One acts akratically when one is aware at some level of the various factors involved but nevertheless acts contrary to one's considered judgment—that is, if one had allowed oneself to deliberate in a considered way. Aristotle wrote extensively, although not always consistently, on the problem of akrasia, especially in his *Nicomachean Ethics*, and a long philosophical debate has ensued.[9]

Moral weakness is a form of akrasia that 'consists in failing to live up to one's sincerely expressed beliefs about what it would be morally best to do'.[10] It arises when we decide to act against our 'better judgment'—when our judgment leads us to conclude that the moral arguments outweigh others but we act selfishly anyway. In this case we can say 'the better judge' resides in the realm of inner freedom and its role is to adjudicate on the best course of action, taking account of one's own interests and those of others represented by our moral values or commitments. These moral interests can include the personal standards of integrity we set for ourselves. The remorse of the compulsive gambler, the violent husband and the absent parent is well understood, and the behaviour is explained by the proclivities or character faults of those concerned. We might, however, just as easily point to the daily disappointment millions of people feel after they have been drawn into an act of 'retail therapy'. Many people who live a life of abundance die regretting their life choices; they did not adhere to their principles or deeper urges. When we succumb to temptation we sacrifice our inner freedom because 'outside' forces have led us to do something we feel is wrong. These outside forces are not other people or the state; they are forces outside what we regard as our 'true' self. A theory of the 'true self' thus becomes even more important.

NINE

A digression on the ethic of consent

THE ETHIC OF CONSENT is the dominant principle of moral behaviour in post-modern society. The rule is used to make judgments about a range of behaviours, from 'deviant' sexual practices to medical experimentation on humans, euthanasia and genetic engineering. It is confined to activities where there are no third parties that could be affected, although debate about some moral concerns often focuses on whether particular third parties, including society in general, are affected. According to the ethic of consent, when third parties are not affected informed consent is the only ground for judging the moral value of someone's behaviour. It is thus a procedural ethic of permission giving, in which the only source of moral authority is our subjective consciousness. There is no 'morality', only an agreed procedure for individuals to decide 'what is right for them'. This radical individualism is the ethic explicit in libertarianism, and it also underpinned the political and social demands of the liberation movements of the 1960s and 1970s, especially those relating to sexual expression and the use of drugs. It permits—indeed, celebrates—moral diversity as an essential aspect of a pluralist society, a position that has received theoretical expression in post-modern theories in which moral judgment is cut adrift from any absolute principle and becomes culturally relative (a topic I return to in section 25).

The ethic of consent is based on a view of human decision making in which adults are assumed capable of weighing up the implications of an action and deciding whether it is in their interest to engage in that action. But once we concede that humans are prone to self-deception and akrasia, and to subtle forms of coercion (considered shortly), cracks open up in the argument for moral judgment based on consent alone. We must admit the possibility that we can act in ways that are contrary to our own interests, something we 'know' at one level but choose to ignore. Although the ethic of consent has broad, if not universal, support as a principle, popular opinion also admits exceptions when self-deception and moral weakness come into play.

Take self-deception as an example. Some people have an irresistible desire to have a healthy limb amputated and are convinced they will not achieve peace and fulfilment in life until they have rid themselves of the offending limb. Known as body dysmorphia, this syndrome has no accepted explanation. Not only do people suffering from it consent to amputation; sometimes they take extreme measures to achieve their goal—such as having a 'backyard' operation or placing a leg on a railway line. When asked whether a surgeon should agree to amputate, almost everyone who does not suffer from the condition says 'no'. So, although consent is informed and explicit, there is nevertheless a widespread view that anyone engaging in such aberrant behaviour must be mentally unbalanced and is therefore in some way deceiving themselves about the benefits of amputation. The answer is not to accede to the wish to amputate; rather, it is to understand why the desire exists and to change it.

The ethic of consent faces its most frequent test in relation to sexual morality. When interviewed, prostitutes and porn stars usually say they are fully consenting and have no qualms about their decision to use their body to earn a living by gratifying strangers. Yet in later years some do admit they feel they have degraded themselves, have difficulty forming loving and lasting relationships, and regret their decisions. Sylvie Kristel, star of the mainstream porn film *Emmanuelle*, made in 1974, spoke 30 years later of the 'melancholic paradox of being desired by everyone but truly loved by very few' and of renting herself out but never giving herself.[1] For some of these people it becomes apparent they were deceiving themselves about the implications of their decision to become a prostitute or a porn actor because their activities were contrary to a moral sense they suppressed.

These considerations are exemplified by Catherine Millet's description of her sexual life in her memoir *The Sexual Life of Catherine M.*[2], since reflection on that book forces us to consider the social context in which consent occurs. Millet provides accounts of dozens of sexual encounters, especially orgies in which she is penetrated in every orifice, in apartments, parks and cars. The anonymity and arbitrariness of sexual partners—she concedes she cannot remember most of them and did not even see many—celebrate sex as an activity devoid of personal contact, and she writes of herself as if she were always available and virtually insatiable, just the way women are portrayed in pornographic videos. But it is not the copiousness or explicitness of the sex in the memoir that makes it obscene: it is the absence of intimacy and affection. In writing the memoir, Millet dared us to judge her and, fearful of mockery, few took up the challenge.

Perhaps the emblematic statement in Millet's memoir is this one: 'Fucking is an antidote to boredom. I find it easier to give my body than my heart.' Millet seems to be arguing that only through sexual abandon can we find full freedom and that any criticism of her sexual choices is neurotic and possibly oppressive. Can her sexual adventurism be interpreted as an exercise in self-deception or as weakness of the will? Although one might easily interpret her incontinence as the result of her own upbringing and character, Millet herself shows no sign of moral doubt and few signs that she could have deceived herself into pursuing a life of sexual licence. She made a conscious choice and, apparently, has no regrets, although one does gain the impression that she must work quite hard at having no regrets. But Millet's memoir forces us to confront quite different questions: Is a cultural environment that entrenches an ethic of consent itself a healthy one? Does the memoir do no more than highlight a pervasive emptiness in which sexual practice becomes just another form of gratification? This suggests that an ethic rooted in inner freedom, in which decisions are based on considered judgment and moral reflection, can take us much further than the superficial notion of 'informed consent' (an argument developed in Part Three).

Finally, it is worth dwelling briefly on the role of subtle coercion in the ethic of consent. Sometimes it is said that everyone is free to sleep under a bridge, but it would be distorting the meaning of the word to suggest that the homeless 'consent' to sleeping rough. Poor people who consent to selling their blood or their bodily organs (both of which sustain a vigorous trade today) can be considered to

A digression on the ethic of consent

have been coerced by their circumstances into doing something a wealthy person would not contemplate. It is dangerous to life and limb—entire communities in China, with no income source other than the sale of their blood, have been infected with HIV as a result of unsafe donation and transfusion procedures—yet, in full knowledge of the dangers, desperate people are willing to take the risk. An imbalance of power and life circumstances deprives the poor of the capacity to consent freely.

Although the poor might be coerced into consent because they lack basic necessities, other familiar situations involve pressure to consent when a choice is in fact available. Doctors are forbidden from having sexual encounters with their patients because the doctor–patient relationship involves an imbalance of power that, by subtle processes the patient does not understand, means the patient might be coerced into having sex. In this circumstance it is agreed that, because they are vulnerable and needy, patients cannot consent freely. This is especially the case with psychiatry, where patients can be rendered very vulnerable by a phenomenon known as 'transference', whereby they fall in love with their therapist, the person to whom they entrust their most intimate thoughts and emotions. In such a situation it is difficult for a patient to assess properly whether it is in their interests to have a sexual relationship with their doctor. A more difficult, but no less real, situation arises when a teenager, succumbing to the weight of social pressure and the need to feel accepted by their peers, consents to engaging in sexual practices or potentially dangerous activities. Peer pressure can be extremely coercive, and the punishment for refusal to conform can leave lifelong scars.

All this suggests that the ethic of consent suffers from an assumption that the only circumstance that matters is the subjective consciousness of those involved at the time of the decision—the point at which 'consent' is given. The context in which the decision is made is immaterial, and subsequent feelings of regret are rendered irrelevant by the freedom associated with the initial decision. It is apparent that, in order to judge whether consent has been freely given, we need to consider both the consequences of the decision and the context in which it was made. In short, we need a theory of regret.

Consent can be defended as an ethical principle only if it is based on inner freedom. In place of the ethic of consent as commonly understood, I argue for an ethic of moral deliberation based on considered awareness rather than superficial awareness; that is, we need an ethic of clear-eyed reflection, so that each decision is guided by one's own considered will, by one's reason or lasting conviction, rather than by impulse or circumstance. Only by means of such reflection can consent be unsullied by self-deception, coercion or weakness of will and thus give expression to one's true intentions and long-term interests. There is no reason such an ethic should not give rise to almost as much diversity of opinion and behaviour as the conventional ethic of consent; in fact, it might give rise to even more diversity since the ethic of consent has in practice promoted a herd mentality in moral decision making.

TEN

Exercising inner freedom

INNER FREEDOM MIGHT BE imagined as a potentiality in each human that takes real form only when it is practised. The foremost capacity that allows us to exercise inner freedom is rational deliberation. Hayek refers to one's considered will or lasting conviction and says that, to assert this will, as opposed to the caprice of passion or desire, requires no more than sober reflection and the courage to see one's actions governed by the conviction formed by it. Of course, it is not reason alone that provides the bedrock: instead, it is a full awareness of our ethical standards and an understanding of what contributes to our welfare in the longer term. These allow us to avoid falling victim to short-term urges and others' manipulation of our desires.

The post-Kantian philosopher John Rawls discusses this process in some detail since it is essential to the plausibility of his celebrated theory of justice.[1] If one deliberates rationally one is led to adopt the plan that maximises the 'expected net balance of satisfaction' or to take the course most likely to realise one's most important aims:

> It is the plan that would be decided upon as the outcome of careful reflection in which the agent reviewed, in the light of all relevant facts, what it would be like to carry out these plans and thereby ascertained the course of action that would best realize his most fundamental desires.[2]

Deliberative rationality requires us to be 'under no misconceptions' as to what we really want, so that when we achieve our aims we do not decide we were mistaken and want something else. In other words, we are fully informed and have clear, unambiguous preferences. This assumes a degree of maturity, minimal intelligence and psychological stability on the part of the decision maker and is, of course, the rationality assumed to be exercised by *Homo economicus* in the neoclassical economics texts, including all the axioms and proofs that have so occupied them. The conflict between the behavioural norms of the economics texts and the evidence from the emerging field of experimental economics should alert us to some difficulties that could arise with Rawls' theory.

Rawls acknowledges that in practice we are rarely fully informed about the likely consequences of our actions but we do the best with the information that is readily available, so that the plan we then follow can be said to be 'subjectively rational'. Gathering information and deliberating involve effort, and the amount of effort to be expended on each decision is itself the subject of decision. In this rational mode we decide at some point that the possible benefit of more information and deliberation is less than the cost of the additional effort required. If we make the wrong decision and regret it under these conditions, it is not because we acted impulsively or with a cavalier attitude toward the facts: it is because we made a decision not to make the effort to gather more information. This is why we are harder on ourselves when things go wrong because we failed to think the situation through rather than for reasons that could not be foreseen.[3]

Although one can raise objections to this conception of deliberative rationality (objections that are canvassed later), something broadly along these lines can be considered one of the grounds for exercising inner freedom. I have, however, said enough to suggest that—far from being the norm some philosophers and economists imagine—this form of rational deliberation is a human capacity that increasingly must be protected from the seduction of impulsive gratification and the manipulation of our preferences.

The discussion thus far describes only a process of decision making; it says nothing about whether the outcomes of that process are desirable. To make the case that rational deliberation leads to the best outcome, neoclassical economists argue that rationality allows consumers to best satisfy their preferences subject to the constraint provided by their incomes. The preferences of consumers—and humans are characterised as either consumers or producers—are taken as given and sacrosanct. Whatever the consumer chooses is, ipso facto, good. Thus for consumers to maximise their utility it is enough that they be free and rational. This is not, however, adequate for the social democrat Rawls, who can readily see that the outcomes generated by the market, no matter how free, are rarely fair because the initial conditions—mainly the distribution of resources—are unjust. In order to separate the actual distribution of resources from consideration of a fair distribution of resources, Rawls wove what he called a 'veil of ignorance', a hypothetical barrier behind which we make decisions about a just society. This veil prevents us from knowing where we ourselves would be placed in society: we remain ignorant of our gender, ethnicity, social class, and so on, so that our judgments about fairness are unclouded by self-interest. For Rawls, the process of rational deliberation says nothing about the desirability of the content of the plans the rational person formulates. Indeed, 'it is not inconceivable that an individual . . . should achieve happiness moved entirely by spontaneous inclination'.[4] But the problem of how to judge this happiness remains.

At this point Rawls introduces a concept of the 'good'. According to the Aristotelian Principle, 'human beings enjoy the exercise of their realized capacities (their innate or trained abilities), and this enjoyment increases the more the capacity is realized, or the greater its complexity':

> Now accepting the Aristotelian Principle as a natural fact, it will generally be rational . . . to realize and train mature capacities . . . A rational plan . . . allows a person to flourish, so far as circumstances permit, and to exercise his realized abilities as much as he can.[5]

This is the good life described by Seligman—or eudaemonism in Aristotle's *Nicomachean Ethics*—although in Rawls' hands the Aristotelian Principle becomes a somewhat desiccated interpretation of Aristotle's idea. Combined with deliberative rationality, the principle allows Rawls to define a person's good as the successful execution of a rational plan of life: 'A person is happy then during those periods when he is successfully carrying through a rational plan and he is with reason confident that his efforts will come to fruition . . . [it is] the fulfilment of the whole design itself'.[6] If one does not develop and implement a rational plan one will not flourish. As a result, exercising our inner freedom (so far as it is done through deliberative rationality) is the necessary condition for human flourishing.

The problem with Rawls' theory of justice is its abstractness. For all its elegance and intellectual appeal, it cannot tell us what we most need to know: *How* can a society be made more just? To be sure, we can imagine a host of humans deliberating behind a veil of ignorance. Yet when they descend from the other world and assume their places in society, what will motivate them to pursue the form of social justice they were happy to agree to? Even the purest among us find intellectual constructs inadequate incentives when real positions must be taken. Yet in Rawls' world we are imagined to return to Earth imbued with the spirit of fraternity that informed our decisions behind the veil. Kantians feel uncomfortable with the heart, preferring always to remain in the head, but all the evidence suggests that an ethic that fails to accommodate both cannot succeed.

Despite these reservations about the limits of reason, there is no doubt that the exercise of reason is essential to the pursuit of inner freedom. It is essential to overcoming self-deception, although its powers fail when the problem is akrasia, or weakness of will.

It is curious that the dominant schools of philosophy and economics tend to define humans by their rationality when it is evident that the essential, and most interesting, characteristic of humans is that they so often deviate from the rational ideal. Indeed, although the capacity to reason might separate humans from animals, it is humans' failure to exercise that capacity that makes them intriguing. Shakespeare could not have written his plays if men and women behaved as the philosophers imagine. This is why psychology, the purpose of which is to understand why we behave the way we do, is so much more appealing to a lay person than philosophy and economics. Perhaps the philosophers, when working at their disciplines, are absorbed in the analytical mode and cannot imagine any other. The economists are guilty of the same failing—but with much more serious consequences. Marketing and modern consumer capitalism owe their existence to people's persistent refusal to mirror the behaviour of rational economic man. It is not our reason the marketers appeal to: it is our weaknesses, prejudices, vanities and neuroses. Free-market economics, which finds its rationale in the form of rational economic man, survives and prospers only because this type of human does not in practice prevail.

These considerations lead to a further observation about the role of rational deliberation. Until now the assumption has been that the person doing the deliberating is of sound mind. The schizophrenic might exercise their rationality but do so on the basis of such a bizarre set of data about the world that the conclusions they draw will be seen as wholly irrational. At a less extreme level, a person suffering from an everyday neurosis, such as an obsession with shoes or an unjustified dislike of a neighbour, might act on decisions that meet all the axioms of rationality, yet they cannot be said to be exercising inner freedom.

Someone who is 'normally neurotic' might well be guided by his own considered will and, respecting Rawls' injunction, follow 'the plan that would be decided upon as the outcome of careful reflection', a plan that 'best realizes his most fundamental desires', although it could incorporate emotions that are long-lasting but 'irrational'. If the person has a shoe fetish, for example, he might hatch a careful plan to steal shoes from a shop. Or a person might refuse to accept a free ticket to visit a dear friend on the other side of the world because she knows this friend lives at the top of a tower block and her claustrophobia prevents her from taking lifts. Once again, if these are isolated incidents that affect only a minority of the population they ought not disturb the notion of inner freedom that has been developed to this point. But if we live in a society where such occurrences are common, and where society by its nature undermines the exercise of cool deliberation in some or all areas of life, then on these grounds alone it can be said that our inner freedom is jeopardised.

ELEVEN
Subtle coercion

THE ARGUMENT THUS FAR is that the absence of inner freedom is something we bring upon ourselves. Sometimes, however, we forgo our inner freedom in response to external pressures, to the point where it could be said we were coerced or deceived into relinquishing it. The enemies of inner freedom are impulsiveness, self-deception and moral weakness, but there are forces working to exploit these breaches. For the individual, the responses to impulsiveness and moral weakness are the application of reason and resolve, which can be used to reclaim our inner freedom. Yet we must also take collective measures to restrain those who would coerce or deceive us.

Hayek notes that his definition of freedom as the absence of coercion begs the troublesome question of how to define coercion. Most simply, he suggests, 'Coercion occurs when one man's actions are made to serve another man's will, not for his own but for the other's purpose'.[1] We are familiar with the role of coercion in denying citizens their civil liberties and refusing people the opportunity to participate in the institutions of democracy. In recent decades libertarians have directed their attacks at what they see as forms of coercion that prevent individuals from pursuing their economic interests—for example, 'onerous' taxes, restrictions on how private property can be used, and limits on trade in certain goods. But there is another, subtler, type of coercion that has received much less attention, and it lies at the heart of modern society. This coercion takes the form of unreasonable attempts to influence people to act in ways that are contrary to their considered interests.

The market itself has in recent times evolved into an instrument of subtle coercion. Examples can also be drawn from quasi-market activity, such as religious organisations that use a 'personality test' as a device for drawing vulnerable people into their webs. This is an attempt to deprive us of our inner freedom, to induce us by deception to act on impulse or from our weaknesses, even though we might take the test willingly. Modern marketing methods and the recruitment techniques used by cults represent others' efforts to pursue their own interests through exploiting our fears and vulnerabilities and so influencing our behaviour. In fact, some of the more blatant methods of doing this have been outlawed or are at least discouraged by injunctions contained in the advertisers' 'code of ethics'; an example is the ban on subliminal advertising.

Hayek acknowledges these difficulties and develops the notion of an 'assured free sphere' where we can be protected from such coercion: 'Since coercion is the control of the essential data of an individual's action by another, it can be prevented only by enabling the individual to secure for himself some private sphere where he is protected against such interference'.[2] This private sphere is one in which an individual can weigh up the consequences of their actions, being confident that the facts on which they make an assessment are not 'shaped by another'. An individual's 'rights' depend on recognition of this private sphere, which, understood in physical terms, is most nearly co-extensive with the home:

> ... the recognition of a protected individual sphere has in times of freedom normally included a right to privacy and secrecy, the conception that a man's house is his castle and that nobody has a right even to take cognizance of his activities within it.[3]

Of course, Hayek wrote before the age of television, telemarketing and the internet and before the introduction of the highly inventive methods marketers, political parties and others use to penetrate the home. As was observed more than a decade ago, 'the lounge room has become a marketing free-fire zone'.[4] But Hayek is cagey when it comes to the nature of the assured free sphere: is it the private home, the whole set of private goods or the various rights to private property? John Stuart Mill was more explicit when defining a similar notion, which he called 'the appropriate region of human liberty'.[5] The notion has three aspects, or domains. Two are the external ones associated with individual and political liberties—freedom of tastes and pursuits and freedom to plan and live out one's life as one sees fit as long as it does not harm others.[6] The third aspect—freedom to combine for any purpose other than one involving harm to others—corresponds in some respects to the 'assured free sphere'; Mill calls it the 'inward domain of consciousness', in which there should be liberty of thought, conscience and opinion.

Although his comments in this regard constitute only a minor digression in his tome, Hayek comes very close to adopting the position taken in this discussion when he declares that, in addition to violence in all its forms, fraud and deception are kinds of harmful action that ought to be prevented, even though it would be 'straining the meaning of words' to call them coercion. 'Deception, like coercion, is a form of manipulating the data on which a person counts, in order to make him do what the deceiver wants him to do.'[7] The deceived becomes the unwitting tool of the deceiver: 'all we said of coercion applies equally to fraud and deception'. Thus:

> . . . freedom demands no more than that coercion and violence, fraud and deception, be prevented, except for the use of coercion by government for the sole purpose of enforcing known rules intended to secure the best conditions under which the individual may give his activities a coherent, rational pattern.[8]

From his 1950s' viewpoint, Hayek could not have imagined the extent to which the neoliberal revolution he spawned would lead to the emergence of societies where fraud and deception are endemic to the reproduction of the system—where pre-teen children without incomes are targeted by corporations in an attempt to build lifelong brand loyalty; where teenagers declare that the brands they wear and otherwise consume determine 'who they are'; where both popular and classical culture are systematically mined for icons and images that can be used to sell products; where the intimate details of our personal lives are secretly collected and sold to marketing organisations; where sporting, artistic, literary and educational institutions have become the playing fields of advertisers; and where the essential data of our actions are provided overwhelmingly by a handful of media corporations.

FREEDOM RECONSIDERED

Hayek would be shocked to discover that his assured free sphere is no longer protected but has itself become the domain of the most powerful form of coercion, the psychological techniques of modern marketing. Even the neurochemical functioning of our brains (the mechanics of our thought processes)—perhaps the most private aspect of each of us—is being mapped by marketers so that they might manipulate our responses for commercial benefit.

In Hayek's innocent era the threats to freedom were seen to be posed by big government and the monopoly tendencies of big business. The response to businesses' accumulation of excessive power in the marketplace was to make laws to prevent the creation of monopolies. Antitrust laws became central to the neoliberal project; this explains why neoliberals who cleave firmly to their principles will at times surprise their critics by turning on big business. Today, however, we see that these laws have done nothing to restrict the influence of corporate values on society and the dominance of marketing ideology, not to mention the symbiosis between corporate interests and the structure of the political process. Democracy has been superseded by a form of executive government increasingly remote from popular influence, and 'free speech' is increasingly the prerogative of paid lobbyists. In capital cities, the nerve centres of government decision making are literally encircled by organisations whose purpose is to promote the interests of corporations. Yet we are told that power today lies in the marketplace and that consumer choice is the ultimate determinant of the social good. We can read the power of consumers from the bottom line, they tell us. In this way democracy itself is undermined by the refusal to consider the nature of power and the assertion that ultimate power lies in the hands of the consumer.

Hilaire Belloc wrote, 'The control of the production of wealth is the control of life itself'.[9] Revolutionary socialists and supporters of laissez-faire capitalism concurred, and competing political philosophies have been divided on the question of how the means of production can best be used for the social good. But in affluent countries it is no longer true that control of production implies control of life itself: now it is much more accurate to say that control of the process of consumption is control of life itself, since it is above all through consumption that people in rich countries define themselves. Control of production once meant control of our capacity to reproduce ourselves physically, whereas today control of consumption means control over our capacity to reproduce ourselves socially and psychologically. It is for this reason that in modern corporations the marketing departments are paramount, and companies are increasingly divesting themselves of the messy task of actually making physical objects, preferring to contract that out to factories in developing countries and leave themselves to concentrate on the creation of abstract value invested in images, styles and brands.

TWELVE
The decline of free will

WE ALL KNOW THAT sudden wealth and lack of self-control make for a hazardous combination. This is why some governments insist that a million dollars won in a lottery is best paid out in instalments over several years. There is, nevertheless, a general assumption that greater affluence is associated with a greater ability to exercise control over our lives. If higher incomes provide more potential choices in life, self-control is needed in order to maximise the benefits of that choice. Indeed, although it is little remarked on, the assumption of greater self-control is essential for people who argue that more choice means greater wellbeing. The child in the sweetshop with $10 in her pocket has a plethora of options, yet few parents would agree that it is in their child's interests to daily have so much choice. Most would accept that the benefits of choice are to be had when the chooser is able to exercise self-control. From this perspective, greater choice is a boon to our wellbeing only when combined with a decline in impulsiveness. But has the increase in consumer choice in affluent countries been accompanied by increased self-control?

Anecdotal evidence suggests that the answer could be 'no', although the question needs further exploration.

Previous sociological work has suggested that rising incomes are linked to greater self-control, but economic historian Avner Offer argues that personal self-control has declined with affluence. He maintains that self-control strategies take time to develop and involve costs that the wealthy can better afford—which helps to explain why poor people in rich countries are more prone to obesity.[1] The evidence suggests that the increase in affluence since the Second World War has outpaced the development of greater prudence, so that self-control has been in decline. Falling rates of national saving and rising levels of consumer debt in the 1990s can be explained by this. It turns out, though, that the increase in consumer debt has occurred mainly among middle-class and wealthy households, for the purposes of funding increasingly extravagant lifestyles.[2]

Perhaps more insight can be gained from the large body of psychological literature exploring the idea of the 'locus of control', which has for decades been one of the most commonly measured personality traits. People with an internal locus of control believe they themselves are responsible for the course of their lives; people with an external locus of control believe outside forces are dominant and, as a result, adopt a more fatalistic approach to life. On the face of it, the rise of individualism and the falling away of the social constraints imposed by class, gender, race, and so on, should have engendered a much stronger internal locus of control in the populations of rich countries. After all, we are constantly told—not least by advertisers and politicians—that the course of our lives is a matter of personal choice. The evidence shows, however, the opposite to be the case. Compared with the 1960s, young Americans today are substantially more likely to believe outside forces control their lives.[3] This perceived loss of control over our lives is associated with weakened self-control and an inability to delay gratification. Even more remarkably, the same studies show that, despite the decline in patriarchal attitudes and institutions and the huge expansion of opportunities for women, the increase in 'externality' is greater in young women than in young men.

Zygmunt Bauman casts further light on the spread of impulsiveness and the decline in self-control in his analysis of the modern individualised 'risk society', where insecurity and contingency have intruded into daily life, even though affluence prevails. He concludes:

> In the absence of long-term security, 'instant gratification' looks enticingly like a reasonable strategy ... The objects of desire are better enjoyed on the spot and then disposed of; markets see to it that they are made in such a way that both the gratification and the obsoleteness are instant.[4]

The very openness of modern life—the demand for independence that has left us with the freedom and the obligation to 'author' our own lives—entails forms of risk to which we were previously immune. For if we must take responsibility for our own lives we are confronted daily with the possibility that we will take the wrong path: what was once in the hands of the gods, the landlord and the boss is now a personal gamble. More choice is accompanied by more stress about making mistakes and ending up a 'loser'; more money means more anxiety about our wealth; more personal freedom imparts more insecurity in our relationships; and our longer life spans still do not afford enough time to achieve all the goals we set for ourselves. The spectre of personal failure haunts us at every turn.

In the risk society impulsiveness is a response that arises not so much from the unpredictability of policy and economic structure; rather, it arises from the entrenchment of individualism and the associated idea that gratification of one's own needs should come before all else. Of course, the marketing industry daily sends us subliminal messages in support of this attitude—that happiness is to be had by buying this product or that (in other words, through a series of momentary pleasures) and that the good life itself is nothing more than a series of hedonic episodes. Likening relationships to consumer durables, Bauman observes:

> ... if the pleasure derived is not up to the standard promised and expected, or if the novelty wears off together with the joy, there is no reason to stick to the inferior or aged product rather than find another, 'new and improved', in the shop.[5]

These are the preoccupations of people who inhabit free but individualised societies. The marketers daily reinforce the promise of instant gratification and stimulate a generalised impulsiveness that works against rational deliberation. The result is that we find it increasingly difficult to recognise and exercise our inner freedom. The marketers' messages have penetrated some of the deepest recesses of our individuality and must be counted, like brainwashing, as a form of coercion. It is virtually impossible today to defend ourselves against the invasion of our private spheres by commercial messages and marketing culture.[6]

Deception is essential to modern marketing. It is not true that a particular brand of margarine will impart a happy family life or that a sports car will deliver sexual allure. Yet the purpose of advertising is to convince us that these things *are* true. Supporters of the market who might suggest that this is just harmless fun and that consumers know to apply a degree of scepticism need to explain why year after year billions of dollars are committed to such a futile activity and why such a large proportion of the world's creative talent is employed by marketing agencies. Advertising and marketing have colonised virtually all public and private spaces. They are impossible to avoid. Schools, universities, hospitals, sporting venues, public and private buildings, landmarks, public transport and skylines are sites for the promotion of products. As a result, the production and consumption of culture have become imbued with commercial values and marketing messages. Brands have become the most powerful means of forming and spreading culture.

In view of all this, it is amusing that Hayek, arch-defender of the free market, wrote that if he were to choose the name of his political party he would choose 'a word which describes the party of life, the party that favours free growth and spontaneous evolution'. This is exactly what I favour, a party that would put human flourishing before consumption, personal fulfilment before economic growth, and authentic human values before a collection of brands. It was Hayek's error to wish that the opposite of socialism—the least restrictive form of free-market capitalism—would give us free growth and spontaneous evolution.[7] What flourished was not the human spirit but the political power of capital and the culture of consumption, forces that have diverted, even corrupted, the urge to spontaneous evolution and turned it into an increasingly crass materialism, a sort of market totalitarianism.

For Hayek, a person's freedom hinged on 'whether he can expect to shape his course of action in accordance with his present intentions, or whether somebody else can so manipulate the conditions as to make him act according to that person's will rather than his own'.[8] Is this not the point we have reached, where in every decision the 'essential data' of our lives have been created or manipulated by the marketers, so that our will is bent to another's purpose? It is a great irony that in a society created to give us more 'choice' the most important choices are forbidden. For individuals, any attempt to withdraw from the market is met with disapprobation and, indeed, accusations of craziness. For citizens, opting for a different sort of society has been declared impossible since, as Fukuyama said, it is not feasible even to conceive of a society that could come after liberal capitalism. History has come to an end; our future is no longer a matter of choice but an iron necessity. The existentialists argued that the essence of human freedom is being able to imagine ourselves to be something other than we are. Like his mentor Hegel, Fukuyama has submerged individual consciousness into the 'grand unity of an ideal mind', except that today the ideal mind takes a form Hegel could not have foreseen—The Market.

THIRTEEN

From political philosophy to metaphysics

I BEGAN THIS BOOK with the observation that, despite all the freedoms they now enjoy, the citizens of rich countries do not seem to be the contented, creative, flourishing individuals imagined by the classical political liberals, the free-market libertarians, and the leaders of the liberation movements of the 1960s and 1970s. The space created by the freedoms gained has been filled by a different form of coercion, one that deprives people of a hitherto neglected form of liberty—inner freedom.

Yet the argument I set out is, in a way, a prologue only. At various stages some of the most tantalising questions are left unanswered and, in some cases, not even properly posed.

The first difficulty concerns the notion of inner freedom, which must have its basis in something more solid than a particular conception of psychological functioning. I have suggested that inner freedom is the prerogative of individuals who have sufficient command of their own reason and moral strength to give them a degree of autonomy in the face of social forces that conspire to deprive them of that autonomy.

To a point, this is a useful way of understanding the phenomenon, but it tells us nothing about the grounds for inner freedom itself, only that, whatever it is, this freedom is vulnerable to erosion as a result of self-deception, moral weakness and subtle coercion.

This suggests a more challenging task. We need to understand the relationship between the nature of inner freedom and the nature of human wellbeing. Can we simply say that greater inner freedom means greater happiness, or does the notion of inner freedom suggest something about the nature of happiness and, in fact, the purpose of life?

The second problem we are left with concerns understanding rationality's contribution to inner freedom. I have said enough to cast doubt on the Kantian view that virtue is to be found in the categories of reason. We might further appeal to Mill's verdict that, for all the achievements of Kant's philosophy, his (Kant's) theory of morality 'fails, almost grotesquely, to show that there would be any contradiction . . . in the adoption by all rational beings of the most outrageously immoral rules of conduct'.[1] The Kantian opinion was expressed more crudely by another product of the Enlightenment, Carl von Clausewitz, when he said, 'Savage peoples are ruled by passion, civilized peoples by the mind',[2] which we might counter with Schopenhauer at his pithy best: 'Reasonable and vicious are quite consistent with each other; in fact, only through their union are great and far-reaching crimes possible'.[3] Since reason can be put to ends good or evil, what are the limits to rational deliberation for achieving inner freedom, and what else must be cultivated if we are to achieve happiness?

This leads directly to the third problem. Although akrasia, or weakness of will, is the enemy of inner freedom, I say

FREEDOM RECONSIDERED

nothing about the moral standards that can be betrayed by that weakness. Must we simply accept that one owes loyalty to a set of moral principles, or is there something more essential to a moral code, loyalty to which is needed in order to attain inner freedom? If we adopt the latter view, what is the basis of this moral sense?

To find the answers to these questions we must go to metaphysics or, more accurately, to a particular metaphysics that has its origin with Kant.

PART TWO
Philosophical foundations

> *There is no greater intellectual crime than to address with the equipment of an older period the challenges of the present one.*
>
> Bruno Latour

FOURTEEN

The need for metaphysics

IN ADDITION TO INDIVIDUAL and political liberties, there is a neglected third form of liberty—inner freedom—and it is the erosion of this freedom that explains the widespread unhappiness and alienation that characterise societies that are otherwise free and wealthy. Moreover, far from being an unfortunate parallel development, the erosion of inner freedom is associated with the social transformations that have given us such unprecedented wealth and privilege. Although the case presented in Part One for the existence, and parlous state, of inner freedom may seem plausible, its plausibility rests on shaky ground. There are some psychological and political reasons for the absence of inner freedom, but if we take away self-deception, akrasia and subtle coercion by external forces are we left with any basis for asserting the existence of inner freedom? In other words, if we are able to exercise sufficient reason and self-control what is it that we experience as inner freedom?

Establishing the grounds for inner freedom—that is, its metaphysical basis—is necessary not least because there is an implicit assumption in the foregoing discussion that, if we took away or neutralised the forces that deprive us of this metaphysical liberty, we would be able to live more balanced, contented and meaningful lives. This assumption, which is a strong one, must be supported if it is to be taken seriously, since it raises a question we have so far avoided: What is happiness? In Part One, I draw the distinction between the pleasant life, the good life and the meaningful life, but I do little other than make a few observations on the characteristics of each, avoiding any exploration of the roots of the differences between them. Once we have established a deeper foundation for human wellbeing the question can be answered more fully, but that task is left for Part Five of this book.

Knowing what the grounds for inner freedom are will provide the basis for answering some other nagging questions. Although rational deliberation is necessary for attaining inner freedom, the curative powers of rational deliberation—including those claimed by Mill, Kant and Rawls—have been exaggerated. Rationality can be an antidote to self-deception, but it can be put to both good and evil purposes. It might save a person from acting impulsively, but that might only make them more effective at bringing to fruition their malevolent intent. As Plato observed, the power of understanding is beneficial or harmful depending on its 'orientation': 'the petty minds of those who are acknowledged to be bad, but clever, are sharp-eyed and perceptive enough to gain insights into matters they direct their attention towards'.[1] What are we to make of paragons of rationality such as Machiavelli or the Nazi doctor? On the other hand, why is Cervantes' clownish Don Quixote held in such affection? And why do judges give lesser sentences to criminals who show genuine remorse? In other words, rationality can be a device for achieving our own selfish ends and, with due deference to Kant, has only a limited influence on how we determine those ends. To explain inner freedom, we must be capable of arguing that an evil action damages not only the wellbeing of the victim but also the interests of the perpetrator. Yet the reasons for believing that committing morally wrong acts is contrary to the perpetrator's interests are by no means obvious. Nor, even when it is put to noble ends, should we rest content in the belief—so dear to some economists and philosophers—that rationality is the highest good. We need to find a place in our scheme for the life-affirming qualities of intuition, spontaneity and aesthetics.

This suggests that what we lack is a moral framework for our rational considerations—a notion of the Good that can provide the basis for judging the value of our actions. I have thus set the formidable tasks of providing the metaphysical basis of inner freedom, understanding the limits of rationality in the pursuit of inner freedom, and locating the place and nature of morality in the same grounds.

For this I turn to metaphysics, the most general sphere of philosophical deliberation. Most people today see metaphysics as alien, difficult and, because of the possible religious connotations, cranky. At its most general, it is the study of the nature of reality, including the ideas of existence, causality and non-physical entities. Metaphysical investigations naturally involve both epistemological questions (those concerning types of knowledge and their validity) and ontological questions (those that bear on the nature and experience of being). In some philosophical systems metaphysics also extends to the realm of understanding that is 'beyond' human experience—an idea that can be interpreted in two ways. It can mean

PHILOSOPHICAL FOUNDATIONS

understanding or knowledge that is of a different, or higher, order compared with everyday experience. Or it can refer to knowledge of the conditions that precede everyday experience and that make everyday experience possible, such as the exploration of the pure ideas of space and causality.

In this part of the book I develop a philosophical basis for inner freedom, drawing particularly on the work of Kant and Schopenhauer—in other words, in the tradition of what is known as German idealism. Immanuel Kant (1724–1804) was the towering figure of Enlightenment philosophy, turning the world on its head with his 'Copernican revolution'. Although many philosophers today define themselves as Kantian in some sense, few of them accept the notion of 'transcendental idealism', which forms the core metaphysics of his philosophy. Arthur Schopenhauer (1788–1860) saw his own work as developing and amending Kant's revolutionary system of thought. Despite being celebrated for a time in the middle of the nineteenth century, Schopenhauer has had an influence much less enduring than Kant among professional philosophers.

Modern 'analytical' philosophy's preoccupation with asserting the authority of rationality explains both the attention given to Kant's rationalist ethics and the reluctance to accept the transcendental aspect of his idealism. The atheist Schopenhauer, on the other hand, took the transcendental aspect of Kant one crucial step further: he recognised the limits of rationality and as a result had a more sophisticated understanding of human psychology, something that allowed him to put forward a much more persuasive moral theory. But we are jumping ahead of ourselves.

These days the word 'transcendent' is generally taken to refer to personal experiences that go beyond the mundane to a level of reality sometimes associated with mysticism. Rejecting this, Kant used the term to refer to that which is 'beyond all possible experience'[2]; by this he wanted to describe concepts that relate purely to our faculty of cognition, concepts of reason that 'exceed any given experience and become transcendent'.[3] These concepts—those of space and time, for example—stand above experience, or the world of the senses, without the need for mediation from experience.[4]

Schopenhauer, too, insisted that his philosophical method be one of rigorous application of reason, but he did not insist that everything be framed in terms of rationality. For him, metaphysics pertains to a world that is 'hidden behind nature, and renders nature possible'.[5] He drew a distinction between two different types of metaphysics—the philosophical and the religious, 'distinguished by the fact that one has its verification and credentials *in itself*, the other *outside itself*'.[6] The first investigates and aims for a truth that conforms to the rules of logic and evidence; the second relies on faith, and the truth it upholds is an allegorical truth in which mystery is an essential ingredient. In this sense, religion does not lend itself to disproof.

What follows in sections 15 to 18 is the most difficult part of the argument in this book. Apart from the fact that some of the ideas might be hard to grasp (although some readers will find them intuitively obvious), Kant and, to a lesser extent, Schopenhauer have been the subject of widely differing interpretations and frequent misunderstanding. Indeed, many philosophers have devoted their professional lives to interpreting their works, to uncovering 'what Kant really meant'. Schopenhauer interpreted Kant in a particular way, one that influences my thinking. So my explanation of some Kantian ideas is filtered through Schopenhauerian eyes, and

PHILOSOPHICAL FOUNDATIONS

I use Kant to enrich and illustrate my view rather than to faithfully represent his. Where I depart from Schopenhauer I try to make this clear.

Contentious philosophical debates underpin much of the discussion that follows. I exclude or skate over most of the controversies if pausing to review them would interrupt the flow of my argument. For readers interested in the contentious questions, I try to deal with, or at least acknowledge, them in the notes.

At various points in the discussion to come I digress to comment on some religious implications of the argument. These digressions are provided for two reasons: they are intrinsically interesting, and some readers might interpret my argument in terms of their own religious orientation. The argument is intended, however, to be understood wholly in philosophical terms and will be, I hope, as accessible to the atheist or agnostic as to the believer. It might be impenetrable, though, to people who are reluctant to step outside the world of scientific rationality and who therefore reject anything beyond that particular frame.

The sections that follow are devoted to establishing the following propositions.

Starting from consciousness immediately creates the distinction between subject and object—the knower and the known.

The world as we know it is a world of appearances or representations and is always mediated by our sensory and intellectual capacities as knowing subjects.

Our capacity to understand the outside world depends on particular conditions of sensibility we bring to the world, including the categories of space, time and causality. At this level of abstraction, instead of our knowledge conforming to the world as it is, the world conforms to the categories of knowledge we bring to it.

The everyday world of appearances can be contrasted with the 'thing-in-itself', which transcends consciousness and 'lies behind' the everyday world of knowledge. I thus distinguish between the phenomenal world of things as they appear to us and the noumenal world of the thing-in-itself, sometimes known as the 'subtle essence' in Eastern philosophy.

This sets up the fundamental distinction between phenomenon and noumenon. The phenomenon is characterised by differentiation and change; the noumenon is characterised by unity and changelessness.

There is a different form of knowledge—a 'non-sensible intuition'—that transcends the subject–object distinction and allows us to 'know' something of the noumenon or subtle essence.

The framework thus developed is then used to form a conception of the self that goes beyond the everyday one, to comment on the question of the existence of a deity and to consider death and its meaning. In Part Three the philosophical foundations developed here are used to create a theory of ethics.

FIFTEEN

Consciousness and the subject

THE STARTING POINT FOR philosophy can be nothing other than consciousness—a being's ability to be aware of the world. Everything we know must be mediated by consciousness; as Schopenhauer wrote, '*Consciousness* alone is immediately given'.[1] Consciousness is the receptacle in which all knowledge lies; nothing can be known outside it. This is true of both the intuitive knowledge that arises from our senses (the sky is blue, the sand is hot) and the abstract or discursive knowledge we construct from concepts (Pythagoras' theorem, the idea of democracy). Consciousness is the precondition of all knowledge, and before its emergence there was no knowledge.[2] Although this first step might seem obvious, it has far-reaching implications.

When consciousness is awareness of something it must reside in a subject, the knower. So the idea that we must begin with consciousness immediately creates the distinction between subject and object, the knower and the known, a distinction that lies at the heart of all that follows here. A subject comes into existence only when consciousness has an object. This presupposes a fundamental division—between the subject (the possessor of consciousness) and the object (that to which consciousness pertains). The object is not that to which consciousness can *potentially* apply: only through application of consciousness does the object become an object. Thus consciousness presupposes the subject–object distinction; indeed, the emergence of consciousness creates the division between subject and object. (Later I consider the possibility of 'pure consciousness', or contentless consciousness, in which the distinction between subject and object disappears.)

The world can be known only through our sensory capacities and the intellectual processes built on them or that condition them. Even our own selves are known to us only through our representations of them, so that we are both object and subject to ourselves. (I modify this in a crucial way later.) Thus, if one person says a tree's leaves are green but another is colour-blind and says they are red, this confirms that the greenness of the leaves is established only by our capacity to perceive it through our senses. A person with synesthesia has neural pathways that send signals picked up by one sense to a region of the brain that processes another sense. They might smell sounds or associate numbers with particular colours, which suggests a certain arbitrariness about what we normally think of as the 'real world'. Schopenhauer observed that what we see and comprehend is nothing but a '*phenomenon of the brain*, and is encumbered by so many great and different *subjective* conditions that its supposed absolute reality vanishes'.[3] As soon as this proposition is put forward it becomes apparent that, in Schopenhauer's words, 'the world is my representation'— that all we can know is the ideal or ideational form of the world inside our own heads. Only our own consciousness is known directly, unmediated; everything else must be mediated by consciousness:

> Therefore no truth is more certain, more independent of all others, and less in need of proof than this, namely that everything that exists for knowledge, and hence the whole of this world, is only object in relation to the subject, perception of the perceiver, in a word, representation.[4]

The implication of this is that the object, and thus the entire 'outside' world, cannot be conceived without the subject; in fact, the word 'conceived' presupposes a conceiver. As a result, contrary to the position of realist philosophers—who regard the objects as 'given in themselves', for whom objects of the senses exist in themselves even apart from sense—no 'real world' can be known independent of the knowing subject. The realist view, shared, it must be said, by commonsense understanding, begins from the assumption that what we know is not mediated by a knowing consciousness. It confuses our perceptions of things with the things themselves and thus asserts the existence of objects without subjects.

I am not saying the only things that exist are appearances: such a view would attribute to 'outside reality' the quality of our inner sense. What I am saying is that all we can *know* about outside reality is what our consciousness allows us to know. If there is a reality beyond our capacity to perceive it, it must be a 'transcendental' one—beyond our everyday consciousness. Thus we cannot know things directly; we can know them only by way of our senses and cognition. And, since we can have sensations only within our selves, the existence of objects outside of us cannot be experienced or captured by concepts. To assume otherwise is to attribute to outside objects all the properties and characteristics that are really part of our sensory or cognitive perception.

In the realist view, everything we know about the outside world we must acquire from the outside world itself, so that we begin as a blank slate, and each human must learn everything anew, including the most fundamental framework of perception and understanding—the notions of space, time and causality. Kant's shattering insight was that human cognition is possible only because of certain 'conditions of sensibility' that are given *prior* to perception itself and on which perception and cognition are based. This ability to order the world as we see it means we are not mere receptors of information but impose a structure of understanding on the world around us.

The idealist way of understanding the world seems to conflict with commonsense, which has the world existing independently and objectively and humans being simply incidental observers who watch, analyse and transform it. When I die the world will continue to be just as it was but with one less human, and if all humans were to die the world would remain the same objective reality but with one less species. This is the essential position of philosophical 'realism': nothing could be more obvious than the independent existence of the world. Commonsense realism assumes there is only one real world—the one 'out there'—and that it is projected onto a kind of screen in our heads. Each of us is just a part of the real world and can be excised without affecting the rest, except that there is one less screen onto which the real world can be projected.

There is, however, a contradiction in this: we can *imagine* a world existing without humans to be conscious of it, but that imagining is itself an act of consciousness—one that presupposes the subject in order to prove the independent existence of the object.[5] The realist view is constructed in the mind of humans; it is a product of consciousness. The world without subject can exist only for a subject, and the realists have therefore proved the opposite of what they intended. The commonsense way of understanding the world is referred to in Eastern philosophy as 'dualism': it does not recognise that the object and subject condition each other. Commonsense realism is comfortable with the idea of splitting the two worlds—the world 'out there' can exist without the world 'in here'—and baulks at the Kantian insight that one cannot exist without the other.

Thus, for the idealist, consciousness creates the world. Schopenhauer conjures up the metaphor of the 'first eye' opening on an unknowable world: 'For such an eye necessarily brings about knowledge, for which and in which alone the whole world is, and without which it is not even conceivable'.[6] The most challenging, and, it turns out, important, objection to the idealist view that the world is one of mere appearances is the observation that the consciousness that perceives the world is located in a body and because of this fact we can be certain we exist, even if no one else perceives us. In other words, we might be no more than 'appearances' for others, but we are the object of our own subject. Our own self-perception is the one thing we can be certain of; hence Descartes' 'I think, therefore I am'. The same argument applies to each person—indeed, each conscious thing.[7] But here again we are confusing, or eliding, subject and object because we can know ourselves only through our consciousness. It is the subject who says 'I know I really exist', the subject who says 'I think', and the body we are referring to is the object, the object of representations. Every perception of my self is mediated by my brain, my senses, my consciousness. Even the pain I feel, which seems to remind me more acutely than anything else of my material existence, is felt through the brain or the senses:

> In no way . . . are there given to me directly, in some general feeling of the body or in inner self-consciousness, an extension, shape, and activity that would coincide with my inner being itself . . . It follows from this that the existence of my person or of my body *as an extended and acting thing* always presupposes a *knowing being* different from it . . .[8]

In section 17 I argue that the world of appearances is the world of time and space. Transcendental idealism allows us to put boundaries on our knowledge by recognising time and space as categories or forms that we impose on the world. This was Kant's revolutionary insight, and it follows that answers to the ultimate questions cannot be found in the world of appearances. There can never be a theory of everything. As Schopenhauer wrote of Kant, 'He showed that the laws which rule with inviolable necessity in existence . . . are not to be applied to deduce and explain *existence itself*'.[9]

In sum, we are incapable of knowing anything beyond the boundaries of our consciousness—that is, beyond the possibilities afforded by our senses and our various forms of cognition. The oft-levelled criticism that for idealists everything is just an illusion comes only from those who imagine themselves stepping outside their own consciousness and, as a third party, positing the separate existence of a 'real world' and a human consciousness affected by it. Of course, this can be done only from within a human consciousness, so that idealism's critics are themselves creating an illusion, the third party, that they imagine to be real. This third party has a 'god's-eye view' of the world; Kant's insight was to make the world human-centred.

SIXTEEN

Phenomenon and noumenon

THE THING-IN-ITSELF

The world as we know it is one of appearances. We do not know it as it really is; we know it only as it is represented in our consciousness, and this must be the starting point for any philosophising. Struck by the unreliability of the senses, Descartes doubted the existence of everything but resolved that, since he was contemplating the world, the act of thinking is the one thing he could be certain of and from that the rest could be deduced. This insight was similar to that of Schopenhauer, who insisted that only our own consciousness is known immediately: everything else is mediated through our consciousness and is therefore dependent on it.

But can reality be nothing more than our representations of it? Is it possible that nothing exists as such? Kant argued that if the world is one of appearances there must be something that appears, 'an object independent of sensibility'. He referred to this as the 'thing considered as it is in itself', or the 'thing-in-itself' for short.[1] The thing-in-itself must be neither object nor subject. And if it transcends the distinction between subject and object it must transcend consciousness and the knowledge that attends consciousness.

If this is so, in addition to being an object of consciousness, everything is also a thing-in-itself. This 'existence in itself' stands outside the subject– object relationship and has a metaphysical existence that has its being in an unknowable world beyond consciousness; it is a 'metaphysical being'.[2] We can know nothing about it because all we know are appearances, and those appearances are structured by our given forms of understanding.

At this stage of the argument it seems reasonable to imagine that the world exists twice—once as an 'objective fact' independent of us and once in our representations as a set of images projected onto some sort of screen in our head. As the argument develops, though, it will become apparent that there is just one world but there are two distinct ways of apprehending it.

The main argument for the existence of the thing-in-itself is that without it we are left with a view of the world as nothing more than the illusion created by human consciousness. Although we know everything we know through our consciousness—including our senses and our cognition—this is not to say there is nothing we cannot know. Our awareness has limits. It is this that allows for the possibility of things existing beyond their appearances, as the thing-in-itself. We can *think* about the world 'beyond' the world of appearances, but that does not mean we know it. To use a theistic analogy, the idea of God can never *be* God.

The approach of transcendental idealism—which considers the problem of reality not from the starting point of object or subject but through the inseparability of the two—differs

PHILOSOPHICAL FOUNDATIONS

from other philosophical approaches, including the common-sense realist one. (I labour this point because appreciating it is central to the argument of this book.) Most philosophical approaches, at least in the Western tradition, recognise only the subject or the object. In particular, realists (or 'materialists') recognised only the object, and the idealists who preceded Kant recognised only the subject. Realists take matter as having absolute existence, independent of consciousness, but they are then confronted with the problem of perception: if I see an object as green but my colour-blind friend sees it as red we are compelled to admit we cannot do without the perceiving subject. As Schopenhauer wrote, 'For "No object without subject" is the principle that renders all materialism for ever impossible'.[3]

Realism, which coincides with the working assumption of everyday life, is therefore based on nothing more than a supposition—the absolute existence of the world beyond our senses—since we can never test the supposition by stepping outside ourselves to see whether it is true. Such a world is not conceivable. Thus, despite its intuitive obviousness, realism is 'the philosophy of the subject who forgets to take account of himself'.[4]

Transcendental idealism has been called 'a doctrine of epistemological modesty': it recognises the limits of our knowledge 'since it denies finite cognizors like us any purchase on the God's-eye view of things'.[5] This might seem odd at first, but on reflection we see that realism imagines there is a world outside us which is then mirrored by a world within us that represents the 'objective' world. In this view we imagine, if only by implication, an all-seeing God above who observes his creation, a God who exists independently of our consciousness. This is implicitly a theocentric model, and

Kant's revolution was to make our understanding of the world human-centred instead of God-centred—perhaps the crucial philosophical insight of the European Enlightenment. The world as we see it is as we see it, rather than as it really is; it is conditioned by our perception; it is a world of appearances. This is the meaning of the often-quoted observation in the Talmud: 'We do not see things as they are, but as *we* are'.

Kant did not turn man into God but took away from man the god-like insight the realists had unwittingly assigned to him. This is why Kant's idealism is modest and why Kant himself was suspected of holding heretical views. Kant's intervention followed a long and intense debate in the Catholic church over the nature of reality, the theologians being divided between nominalists, realists and conceptualists. As the Enlightenment dawned the consensus converged on what was known as 'moderate realism' (especially as formulated by Thomas Aquinas), which allowed the church's teachings to coexist with the new science. Kant's assertion of a form of conceptualism laid the groundwork for the emergence of humanism. In particular, the anthropocentric model gave humans responsibility for their moral laws and their destiny, rather than these things being handed down by God, with the clerics acting as middlemen.

REASONS FOR THE EXISTENCE OF THE THING-IN-ITSELF

Kant adopted the terms phenomenon and noumenon to distinguish between the thing as it appears to us and the thing as it is in itself. I use the same terminology here.[6] Thus 'phenomenon' applies to the world of appearances, the phenomena that inhabit our consciousness, and 'noumenon' describes the world that 'lies behind' the world of appearances. I later argue that, in addition to providing two ways of thinking about the world, phenomenon and noumenon reflect and represent different ontological concepts—that is, distinct modes of being—an idea closer to Schopenhauer's view than to Kant's.

For Kant, the difficulty lay in establishing the need for the existence of something about which we can know nothing.[7] Positing the existence of the noumenon was pivotal because if the world were nothing but appearances it would be indistinguishable from a dream. But if there *is* another side to the world we can know nothing about it, since anything we do know takes the form of a representation, a phenomenon.

So far I have been following Kant and using only negative reasons for the existence of the noumenon. Appearances must be appearances of something. Then the noumenon is a thing 'so far as it is *not an object of our sensible intuition*'. But there could be a positive reason for establishing the existence of the noumenon. At one point Kant entertained the idea that there might be a special kind of awareness, beyond our ordinary consciousness, that allows us special knowledge of the noumenon. He suggested 'a peculiar mode of intuition . . . the very possibility of which we have no notion' that would allow us to understand the noumenon positively, as 'an *object of a non-sensible intuition*'.[8] But he then rejected such a notion and reverted to negative arguments for the noumenon.

Although declaring that 'we are not entitled to maintain that sensibility is the only possible mode of intuition'[9], the Sage of Königsberg, as Kant became known, adopted a position of philosophical humility, shying away from this postulated form of non-sensible intuition because such a notion 'lies absolutely beyond what we could know'.[10] He conceded the possibility of a form of intuition beyond everyday senses and cognition but argued that since our faculties can know nothing of this it is legitimate to motivate the existence of the noumenon only in the negative sense.

Kant's 'distinctive concern was to vindicate the authority of reason'[11] after centuries of superstition and ecclesiastical dogma. He was determined to stay true to the Enlightenment value of stringent rationality and resisted the temptation to resort to notions that seemed dangerously close to theology or, worse, mysticism. So, despite professing to be a Christian throughout his life, he used the existence of the noumenon to structure the void left by the boundedness of the world of appearances—as if to prevent theists from filling it with God. Thus, in the end he insisted that the division between phenomenon and noumenon can be supported only in the negative sense. The willingness to argue for the existence of a form of 'non-sensible intuition' was the decisive break from Kant that Schopenhauer made. It is also at the centre of the argument put forward in this book.

SEVENTEEN

The 'legislation for nature'

HERE I EXPLORE SOME of the implications of the distinction between phenomenon and noumenon and what this tells us about how we understand the world.

First, a question. If we cannot know the world as it is in itself but can know it only through our perceptions, how is it that our perceptions are so uniform we can communicate with each other effectively through a shared view of the world? Kant maintained that humans' capacity to perceive the outside world and thus form representations of it depends on certain 'conditions of sensibility' that exist before the experiences themselves, notably the forms of space, time and causality. These are inbuilt forms of the human mind, and they provide the structure that allows us to receive in an intelligible way the sensory data of the outside world.[1] They are a priori—that is, present before experience. As a result, instead of learning the forms of space, time and causality through experience of the world, we in fact *impose* them on the world.

This is a mind-bending idea. Putting causality aside for the moment, in this view space and time are the two pure forms of sensory intuition. Space is the property of the mind by which we represent objects outside ourselves, whereas we represent everything that relates to our inward mental or sensory consideration in terms of time.[2] Space and time thus provide the pure forms by which we apprehend the world; they do not belong to things in themselves. In the case of space, we do not learn by experience to understand and use the concept because it already structures our capacity to perceive the world. It is 'the foundation of all external intuitions' or appearances. Indeed, the a priori form of space makes all external appearances possible. Geometry is the science of space that developed wholly independently of any real object and does no more than apply intelligence to the form of space. If we imagine an object from which we progressively strip away all features—colour, hardness, weight, and so on—we would still be left with the space it occupies, 'and this it is utterly impossible to annihilate in thought'.[3]

So, rather than being properties inherent in the 'object' (the material world outside us), these a priori forms are brought by the subject to the world and used to structure representations of it. Indeed, these forms are essential to allow communication between subject and object—that is, the opportunity for the subject to structure the world in a useful way.[4] This is a radical and counter-intuitive position since Kant is arguing that, instead of assuming that 'our knowledge must conform to the objects' as they are actually given outside of us, 'the objects must conform to our knowledge'.[5] Kant compared this reversal of commonsense with Copernicus' revolutionary assertion that the Earth-bound observer rotates around the sun, rather than the sun revolving around the observer. Kant's is the pivotal insight of transcendental idealism and accounts for its transcendental aspect, since if nothing can be known about the thing-in-itself it can be only the subject who imposes particular forms on the object.[6]

PHILOSOPHICAL FOUNDATIONS

Although this might seem monstrous hubris, because humans are seen to 'create' the world, the opposite is the case. Instead of humans being able to capture reality as it is, we are captives of our representations of the world and cannot know it as it really is. Just as Copernicus demoted humanity to cosmic specks instead of gods around whom the universe revolved, so Kant turned humans into mere subjects.

According to Kant's Copernican revolution, humans provide the rules by which we understand the world. Kant called these rules we bring to the world the 'legislation for nature'. They allow us to order our perceptions. And they make possible pure understanding—cognition that depends on concepts alone, such as pure mathematics. The rules we bring to the outside world are common to all of us and therefore give our understanding objectivity. Realists, on the other hand, do not recognise these rules as a priori conditions; instead, they attribute them to the outside world as inherent qualities of it that each human must learn anew through experience.

SPACE AND TIME

Let us explore this further. I argue that we must start from the fact of consciousness and that consciousness creates the world for our knowledge, the world of appearances. The properties of the world as we perceive it do not belong inherently to the world but are 'imposed' on the world by our perception of it. This does not mean the only reality is the world of appearances; rather, it means that, to the extent that we perceive and think, we do so only in terms of appearances. There is a reality 'behind' appearances, or at least it is necessary to posit such a world because appearances presuppose things that appear.

The 'legislation for nature'

In order to sustain the argument that the properties of the world of appearances are not inherent but are imposed by consciousness (the knowing subject), Kant argued that we must be capable of certain intuitions that are independent of any experience.[7] In the realist view, intuitions emerge from things as they actually are and somehow 'migrate' across to our representations of them. But if we function in a world of appearances the intuitions in question are the 'forms of sensibility' we use to apprehend and make sense of the world outside us. Thus, in the subject–object situation, instead of imagining the object has all its properties inhering in it, so that we simply reflect them in our minds, the subject imposes those properties on the object. The subject already comes to the object with the capacity to impose form on the object. As noted, these forms of sensory intuition include those of space, time and causality.

Space and time are the most general sensory forms that allow us to create and understand a consistent and stable world of appearances. In Kant's words, 'this space in thought itself makes possible physical space, i.e. the extension of matter . . . [it] is by no means a property of things in themselves, but only a form of our power of sensory representation'.[8] This explains why the world is stable, so that each of us perceives it similarly. It seems clear that the reason the world is anchored in such a way as to ensure we all see roughly the same thing is that the a priori forms of sensory and intellectual intuition we bring are common to humanity.

Why this should be so is another question. To speculate, if we move from the metaphysical to the physical (perhaps an unsafe move), human beings might have evolved to be hard-wired with the forms of space and time, so that our metaphysical tools emerged from the biological—in the way envisaged by Rupert Sheldrake with his idea of morphic fields.[9] The a priori forms of time and space could then be inherited after being developed through the history of the species. Thus, like the body, the mind would carry with it the metaphysical forms that have been acquired throughout the species' history. If this is so, the perceptual habits of our ancestors are born into us, and none is more fundamental than those associated with space, time and causality, which we then use to interpret the world. They provide the basic framework within which our personal memories are stored.

So, for the transcendental idealist, if the world is one of appearances then time, space and causality are the 'arrangements of the intellect' we need in order to process the inflow of sensations. They are not features naturally inherent in the world; they are 'imposed' on the world by our perception of it. This underlying insight of Kant can also be found in Plato.[10] Schopenhauer realised that transcendental idealism is remarkably similar to Eastern philosophy's conception of the world and the place of humans in it. But before considering this similarity we need to return briefly to the idea of causality.

CAUSALITY

Eighteenth-century British philosopher David Hume was the first to argue that the Newtonian assumption of causation as a natural property of the world 'out there' is unsustainable. If we observe event B following event A and doing so with great regularity, it seems natural to conclude that A causes B. Yet this is mere induction: we cannot be certain that at some point an event A will not be followed by an event B. If we act with complete certainty that A causes B—something we do constantly—this tells us something important about human psychology but proves nothing about the laws of the world out there.[11]

Instead of ascribing knowledge formation to the world out there, transcendental idealists emphasise the forms of understanding we bring to the process of perceiving and thinking about the world. The law of causality we bring to the world ensures that the world 'hangs together'[12]:

> The concept of cause is therefore a pure concept of the understanding, which is completely distinct from all possible perception, and serves only, with respect to judging in general, to determine that representation which is contained under it and so to make possible a universally valid judgment.[13]

This means that, since all differentiation between objects and all change are possible only through space, time and causality, differentiation and change are of the phenomenal world. The noumenon, or thing-in-itself, must be characterised by the absence of these characteristics—that is, by unity instead of differentiation and constancy instead of change. The noumenon must be beyond causality and be itself uncaused. This idea has two important implications that form the basis for much of the rest of this book.

First, it means that rationality—being the process whereby we order and understand events using the law of causality—belongs to the phenomenal world (or at least to the forms we bring to the phenomenal world to make sense of it) and has no place in the noumenon. Thus, as I argue in Part Three, if we are to seek a source of moral authority outside the subjective world of appearances, in the noumenon, we cannot rely on the laws of rationality to take us there.

Second, reason cannot be the ground from which inner freedom grows. In the world of appearances every event must have a cause. If causal forces (compulsion, persuasion, inducement) lead us to act, we cannot be said to be free, since we are under the influence of outside forces. Freedom, 'the faculty to begin an event by oneself',[14] must have its own cause, which means that the source of freedom must lie outside the realm of causality—that is, in the noumenon, the domain of first causes.[15]

SOME PARALLELS WITH EASTERN PHILOSOPHIES

Readers might have concluded that the noumenon can be thought of as the place religious thinkers have reserved as the domain of God. If this is so, and time being alien to the noumenon, 'knowing' God must be an experience beyond time. Many spiritual masters have reached this conclusion. A Sufi sage observed, 'Past and future veil God from our sight'.[16] In the Christian tradition Meister Eckhart wrote, 'Time is what keeps the light from reaching us' and 'Three things prevent man from knowing God. The first is time, the second is corporeality, the third is multiplicity'.[17] This means that to know God we must first free ourselves from the shackles of time. For realists, time and change are fundamental to how the world is; for transcendental idealists, in contrast, they are no more than forms the subject brings to the world. That which is fundamental, the thing-in-itself, is timeless and changeless. In Hinduism this changeless entity, or universal 'substance', is known as Brahman.

Schopenhauer was the first Western philosopher to appreciate the deep insights of the East, where it has been understood for millennia that the world as we experience it has no real being but is instead 'a ceaseless becoming'. In the Hindu Vedas—the oldest books in the world—the idea can be found in the doctrine of Maya, the chimera of the everyday world, 'an unstable and inconstant illusion without substance . . . a veil enveloping human consciousness'. These ideas, Schopenhauer noted, were produced not from philosophising by the sages but from 'the direct utterance of their consciousness'.[18]

As with time, so with space: both are forms that inhere not in the world itself but rather in our representations of it. Thus in the *Upanishads* (a later distillation of the Vedas), space is, in addition to being a property of things, the 'creator' of things, and all things are contained within space as Brahman: 'Space, as it is called, is the bringer into being of name and form. That which contains them is *brahman*, the immortal.'[19] All phenomenal forms exist 'inside' the boundless and timeless ground. When the subject brings the form of space to the world, differentiation is created since the spatial coordinates of a thing distinguish it from another thing. In the Kantian view, the phenomenon is characterised by multiplicity but the noumenon is undifferentiated; in Schopenhauer's words, 'only the one and identical essence can manifest itself in all those phenomena'.[20] This idea reappeared across the ancient and modern worlds, in the writings of the Platonists and the Sufis and the works of Spinoza and various Christian mystics, before Kant took it up and argued it using the rules of logic rather than direct realisation.

In the *Upanishads* the idea of oneness from which all else is manifest is explicit in the idea of Brahman. The unifying or subtle essence can be interpreted as the sacred power of the whole universe—that is, the universal 'energy' that is the essence of the noumenon. It is the source of creation yet is

PHILOSOPHICAL FOUNDATIONS

uncreated. Thus Brahman is said to be 'self-born'. In Buddhist teaching, which is atheistic, this is captured in the notion of the 'suchness' of the world, the essential quality that infuses all things and reflects the oneness of the whole creation: 'When the Ten Thousand things are viewed in their oneness, we return to the Origin and remain where we have always been'.[21]

Aldous Huxley summarised the insight of the sages of all traditions by describing a hierarchy of the real:

> The manifold world of our everyday experience is real with a relative reality that is, on its own level, unquestionable; but this relative reality has its being within and because of the absolute Reality, which, on account of the incommensurable otherness of its eternal nature, we can never hope to describe, even though it is possible for us directly to apprehend it.[22]

EIGHTEEN

Scientific thinking

A PARALLEL CAN BE drawn between the philosophical shift from realism to transcendental idealism and the change in the way modern physics understands the world. In the early decades of the twentieth century developments in physics led to the overthrowing of the Newtonian world view, in which the universe was considered to be an external reality consisting of three-dimensional space and continuous, uniform time. Einstein's relativity theory recognised space and time not as absolute but as relative—no longer bound to something fixed and immovable. As Stephen Hawking wrote, 'the theory of relativity put an end to the idea of absolute time'.[1] Although the Newtonian view is a good approximation of the world for most purposes, in modern physics space and time do not have independent existence but are dependent on the observer. The belief that geometry is an integral part of nature was thus shown to be erroneous: geometry consists of spatial concepts we use to interpret nature; it is a construct of the human mind. Writing in *Physics Today*, physicist Mendel Sachs put it this way:

> The real revolution that came with Einstein's theory ... was the abandonment of the idea that the space–time coordinate system has objective significance as a separate physical entity. Instead of this idea, relativity theory implies that the space and time coordinates are only the elements of a language that is used by an observer to describe his environment.[2]

Most strikingly, the rigid division between the observer and the observed, which Newton inherited from Descartes, does not apply at the atomic level. Thus Kant planted a philosophical seed that germinated elsewhere a century after his death, and it is perhaps no accident that it sprouted in the very country in which it was planted. The seed grew into the idea that the human subject creates the arena in which Newtonian physics applies, and that arena does not coincide with the world as it is in itself. In contrast with everyday realism and Newtonian science, knowledge of the material world is always and everywhere conditioned by the perceptions of the observer.

Some critics argue that transcendental idealism relegates cognition to a purely subjective realm, undermining the 'objectivity' of science. This, of course, is anathema to all who support a realist view, from which vantage point one can make all sorts of criticisms of the apparent contradictions in Kant. Transcendental idealism seems to render all things relative and subjective, which seems to rule out the 'objectivity' of science.

Although this is a valid criticism of pre-Kantian idealism, it is a misreading of transcendental idealism. The latter does not undermine science. It asserts that, for most purposes, it is appropriate for science to assume there is a real world outside human consciousness. But it insists that is no more than a convenient presupposition, in the same way that it is useful to

Scientific thinking

assume that, for most purposes, the laws of Newtonian physics are true.* When it comes to philosophy, though, the assumption that the everyday world has an absolute existence leads directly to error—the error of realism. As Schopenhauer reminds us:

> Realism, which commends itself to the crude understanding by appearing to be founded on fact, starts precisely from an arbitrary assumption, and is in consequence an empty castle in the air, since it skips or denies the first act of all, namely that all we know lies within consciousness.[3]

In contrast with the realist view that the world can exist independently of knowledge of it, the emergence of consciousness, and thus the subject–object dualism, actually creates the world. As a result, because of its epistemological boundaries, science cannot get beyond the phenomenal world to the 'inmost nature of the world'.[4]

So what exactly do the developments in quantum physics tell us? Just as in philosophy, it is possible to arrive intellectually (that is, from within the phenomenon) at the limits of the phenomenal world, so in science it is possible to arrive intellectually at the limits and contradictions of the natural world as science conceives it. Quantum physics' insights into the relativity of space and time do not represent the irruptions of the noumenon into the phenomenon. Quantum physics is not the physics of the noumenon—there can be no such thing—but simply the physics of the phenomenon understood as conditioned by the noumenon. Quantum physics

---

* This is not quite accurate. It is valid to assume a real world because we bring a common set of a priori concepts and forms to the interpretation of it; it is valid to assume Newtonian physics holds true over a certain range because empirically it is an excellent approximation.

PHILOSOPHICAL FOUNDATIONS

does no more than confirm the ideality of time and space that Kant proposed.

For some readers, especially those schooled in the sciences, the cognitive leap from commonsense realism to transcendental idealism might be hard to make. It is like looking at a picture of a candlestick that from 'another perspective' turns into a silhouette of two faces looking at each other. To see the two faces requires a perceptual shift, and if one can't make this shift the faces will remain elusive, no matter what. In fact, it is sometimes easier to see them by not trying.

A cosmological analogy might be useful here. When we think of the universe from our position here on Earth it is natural to imagine that space goes on forever, that it is infinite. Even if our own universe has a boundary, there must be something beyond that. But this is the wrong way to think of it. If, as seems accepted, the universe was created from the Big Bang and is expanding continuously, it creates 'space' as it expands. So beyond the boundaries of the universe there is not another universe, or even just 'nothing', a vacuum that goes on forever, because in thinking this way we are creating the space that 'nothing' occupies. Rather, we should not even think about what is beyond the boundary of the universe: it is beyond thinking. Some cosmologists who are uncomfortable with this approach argue for a multitude of universes in which ours is enfolded. This seems to me no more than a convenient construction for people who have trouble admitting the limits of scientific reason.

The point here is that sometimes comprehension comes from making the move to 'not thinking', because thinking gives the wrong answer. Similarly, the Kantian 'inner world' cannot be comprehended by thinking—or, rather, it can be comprehended only in its superficial aspect, by its reflection in the world of appearances. Although not devoid of usefulness, this superficial aspect can by definition never reveal its true nature.

These ideas have entered into modern cosmological debate by way of the 'anthropic principle'—the notion that our nature as observers influences how we see and understand the universe. The principle was generated by the observation that life as we know it is possible only if a number of physical parameters, such as the gravitational constant, take the values they do. If any of these parameters were significantly different we would have a different universe, or no universe at all, and we would not exist. Physicist Brandon Carter put forward this proposition to counter the Copernican principle according to which there is nothing special about the position of humans in the cosmos.[5] The weak version of the anthropic principle says simply that we are around to observe the universe only because certain conditions prevailed and allowed human life to evolve. The strong version suggests there are many, many universes, a multiverse, and we live in one that allows for the possibility of our existence. Our universe is thus 'fine-tuned' for human consciousness.

Although suggestive of idealism, these formulations remain philosophically realist. The physicist who imagines an infinite number of universes to allow for the possibility of our existence still takes a 'god's-eye view' of those universes and our place in them. In contrast, a 'Kantian principle' would assert that the universe we observe is the only possible universe because we create it through our participation in it. This stance rejects the implicit god's-eye view and places humanity at the 'centre' of the universe. Our consciousness as observer is not a lucky accident made statistically likely by the

PHILOSOPHICAL FOUNDATIONS

proliferation of universes; nor is it the expression of God's will, as in pre-Copernican cosmology. It creates the universe as a world of appearances. The idea of a multiverse allows us to avoid confronting the mystery of our existence.

Some expressions of the anthropic principle come close to recognising this. The formulation *Cogito ergo mundis talis est* (I think therefore the world is as it is) could be understood this way. But the world is as it is not because the laws of physics happened to be tuned in a particular way; it is as it is *because* I think. The eminent physicist John Wheeler seems to have reached this view in his idea of a 'participating universe', in which the boundary between the world 'out there' and our consciousness of it becomes blurred. Further, the idea finds almost direct expression in the notion of the 'implicate order' advanced by quantum physicist David Bohm.[6] Here the 'explicate order' (the world of appearances with its everyday dimensions of space and time) is manifested out of the underlying implicate order, which contains the ground of all existence, considered to be an 'immense background of energy'. Humans are not mere observers: they are an 'intrinsic feature of the universe, which would be incomplete ... in some fundamental sense' if they did not exist. It is in this much deeper sense—rather than relativity's conception that the observer's presence can influence the behaviour of a particle—that we through our consciousness participate in the universe.

NINETEEN

Knowing and being

Philosophers differ when it comes to how we should understand the distinction between phenomenon and noumenon. On one view, they should be understood as two different worlds in which things are ontologically distinct; then the noumenon is either knowable or beyond the reach of consciousness and thus unknowable. Alternatively, phenomenon and noumenon are but two aspects of one world; they are not different kinds of thing but are different ways of considering things.* In this book I go directly to a

---

* Kantian scholars have debated whether the distinction between appearances (phenomenon) and the thing-in-itself (noumenon) should be understood as two worlds or two aspects of one world. The most common interpretation, the 'two worlds' view, relies on 'a straightforward ontological distinction between two classes of entity: knowable and mind-dependent appearances and unknowable and mind-independent things in themselves'. The second interpretation, the 'two aspects' view, centres on the *ways* in which empirical objects can be considered using philosophical reflection, rather than the *kinds* of things that are considered philosophically: 'Things can be considered either as they appear, that is, as they are in relation to the subjective condition of

quite different way of seeing the distinction. I posit for the noumenon a distinct form of knowledge that is beyond everyday consciousness and therefore outside the normal forms of space, time and causality. As noted, Kant hypothesised, in passing, the existence of a form of 'non-sensible intuition', something he then rejected. But if there were such a form of intuition it would allow us to know the noumenon directly, unmediated by everyday consciousness and transcending the subject–object relation and all other forms of intuition. This is such a radically different state of consciousness it might even constitute a different mode of being. Let us explore the idea through a thought experiment and then, in the next section, through examples.

Imagine it is possible to pass along a secret passage into the citadel of the noumenal world, the inner world of the thing-in-itself. Here there is a wholly different way of 'knowing', one in which everything is known directly—that is, completely unmediated by our senses, feelings or cognition. In this world the distinction between subject and object is dissolved, and there is no sensory or intellectual barrier between our selves and the world around us. In other words, there is no personal consciousness. In the citadel we do not know something because we form a mental picture of it, experience it through our senses or create a concept of it: we 'know' it directly. Space and time have no meaning because

---

* *Footnote continued from page 119*

human knowledge, or as they are in themselves, independently of these conditions'. Human knowledge is limited to objects as they appear because it is only by way of our senses and intellectual understanding that we can know about things. See Henry Allison, 'Transcendental idealism: the "two aspects" view', in Bernard den Ouden (ed.), *New Essays on Kant*, Peter Lang, New York, 1987.

we left those concepts at the door, and in this timeless world we 'understand' that the multiplicity dissolves into oneness. In the citadel, knowledge does not appropriate things: it participates in them.

Once we are inside the citadel of the noumenon, the moment we begin to think about it, consider it or sense it we are bounced out of it, back into the world of appearances. We are ejected, that being the penalty for thinking. Of course, once we are back outside, in the world where everything is necessarily mediated through our consciousness, we might have a memory of what it felt like to be in the citadel, but we will know it in a completely different way—in a phenomenal way, as a thinking subject conditioned by space and time. We might use metaphors or images to conjure up a sense of what it is like in the citadel, but these devices belong to the phenomenal world and can be suggestive only.

The two modes of awareness are radically different. The existence and nature of the noumenon can be established only from within the noumenal mode of awareness, from within the citadel. From outside, in the phenomenal world, we can infer certain characteristics of the noumenon, as Kant did, but it will always be obscured, if only by the 'lightest of veils'. We can know the noumenon only from within, by abandoning our normal mode of awareness and its subject–object dualism. In this view, the thing-in-itself is not just a concept: concepts belong to the phenomenal world. The thing-in-itself is a distinct realm with entirely different rules. It can be thought of as an eternal, undifferentiated 'substrate' out of which the phenomenon is manifested. Obviously, in order to know the thing-in-itself directly, rather than by inferring it from the phenomenal world, it is necessary to cast off the forms that define the phenomenal world, and that means

PHILOSOPHICAL FOUNDATIONS

setting aside the a priori concepts of space, time and causality.

I am thus arguing that the existence of things and the means of establishing that existence are inseparable. We have to live it to understand it.

This thought experiment is similar to the famous cave example Plato developed, which he described as an 'analogy for the human condition'.[1] Here I simplify and adapt it a little. Imagine a society of people who live in a cave. The cave dwellers are tied to a bench, unable to move or turn their heads, even to look at those sitting next to them. Behind them is the entrance to the cave, allowing daylight in, and just outside the cave is a road where people pass by carrying a variety of things. The cave dwellers can see on the wall in front of them their own shadows and the shadows of the passers-by—nothing more. For them, the shadow world is the only reality, and the voices of the passers-by are understood as the shadows speaking.

But one among the cave dwellers frees himself and turns to see the people whose shadows alone he had seen before. Stepping out of the cave, he learns there is another world, three-dimensional and brilliant, illuminated by the sun, a light much more intense than in the world of the cave dwellers. He realises he and his fellow cave dwellers have mistaken the world of shadows for the world of substance. He has acquired an insight—a special knowledge that distinguishes him as a 'philosopher'.

For Plato, the transition between the world inside the cave (which he calls the 'visible realm') and the world outside ('the intelligible or divine realm') is an ontological shift; he refers to two 'modes of existence'.[2] Although the philosopher with the knowledge might meet scepticism, Plato says 'the capacity for knowledge is present in everyone's mind'. It is just a question of orienting the mind so that it is able to open itself to 'real being and reality at its most bright'. For Plato, education should be the 'art of orientation' so that we are facing the right way—a faculty that allows us not merely to gather information but also to cultivate this special knowledge.

TWENTY

Instances of non-sensible intuition

BOTH KANT AND SCHOPENHAUER established the distinction between the phenomenon and the noumenon by deduction, but the same insight can be gained by way of direct, or 'non-sensible', intuition. The difficulty with employing the latter, however, and the reason most philosophers have a strong preference for the former, is that the latter can be used to justify fantasies. Kant warned of the dangers of amateur metaphysicians who, on the basis of 'sound common sense', actually 'stumble unawares out beyond the objects of experience into the field of chimeras'.[1] He observed that what can be deduced by reflection can also be found in the common understanding, which sees mysterious forces lying behind the phenomenon, but then spoils the insight by turning the intuition of the noumenon into phenomenal forms.[2]

In other words, people have a predisposition to smuggle deities—or, worse, ghosts, apparitions and spirits—into the phenomenon. This helps explain the extraordinary popularity of novels such as *The Da Vinci Code* and books that exploit the public's credulity and sense of something beyond the mundane.

Among the latter, the most exploitative of recent years is a best-selling 'book of wisdom' known as *The Secret*, the pages of which contain as much spiritual truth as a battery-powered plastic heart of Jesus.

Although he, too, recognised the dangers, Schopenhauer went a step further than Kant, arguing that the deepest insights can be had only from intuition:

> If, by way of exception, it happens that we experience a momentary enhancement of the intensity of our intuitive intelligence, we at once see things with entirely different eyes, for we now apprehend them no longer according to their relations, but according to what they are in and by themselves.[3]

Direct knowledge of the noumenon is accessible only through immersion in the noumenon—when consciousness takes on a different form or, rather, takes the form of 'pure consciousness'.[4] Space and time belong in the phenomenal world; the noumenon is undifferentiated and timeless. Immersion in the noumenon therefore requires dissolution of the self, if only fleetingly.

Despite the philosophical difficulty of aspects of transcendental idealism, for some people the essential distinction between appearances and the thing-in-itself is, as noted, intuitively obvious. If the existence of the noumenon is to have any meaning at all in the world, it cannot be the preserve of philosophers. In some form it must be accessible and, indeed, deeply affect ordinary people without them having to wade through the *Critique of Pure Reason* or *The World as Will and Representation*, volumes I and II. The understanding arises from numinous experiences, which, big or small, are to be had every day. (Despite their similarity, the words numinous and

PHILOSOPHICAL FOUNDATIONS

noumenon have different roots. Numinous means revealing or indicating the presence of the divine.) Numinous experiences often occur in connection with nature—sunrises, mountains and especially the ocean, which is seen by many as the symbol of the unconscious. A book could be filled with examples of numinous experiences, but four will suffice here.

When the French naturalist Jacques-Julien Labillardière sailed into Tasmania's Recherche Bay in 1792, he went ashore and spent a night sleeping in the splendid eucalypt forest there. He later wrote, 'I felt myself penetrated with a sentiment of admiration of the grandeur of nature, which is beyond my power to express'.[5]

One of the most famous literary descriptions of a flash of insight into the noumenon occurs in Jean-Paul Sartre's early novel *Nausea*.[6] (It is reasonable to assume Sartre's words reflect his own experience, since it would be impossible to imagine what he describes.) After a long period of feeling intense alienation and having suicidal thoughts, the protagonist has an encounter with the root of a chestnut tree in a municipal park:

> And suddenly, suddenly, the veil is torn away, I have understood, I have *seen* ... Then I had this vision.
>
> It left me breathless. Never, until these last few days, had I understood the meaning of 'existence'.

In his use of the word 'existence' Sartre is clearly referring to the thing-in itself:

> ... usually existence hides itself ... And then all of a sudden, there it was, clear as day: existence had suddenly unveiled itself. It had lost the harmless look of an abstract category: it was the very paste of things, this root was kneaded into

existence . . . the diversity of things, their individuality, were only an appearance, a veneer . . . I realized that there was no half-way house between non-existence and this flaunting abundance . . . neither ignorance nor knowledge was important: the world of explanations and reasons is not the world of existence.

Sartre then describes the process of immersion and the dissolution of self:

I *was* the root of the chestnut tree. Or rather I was entirely conscious of its existence. Still detached from it—since I was conscious of it—yet lost in it, nothing but it . . . Existence is not something which lets itself be thought of from a distance: it must invade you suddenly, master you, weigh heavily on your heart like a great motionless beast—or else there is nothing more at all.

The third example also involves a tree and is described by a 40-year-old office worker:

I was sitting in my office on the third floor of an office block reading a book on Zen Buddhism. Responding to a suggestion in the book, I looked out the window at a tree in the park and as I did I cast off all aspects of the tree and just considered it, not for its size or colour or type, or whether I liked it or what its function was. I just considered it for what it was. And as I did I felt an intensely direct connection with the tree, an unmediated connection, almost a physical bond. I felt in a strange internal way that the tree was no different from anything else, including myself; the tree was the same as everything else yet it remained a tree.[7]

PHILOSOPHICAL FOUNDATIONS

In going through the process of casting off various ways of considering the tree, the office worker arrived at a point of 'pure consideration', transcending everyday awareness and apprehending the tree directly, unmediated by any phenomenal form.

The final example is Wordsworth's well-known poem 'Tintern Abbey'. Wordsworth begins by describing a state of meditative consciousness that is conducive to insight into the nature of the noumenon:

> *. . . that serene and blessed mood,*
> *In which the affections gently lead us on,—*
> *Until, the breath of this corporeal frame*
> *And even the motion of our human blood*
> *Almost suspended, we are laid asleep*
> *In body, and become a living soul . . .*

The 'serene and blessed mood' Wordsworth describes is one that advanced meditation and prayer are designed to achieve, a state in which the functions of the body can be literally suspended. In this state the appearances of the world are stripped away, and the normal boundaries of time and space are loosened so that we perceive the world anew. Thus:

> *While with an eye made quiet by the power*
> *Of harmony, and the deep power of joy,*
> *We see into the life of things.*

When the phenomenal form of the world is dissolved Wordsworth is left seeing into the essence of the world around him, 'the life of things', which can be nothing other than the thing-in-itself. The 'life' he apprehends is a pure life force that pervades all things, including the 'mind of man'. He describes 'a sense sublime':

> *Of something far more deeply interfused,*
> *Whose dwelling is the light of setting suns,*
> *And the round ocean and the living air,*
> *And the blue sky, and in the mind of man:*
> *A motion and a spirit, that impels*
> *All thinking things, all objects of all thought,*
> *And rolls through all things.*

Wordsworth writes of an experience of radical insight into the nature of things, where he divines 'a motion and a spirit' that binds and impels all things, something Schopenhauer called 'the Will'.

This non-sensible intuition finds expression in many forms of aesthetic experience and in some forms of consciousness that are not uncommon but are rarely analysed. Understood properly, such intuition provides the positive reason for the existence of the noumenon, going beyond the negative reasons we have relied on so far. Providing some instances of this intuitive insight helps base the discussion in readers' experience, but it should be stressed that this intuitive evidence is only suggestive of the noumenon and does no more than reinforce its existence and nature as arrived at by analytical means.

Even so, this procedure might be challenged on the grounds that Kant established the existence of the noumenal world by rigorous application of the powers of deduction and that the examples just given lie outside the sphere of reason and in the sphere of 'sensation'. True. But, as we have seen, Schopenhauer took a more adventurous approach, arguing

PHILOSOPHICAL FOUNDATIONS

that the kernel of truly new knowledge—and there have been few more important breakthroughs in the Western history of ideas than Kant's transcendental idealism—can arise only from 'sensation'. Reason alone cannot provide access to the noumenon: it can provide access only to the *concept* of the noumenon.

We are now in a position to revisit the proposition I put forward at the beginning of Part Two—that the starting point for all philosophy must be the positing of consciousness. Against this, Max Scheler asserted, 'Only a very definite historical stage of overreflective bourgeois civilization could make the fact of consciousness the starting point of all theoretical philosophy, without characterizing more exactly the mode of being of this consciousness'.[8] He also argued that it is erroneous to imagine consciousness as the 'receptacle' in which knowledge is held because knowledge precedes consciousness. In arguing this, he jumps ahead of himself, defining knowledge more broadly than the everyday knowledge that characterises the phenomenon. We can see now, though, that Scheler was referring to what I call the knowledge peculiar to the noumenal world:

> We will call this knowledge *ecstatic* knowledge. It is found quite clearly in animals, primitive people, children, and, further, in certain pathological and other abnormal and supra-normal states . . . I have said elsewhere that an animal never relates to its environment as to an object but only *lives in it*.[9]

With the dramatic expression 'ecstatic knowledge' Scheler was referring to what has otherwise been called 'participating consciousness'—the form of knowledge peculiar to the citadel, where the distinction between subject and object breaks down. In Eastern philosophy the idea is better reflected in the term 'pure consciousness', the term I prefer. I return to this when we consider the metaphysics of morality.

Before moving on, it is useful to summarise the argument thus far.

The search for the grounds for inner freedom begins with the fact of consciousness, the only thing that is immediately given. Consciousness creates the division between subject and object—the knower and the known—and from this it is argued that the everyday world in which we function is unreliable and contingent: it is a world of appearances wholly dependent on our sensory and cognitive capacities. In contrast with the assumption of philosophical and commonsense realism, consciousness creates the world. Thus, instead of the world having an independent existence that we learn to interpret, the inbuilt forms of human perception and cognition impose on the world structures that enable us to make sense of it. Space and time are forms of intuition that precede all experience and provide the 'legislation for nature'. The transcendental idealism I outline is human-centred, casting aside the implicit 'god's-eye view' of the world of realism.

But behind the world of appearances must lie the thing-in-itself—a world that transcends consciousness and the subject–object relation. In contrast with the phenomenal world, which gains its existence from our consciousness, it is not obvious that we can have knowledge of the noumenal world of pure existence.

The noumenon is not, however, wholly unknowable. Certainly, it is not accessible to ordinary forms of consciousness,

PHILOSOPHICAL FOUNDATIONS

but there is a form of 'non-sensible intuition' that allows us an insight into the thing-in-itself. In suggesting there is a form of knowledge that transcends ordinary consciousness, I use the analogies of the citadel and Plato's cave and then provide some examples that seem to support its existence. It turns out that the descriptions by those who would appear to have found their way into the citadel bear a remarkable similarity to the features of the 'subtle essence' of things to be found in Eastern philosophical traditions, a topic to which we soon return. Before doing so, though, let us look at the noumenon from another perspective, one that forms the foundation of the theory of morality I develop in Part Three of this book.

TWENTY-ONE

The noumenon and the Self

THE FOREGOING DISCUSSION EXPLORES the distinction between the phenomenon and the noumenon by focusing on the nature of the object. Now we change our orientation and consider the question from the point of view of the subject; in other words, we turn our gaze away from the known and towards the knower. Conceptually, we have been thinking of the thing-in-itself as the 'inner nature' of the phenomenon, as perceived by the subject. But what about the inner nature of the subject? Strictly speaking, this is not a valid question: the 'inner nature' of the subject presupposes there is no subject because the subject–object distinction is dissolved. Posing the question this way does, however, help us make progress.

Schopenhauer's insistence—against Kant's 'epistemological modesty'—that the deepest insights emerge from sensations rather than intellectual understanding marked a fork in the road for Western philosophy. It is no surprise to learn that the inner nature of the subject is revealed by the 'non-sensible intuition' hypothesised but rejected by Kant. On Kant's view, if we search 'inside us' for a self that is not part of the

PHILOSOPHICAL FOUNDATIONS

phenomenal world, we will be disappointed because we can find nothing but thoughts, feelings, emotions and images, all of which belong to the world of appearances. Put another way, if we search for the inner nature of the subject we always find that it is consciousness of something and is therefore a phenomenal form.

Brian Magee argues that Hume, Kant and Schopenhauer 'would have agreed, albeit for different reasons, that if all objects of perception were taken away the self would vanish'.[1] This is not so for Schopenhauer, who tentatively postulated the existence of a 'metaphysical self' that, as neither subject nor object, transcends the perceiving self. If, as Kant insisted, all knowledge arises from a priori concepts and the data of sensory experience, then, as Schopenhauer observed, 'we can never get at the inner nature of things *from without* . . . We are like a man who goes round a castle, looking in vain for an entrance, and sometimes sketching the facades. Yet this is the path that all philosophers before me have followed'.[2]

We should not overlook the difficulty of my argument. After all, we know the world of appearances is created through the perceptions of our consciousness, so the only way to find the noumenon in the subject is to dissolve the distinction between subject and object, something the rational mind fears. When faced with this task, we come up against an almost insuperable problem because we can conceptualise the noumenon in the subject only from within the world of appearances and so must use words and concepts to think about and describe it. Yet we know it is beyond description and evades all concepts. As a result, we can only speculate and use metaphor to elicit a sense of what it might be.

To know the thing-in-itself requires a different kind of knowledge, one that transcends the space, time and causality that characterise the phenomenal world. It was finding an exceptional case in which this different kind of knowledge could arise that led to Schopenhauer's decisive insight.[3] The 'most characteristic and important step' of his philosophy was to argue that we *can* know something about the inner nature of things: 'this whole work is only the unfolding of a single thought'.[4] He discovered the secret passage into the citadel of the noumenon, and his stepping through that passage caused his philosophy to diverge from Kant's. His insight was simple: since each knowing subject exists inside a body, and each body has a double existence—once as phenomenon and once as noumenon—we can know the thing-in-itself directly, unmediated by the senses and the intellect. Unlike external objects (including the body as phenomenon mediated by our senses and our intellects), the body is also given to us in an entirely different way, without any mediation, without sense, without feeling and without thought. In contrast with the body as phenomenon, this 'inner being' does not require any other being to perceive or know it in any way in order for it to come into existence.

This intuition led Schopenhauer to believe he had found the pure motive force that causes the body to act and in which the distinction between subject and object can dissolve.[5] He called it the Will. The choice of the word 'Will' has led to many difficulties in interpreting Schopenhauer, not least because he used the word in different ways. Moreover, he seemed to apply the idea of special insight to the physical body, a move that lacks coherence and is not persuasive. It would have made more sense if he had adopted an idea like the 'subtle body', the Vedic concept approximating a noumenal state of awareness. Nevertheless, the distinction between subject and object disappears in the identity of Will

PHILOSOPHICAL FOUNDATIONS

and body. It arises from a special sort of knowledge and can never be demonstrated any other way. When considered from the perspective of everyday knowledge, our bodies are no more than phenomena, but when considered using this special knowledge, they are manifestations of the Will. This 'double knowledge' gives us a very particular insight, the most important philosophical truth of all—a knowledge of the thing-in-itself, something Kant had declared impossible.

Schopenhauer maintained that his great insight was not any sort of divine revelation but was instead a profound intellectual intuition.[6] This hardly seems plausible, not least because the philosopher himself insisted that breakthroughs such as this can never be purely intellectual. He did not explain how he arrived at this 'philosophical truth *par excellence*', but he did comment on what can only be Kant's postulated non-sensible intuition: 'it is a direct and intuitive knowledge that cannot be reasoned away or arrived at by reasoning; a knowledge that, just because it is not abstract, cannot be communicated, but must dawn on each of us'.[7]

Elsewhere he referred to the knowledge that appears only by way of exception and 'temporarily under specially favourable conditions'.[8] Perhaps one day he was sitting at his desk, reading Kant's *Critique* and pondering the nature of the thing-in-itself. He put down the book, closed his eyes, shut out the sounds of the street (which we know bothered him greatly), and in this reverie sank into his own self. Suddenly he had an intuition. Casting off all sensible perceptions, all thoughts, feelings and sensations, he found himself suspended in pure awareness. As he emerged from his reverie he realised he had had an experience of himself not as an appearance but as he 'really is'. Moreover, he saw that if he could step inside any other living thing he would find exactly the same 'essence'. This inner essence cannot correspond to any feeling, concept or activity and therefore requires no other being to manifest itself or give it validity.[9] Eastern philosophers had grasped this long before and by a more deliberate route, one that bypassed the intellectual entanglements of European philosophy.

Schopenhauer looked beyond the precipice but could not bring himself to leap. This might have been because he wanted to concede nothing to the theologians. He wrote, 'my path lies midway between the doctrine of omniscience of the earlier dogmatism and the despair of the Kantian critique'.[10] He was bolder than Kant's epistemological modesty would allow. I take a still riskier step and assert that we *can* know the noumenon, although we can know it only in a special way—as a form of consciousness peculiar to the citadel and unknowable outside.

Kant deployed intellect to deduce the necessity of the noumenon's existence. But intellect could take him no further than identifying the necessity. To take the next, crucial step, into the citadel, to use our metaphor, requires a form of supra-rational knowledge that transcends all concepts. Thus it is not our capacity for reason that distinguishes human beings from other living things; it is the possibility of understanding ourselves as both an appearance and a thing-in-itself—as phenomenon and noumenon—and the moral sense this engenders.

Yet it is by no means guaranteed that the existence of the noumenon in others will be recognised and acted on. Indeed, there are some who seem never to acknowledge that others are anything more than appearances and think only they themselves have a real existence and that as a result the rest of the world exists only for them and never for itself. This is the definition of pure egoism.* In Part Three I argue that the degree to which we act morally depends, at its core, on the extent to which we live according to the understanding that we have an existence beyond appearances. In other words, when we adopt a moral attitude to another person, we relate to them noumenally rather than phenomenally, a position on which Kant and Schopenhauer were in basic agreement despite the divergence of their moral theories beyond that point. This understanding of others as noumenon might not be at the forefront of our conscious minds but may nevertheless determine our behaviour unconsciously. In fact, Schopenhauer prefigured some of Freud's insights to a striking degree:

> [W]e are often unable to give any account of the origin of our deepest thoughts; they are the offspring of our mysterious inner being. Judgements, sudden flashes of thought, resolves, rise from those depths unexpectedly and to our own astonishment ... Consciousness is the mere surface of our mind, and of this, as of the globe, we do not know the interior, but only the crust.[11]

In section 17, when discussing parallels with Eastern philosophies, we considered the nature of the noumenon from the perspective of 'object'. Now we look at it from the perspective of 'subject'. In the Eastern traditions it has long been accepted that there is a form of knowledge that permits an understand-

---

* While everywhere apparent in practical life, such a view is rarely advanced as a philosophical truth. 'As a serious conviction', wrote Schopenhauer, such theoretical egoism 'could be found only in a madhouse; as such it would then need not so much a refutation as a cure' (*The World as Will and Representation*, vol. I, p. 104).

ing of the noumenon directly. This means the distinction between subject and object, knower and known, can dissolve. Although sharply different in some respects, Hindu and Buddhist teachings share this core insight. The search for the true or universal Self takes us deeper and deeper as we strip away more phenomenal layers; instead of our bodily forms, senses, feelings and ideas we must discover what it is that makes them all possible. The seers discovered the 'ultimate subject' that can be known only by pure awareness.[12]

The seers then realised that the subtle essence, or undifferentiated energy, that imbues the world of objects, Brahman, is identical to the universal Self, which they call Atman. Brahman and Atman are one and the same. They seem different only because we can approach the question of the nature of existence by looking for the ground of things (the question Kant grappled with) or by looking for the ground of the self. Atman is subject without object; Brahman is object without subject: neither can be known by everyday knowledge.

Recognising that Atman and Brahman are one immediately provides a path to discover the nature of ultimate reality. Finding the universal Self, the ultimate subject, is the secret door to the citadel. This is the most profound discovery of the *Upanishads*. When Schopenhauer wrote that his entire philosophy is the elaboration of a single insight, it was this insight he was referring to.

To understand the identity of the subtle essence and the universal Self is the purpose of life, as captured in the emblematic principle of Hindu philosophy 'Thou art that'. 'One must seek for and want to know the self, which is free from evil, ageless, deathless, sorrowless, without hunger, without thirst, of true desire, of true resolve. The one who has found and knows the self attains all worlds and all desires.'[13]

PHILOSOPHICAL FOUNDATIONS

Perhaps it was expressed most succinctly by the ninth-century sage Shankara: 'The wise man is one who understands that the essence of Brahman and of Atman is Pure Consciousness and who realizes their absolute identity'.[14]

The philosophy underlying various schools of Buddhism is quite varied. Yogacara Buddhism, one of the two major Mahayana traditions, comes closest to the Vedic view just described.[15] Consciousness usually functions in a dualistic way, where subject and object condition each other. But knowledge can also transcend the subject–object dualism and become direct, or unmediated. A similar idea is captured in the modern Zen notion of 'big mind':

> Usually we think of our mind as receiving impressions and experiences from outside, but that is not a true understanding of the mind. The true understanding is that the mind includes everything . . . This mind is called big mind.[16]

The same essential truth of one all-encompassing reality is present in Tibetan Buddhism: 'to realize the nature of mind is to realize the nature of all things'.[17]

Moving west, one finds the same idea at the core of Sufism. Ibn' Arabi wrote, 'At last the Gnostic understands that whether it be in the interior or whether it be in outside existence, whatever is manifested is the Absolute Being; that existence is One Existence, One Soul, One Body; it is neither separated nor individuated'.[18] Of course, this is central to the Christian tradition, too, as attested to by the saints and mystics. The god within and the god without are united; in the words of William Law, 'in the deepest and most central part of thy soul'.[19] The immanent deity and the transcendent deity are separated only by incomplete understanding. The last word goes to Christian mystic Meister Eckhart: 'The knower and the known are one. Simple people imagine that they should see God, as if He stood there and they here. This is not so. God and I, we are one in knowledge'.[20]

For all these sages, God is no more than a metaphor, a concept derived from the phenomenal world to evoke the ineffable force of the noumenon. Those who mistake the metaphor for what it applies to misunderstand.

According to the perennial philosophy—a phrase coined by Leibniz to describe the understanding that the ground of being unifies each of us with all things[21]—the noumenon is not blind but instead is intentioned, and it is this intention that imparts purpose to life on Earth. That purpose is the realisation of the noumenon in the phenomenon, expressed in Christian theology as God's desire to glory in his own creation and to do so through us; it is to feel, in Wordsworth's evocation, the motion and the spirit that impels all thinking things. This is what gives value to life—especially to human life, the unique life form that, after being separated from the noumenon by the intrusion of consciousness, has the opportunity to merge once more with it.

TWENTY-TWO

A digression on the existence of God

AT THIS POINT IT is worth applying the distinction between the two fields of knowledge, the phenomenal and noumenal, to one of the great intellectual questions: Is it possible to prove or disprove the existence of God? In Kant's era the school of rational theology adduced a series of arguments to demonstrate that God must exist. In recent times atheists such as Richard Dawkins have used rational argument to prove that God cannot exist. The framework of transcendental idealism allows us to answer the question more satisfactorily. In short, one cannot use the methods of the phenomenal world to prove or disprove a proposition that belongs to the noumenon.

Kant tackled the question of proving or disproving God's existence in a well-known section of *The Critique of Pure Reason* entitled 'The impossibility of an ontological proof of the existence of God'.[1] The section, in which Kant sets out to disprove the arguments of rational theology, was essential to Kant's project, which was to 'eliminate theism from philosophy' and to rescue philosophy as a science.[2] The argument is notoriously

A digression on the existence of God

opaque—technical without being precise—so I try here to present it simply.

As a leading Enlightenment thinker, Kant wanted to liberate philosophy from religious dogma and to pour cold water on the claim that reason can be used to prove the existence of God. In essence, all phenomenal knowledge arises in consciousness and is necessarily conditioned; there can be no absolutes. Since God is, by definition, the absolute, it is impossible to argue from the phenomenal world, which is also the domain of rationality, for the existence of a supreme being. Rational theology is an oxymoron; indeed, so is 'rational atheism'. The concept of God can reside in the phenomenon, but the existence of God as such cannot be deduced therefrom.

Kant refers to God variously as the 'primal being', 'the Supreme Being', an 'unconditioned and necessary being' and the 'absolute necessity'. Whatever the name, God must have the characteristics of the noumenon and be akin to the idea of the 'reality' that underlies all appearances. Despite the human need to find an explanation of the absolute underpinning of concepts, including the concept of God, reason alone, merely through the creation of its own thoughts, cannot be the basis for knowing the supreme being.

Throughout his discussion Kant does not liken the unconditioned or absolute nature of God to the thing-in-itself, the noumenon. But when we recall his insistence that we can know nothing of the noumenon we understand why. He wants to show that within the realm of reason one cannot prove the existence of God, and to do so he must of course remain within the realm of reason—that is, within the phenomenon. It is no surprise then that he should conclude, 'reason looks round for the concept of a being that may be admitted as worthy of the attribute of absolute necessity'.[3] Kant admits that reason must regard the existence of a supreme being as a truth already established by experience and that the task of reason is to find a concept that can do justice to this being. Merely positing the existence of God is no proof.

An equivalent argument applies to the thing-in-itself, the existence of which, for Kant, was deduced as a necessity. He argued persuasively that the absence of the thing-in-itself would generate a contradiction. He must have believed that somehow God resides in the realm described by the thing-in-itself, but it is one thing to deduce the necessity of the noumenon and quite another to maintain that God is alive and well and living there. Indeed, Kant argued that it is not even clear how one can think of or conceptualise the existence of an unconditional or supreme being. The processes of thought must always fall short.

The idea that thinking is hostile to absolute reality is consistent with the Eastern philosophical idea that thought and sensation destroy knowledge of and connection with the supreme being—an idea already encountered in the analogy of the citadel. And if we cannot think its reality we are certainly limited in our capacity to prove its reality. The only way to conjure up the idea in consciousness is to use metaphor and analogy, which is in fact the language of religious literature. Here, too, Kant affirms that it is fruitless and misleading to try to prove the existence of God by way of examples.[4] In the end, the argument comes down to the distinction between proving that something exists and merely positing it. Reason cannot provide access to the transcendental 'object'. To imagine otherwise means the existence of the supreme being is smuggled into the argument and in the

A digression on the existence of God

course of the explanation pops out, as if what was temporarily hidden in the concepts is demonstrated. Reason allows itself 'to be persuaded that a mere creature of its own thought is a real being'.

In summary, using reason we can establish the necessity of the existence of the thing-in-itself, that something must exist beyond appearances. The question then is whether this something can be shown to be God, understood as the 'most real being'. Consistent with his belief that we can say nothing about the noumenon, Kant showed that arguments attempting to establish the identity of God and the noumenon must be fallacious.

The situation can be resolved only if one takes the extra step of recognising that it is possible, through a special awareness, to have an insight into the noumenon. Schopenhauer took this step tentatively but ultimately remained just short of the divide between appearances and the thing-in-itself, peering through the 'lightest of veils' and discerning something of the noumenon's nature. If we are willing to be slightly less cautious we can accept that the noumenon is its own realm, one that can be the only home for God or the godhead. In the phenomenal world of ordinary consciousness we can know only the concept of God, an existence for the subject. But if we can imagine ourselves inside the citadel, as it were, we can 'know' being directly, and existence becomes absolute because it is no longer contingent on the subject. And it goes without saying that there we cannot have any concept of being—or, indeed, any concept. Thus in the phenomenal world to say 'God exists' is no more than to say 'I embrace a concept that I call God'.

This positing of God seems to be the tenuous foundation of religious belief for some of the faithful. Within

PHILOSOPHICAL FOUNDATIONS

the phenomenal world it is impossible to prove the existence of God, and all attempts to do so are trivial. To argue that the word of the Bible or the Koran proves the existence of God is in every way equivalent to arguing that *The Lord of the Rings* proves the existence of Bilbo Baggins. On the other hand, a reader of scriptures who has been persuaded of the existence of God through experiencing the noumenon might find that the consistency of the Bible's words with his or her own experience evokes and perhaps deepens the understanding of the nature of God. One would need to spend some time living in the Shire to be equally certain of Bilbo Baggins' existence.

Biblical literalism thus confuses the concept of God with the supreme being itself; it makes the mistake of idolatry, projecting the phenomenal form onto the noumenal essence. In this way the creation story was no more than a pre-scientific metaphor designed to explain the mystery of human existence. Someone who takes creationism as a literal truth thereby puts the phenomenal in the place of the absolute— the metaphor in the place of the thing it is supposed to represent, the concept instead of the reality—and shows that he or she has lost touch with the true basis of belief. Creationism uses the images of the phenomenon to explain the noumenon in the same way rational theology uses the forms of reason taken from the phenomenon. Neither has found the citadel; both have instead built a castle in the air.

In his refutation of rational proofs of God's existence, Kant succeeded in banishing theology from philosophy. Neither philosophy nor science can provide the evidence needed to establish the existence of the supreme being. The evidence can be had only from a form of non-sensible intuition, if such a thing exists; without the intuition one can be no more than an agnostic, someone who remains uncertain about the possibility of a form of knowledge that transcends the phenomenon.

This provides context for understanding the recent proliferation of books denying religion and asserting atheism. The books by Richard Dawkins, Christopher Hitchens and Michel Onfray stand out. The authors' attacks, although in one respect a welcome antidote to the outbreak of religious fundamentalism that blights the present era, are based on a naive metaphysics. Take Dawkins, a biologist, for example. He insists that the existence or otherwise of God 'is a scientific question',[5] and he therefore adopts precisely the epistemological stance of rational theology that Kant dismantled so effectively. That the existence of God is a scientific question is an assertion that must itself be proved, yet, innocent of epistemology, Dawkins sees it as self-evident. He admits he shares with creationists the refusal to place science and religion in separate spheres. This leads him to displace the mystery: his argument that God is equivalent to the tooth fairy leaves him baffled as to why large numbers of intelligent and sophisticated people believe in some form of deity,[6] and his lack of humility prevents him from asking whether perhaps they are willing to concede that there could be an order of knowledge beyond the science to which Dawkins is wedded.

Scientific rationality is Dawkins' deity, and he deploys it to disprove the God of his opponents. He sets himself the easiest task—to ridicule the fantasies of religious dogmatists—and produces a sustained polemic against the truth of metaphors, a denunciation that gains only a little value by virtue of the fact that those he assails also mistake the metaphors for the things they are designed to evoke. Dawkins seems intoxicated by the power of scientific rationality. For all its achievements, scientific rationality taken as the only way to comprehend the world is a phase of intellectual development that most people pass through in adolescence. Beyond that phase, they no longer ridicule the idea of a virgin birth as a medical impossibility but accept that the story must symbolise something more. Yet Dawkins is still preoccupied by the literalism of youth.[7]

In fact, from the outset Dawkins defines the real question out of his book. He does so in his attempts to reclaim Einstein for his own narrow form of scientific rationality. Einstein declared that he rejected the idea of a personal god but believed in 'Spinoza's God'. So Dawkins distinguishes between 'Einsteinian religion', which he equates to a feeling of awe at the beauty of the universe, and 'supernatural religion', which is a dangerous delusion. A bit more research would have revealed that—however the idea might be metaphorically captured and theologically elaborated—Spinoza's God is the seed of every religion; it is the self-conceiving infinite 'being', the immanent substance preceding all manifestations in the universe.[8] For those people who are exasperated by the influence of religious fundamentalism, reading Dawkins and the other defenders of atheism can be cathartic, but they would be better armed for a fight if they read Nietzsche's devastating and profound attacks on Christianity in, for example, *The Genealogy of Morals*.[9]

I observed earlier that transcendental idealism saw a transition from a theocentric model of the world to an anthropocentric one in which the world is created by consciousness, where we ourselves bring to the world the 'legislation for nature'. The god Kant banished from the everyday world was one separate and remote from humanity, yet omnipotent. This might be called an 'exotheocentric' model, in which God is conceived as an external power or entity. In accepting that the noumenon can be found in the subject (thereby joining the subject with all things), we have, depending on how one prefers to interpret it, arrived at what might be called an 'endotheocentric' view, in which the divine is immanent, a position that corresponds closely with that of Spinoza and an Eastern view of cosmology. In the view put forward here, to find 'god' you need only find yourself.

TWENTY-THREE

On death

> *. . . the dread of something after death,*
> *The undiscovered country from whose bourn*
> *No traveller returns, puzzles the will,*
> *And makes us rather bear those ills we have*
> *Than fly to others that we know not of . . .*
>
> Hamlet

Socrates described philosophy as preparation for death. The ability to contemplate death makes humans unique. It is accompanied by a terrifying awareness of our inescapable annihilation. Even an atheist cannot wholly suppress thoughts of what lies beyond. Yet our capacity for contemplation provides a compensation for death-terror: it offers us the opportunity to understand life and death metaphysically and to console ourselves with this knowledge. As Schopenhauer wrote, 'All religions and philosophical systems are directed principally to this end, and are thus primarily the antidote to the certainty of death . . .'[1]

Before Kant, the churches had provided their own form of consolation, the promise of ascension to heaven under the loving but terrible eye of God. It was a crude metaphysics well suited to the uneducated. Kant showed that the deity, were it to exist, could not belong to the everyday world of understanding. He lit the way, illuminated further by Schopenhauer, for a more satisfying metaphysics, knowledge of which can provide solace in the face of the certainty of death. For there is more to us than mere appearances: the inner nature of each individual is the same subtle essence that infuses the world as a whole; it is the thing-in-itself manifest in each of us. Schopenhauer called it the Will, Hindus refer to Atman, Christians call it the soul. Generically, we might refer to it as the universal Self, or just the Self, understood as the expression in the individual of the universal 'energy', or subtle essence.

Permanence and transience are ideas based in time, yet the noumenon is beyond the temporal. It is therefore erroneous to believe that the universal energy lives forever, because forever is a concept that assumes time. It is also inaccurate to say that the Self is immortal, because immortality assumes mortality, whereas the universal essence exists outside time and beyond living and dying. Thus the individual existence, our phenomenal self, disappears on death, dissolving into so many atoms, but our noumenal Self, the universal Self, is untouched. As phenomenon we perish, but as noumenon we are indestructible: 'with death consciousness is certainly lost, but not what produced and maintained consciousness; life is extinguished, but with it not the principle of life which manifested itself in it'.[2]

To the extent that we live with the illusion that our real existence is in our bodies, our minds and our personalities, this image is shattered by death because with our physical passing everything we thought we were is no more. Yet what we truly are, in our essence, the timeless universal Self, is freed to return to its source. The personal consciousness that is the cause of our separation from the whole is no more, and we are free to be 'reabsorbed'. Understanding this primal unity of the Self with the universal essence 'prevents the thought of death from poisoning the life of the rational being',[3] since we can then go

PHILOSOPHICAL FOUNDATIONS

gentle into that good night in the knowledge that annihilation will not be our fate. For people who more closely identify themselves with their phenomenal manifestations—their physical appearance, their possessions, their achievements, their intellects; in short, their egos—death does appear fearsome because it presents itself as extinction.

Metempsychosis—the transfer after death of one's soul to another person or animal—seems possible only if one imagines the noumenal Self to take on some of the characteristics of the individual, something on which I take an agnostic view. As one's subtle essence already exists in others, so the doctrine of metempsychosis transfers to the future an identification that prevails now; perhaps it is the realisation of this at the moment of death that explains the oft-remarked calm that comes over the dying person. We can liken the course of a human life to the rising and setting of the sun, a sun whose brightness prevents us from seeing the host of stars above our heads.[4] Our individual existence stands as an impenetrable obstacle between ourselves and the true nature of our being. If we are lucky, though, at some point in the day of our life, an eclipse will momentarily darken the sun and we will catch sight of the firmament beyond. Armed with this insight, we are prepared for the passing of our day and we understand that the dark side of the Earth is the only vantage point from which to see our true home.

In Hindu thought Atman, or the universal Self, is conceived as a permanent entity, existing even after the fall of the body. Reincarnation is considered possible because the universal Self is somehow seen to be stamped with aspects of the character of the phenomenal subject, and it takes on the sins and virtues of its bearer. That the Self is presumed to retain some characteristics of the person after he or she dies gives rise to the possibility of reincarnation. Yet, for a metaphysical system that understands so perfectly the unitary nature and timelessness of the noumenon, this notion can be nothing more than a metaphor created to communicate the idea of guilt and punishment for wrongdoing in this life. The reincarnation story thus serves the purpose of social regulation more than spiritual truth. The Christian God, who doles out retribution, deciding which mortal should be rewarded and which punished in the afterlife according to the virtuousness of a life lived, serves the same social function.

Schopenhauer's well-known pessimistic view of human life is inseparable from his belief that the Will—the essential force of the noumenon that expresses itself in the will to live—is blind and purposeless. Yet this is not the mood of the ultimate that emerges from the texts of Eastern philosophy or, indeed, from the writings of the Christian mystics. There the mood is one of hopefulness, because experience teaches one to trust in the power of enlightenment or salvation. The supreme being, Brahman, is not blind, purposeless, unintelligible, austere or remote; it is neither uninterested nor disinterested when it comes to humanity's travails. Although the mysterious nature of the universal consciousness cannot be gainsaid, in this view it is understood that humankind was created for a purpose, that creation in its entirety is given meaning by the existence of humankind, that our role is somehow to validate the universal consciousness and to do so by acknowledging the primacy of the manifestation of the noumenon in each of us. In other words, by using our few decades on Earth to enter the citadel while still in phenomenal form—before death sees us withdraw permanently to that place we came from—we not only pursue our own 'salvation' but also pay homage to that which gives rise to our existence. Nothing else can give a human life meaning. According to the *Upanishads*:

PHILOSOPHICAL FOUNDATIONS

> If someone in this world makes offerings, performs sacrifices, and practices asceticism without knowing the imperishable, that work of his comes to an end. If someone passes on from this world without knowing the imperishable, he is pitiable. But if someone passes on from this world knowing the imperishable, he is a Brahmana.[5]

If this is so, all those philosophical and religious systems that ask us to keep faith in life with the promise of going to a better place after death betray our real purpose. Any notion of a better place immediately evokes thoughts of experiences, objects and relationships that are known by the senses, which are, of necessity, extinguished. The reification of the noumenon as 'heaven' is thus a contradiction.[6] Religions that promise life after death carry out a hoax on people who can think only of the survival of their phenomenal selves as taking some form, particularly because they are more likely to be seized by the fear of annihilation. It is an error to associate the 'soul' with some aspect of ordinary consciousness. The soul—understood as the spirit-being that inhabits the body and survives physical death—is really the universal Self personified, yet each form or quality attributed to it can reflect only an aspect of the phenomenal self and, as such, is mere metaphor. The metaphor might make the truth clearer, but more often it obscures it. On the question of immortality, Meister Eckhart was iconoclastic: 'I already possess all that is granted to me in eternity'.[7]

None of this means a person who has come to understand the unity of the Self with the whole will no longer have the will to live: it is impossible to imagine that the creation could come into existence without being imbued with the urge to perpetuate itself. But the life so willed is a different life, serene and purposeful to the degree that consciousness of unity is held at the forefront of awareness. Every true sage has only one teaching—that, as far as we can, we spend our lives moving our identification away from our personal selves, taking it as close as we can to the universal Self, however that might be conceived. The egotist who wants to live beyond his physical passing can draw little consolation from this understanding because everything he believes about himself and of which he is proud will surely be extinguished on his death. Buried deep within each of us, though, there does seem to be an inborn recognition that on death we will not be entirely extinguished; it is as though we have a vestigial memory that we will return to where we came from:

> He who conceives his existence as merely accidental, must certainly be afraid of losing it through death. On the other hand he who sees, even only in a general way, that his existence rests upon some original necessity, will not believe that this necessity, which has produced so wonderful a thing, is limited to such a brief span of time, but that it is active at all times.[8]

The conviction that there is life after death was once widely held but has waned along with the waning authority of the churches. What is to be put in its place to comfort us in knowing the certainty of our deaths? If no metaphysical answer is to hand it seems natural to devote oneself entirely to a celebration of life in the present, all the more so for its brief duration. Thus in the West, and especially the Anglophone nations, the marginalisation of the churches since the 1960s—

a move to the edges hastened by the clay-footedness of the clergy—has been compensated for by a mounting orgy of consumption and pleasure seeking. This seems to be the only plausible explanation for the reverence with which all segments of society regard economic growth. It helps us understand the great contradiction of the modern world—that the richer we become the more, rather than the less, obsessed we are with growth. Perhaps, too, the alarm that has spread about the ageing of the population can be attributed to an intensification of the fear of death as contact with the noumenon recedes in the popular consciousness, so that we shrink from ageing more than ever, even though in rich countries we have more years than before and can live them more healthily.

Sadly, the gap left by the redundancy of the church has not been filled by advances in secular philosophy, which has seen more or less continual regress over the last century, marked by a retreat to arid scholasticism and a reluctance to explore the ultimate questions. In a statement about pre-Kantians that applies equally to post-Kantians, Schopenhauer wrote, 'All philosophers have made the mistake of placing that which is metaphysical, indestructible, and eternal in man in the *intellect*'.[9] Strangely, this turns out to be more true for modern philosophers who claim to be Kantian, notably John Rawls.

The obverse of death is the generation of life. If the phenomenal self ceases to exist when we die and the universal Self is 'absorbed' back into the noumenon, it must also be true that the creation of each individual represents the manifestation of the noumenal in the phenomenal at or soon after conception.[10] This invests the act of creation—sexual intercourse—with great metaphysical significance, something explored when I consider sexual morality in Part Four.

So time begins with conception and ends with death. This is the cognitive construction that, above all, prevents us from recognising the eternal, changeless nature of the universal essence. If the noumenon is the citadel, it is the place of our birth and the place of our death. Diderot wrote of a chateau above whose entrance were the words 'I belong to no one, and I belong to all the world; you were in it before you entered it, and you will still be in it when you have gone out of it'.[11]

Schopenhauer reflects on nature's apparent indifference to life and death since nature sends organisms large and small into the world to face risks at every turn and, indeed, for one life to snuff out another in a merciless natural order. Anthropomorphising, he observes:

> Now if the universal mother carelessly sends forth her children without protection to a thousand threatening dangers, this can only be because she knows that, when they fall, they fall back into her womb, where they are safe and secure . . . With man she does not act otherwise than she does with the animals . . . the life or death of the individual is a matter of indifference to her.[12]

The destruction of phenomenal forms has no effect on the noumenon. The continual arising and passing away of living things means nothing to the inner core of existence. It is only by superimposing a personal god on the universal energy, a penchant of Westerners, that the grieving family can cry out 'Why?' Only people who have been taught to believe in such a superimposed god can lose faith when a great natural disaster destroys ten thousand lives. Christ's anguished cry on the cross—'My God, my God, why hast thou forsaken me?'—reverberates through the ages.

PHILOSOPHICAL FOUNDATIONS

Perhaps the greatest folly of Christianity has been to instil deeply in the popular psyche the belief that virtue is rewarded with happiness. In the popular understanding God serves as a stern judge and, just as the legal system in the phenomenal world punishes the wicked and rewards the virtuous, metes out the same sort of justice. Yet the common understanding is confronted every day with monstrous injustices—the child struck down by a terrible disease, a tsunami that drowns three hundred thousand souls going about their work or relaxing on the beach, and evil men dying in their palaces smug and unpunished to the end. If we abandon the idea of a God who rewards and punishes deeds in the phenomenon, we are free to accept a more sublime notion of justice, eternal justice, an idea that emerges from the philosophy of morals to which we now turn.

PART THREE
Towards a post-secular ethics

Give me one fixed point and I will move the Earth.

Archimedes

TWENTY-FOUR
Modern moral anxiety

THERE IS A WIDESPREAD belief among the people of Western countries that we have lost moral direction, that the rules and expectations associated with moral behaviour have become diluted or blurred. Moral confusion is a corollary of the demand for self-determination since personal autonomy has meant, to a greater or lesser degree, rejection of traditional sources of moral authority. With the removal of economic constraints as a result of widespread affluence, the demand for self-determination was a natural extension of the challenge to all forms of authority arising from the democratic impulse.

Moral confusion has been inseparable from the success of the various liberation movements of the 1960s and 1970s—the sexual revolution, the women's movement, gay liberation and civil rights. The women's movement, in particular, was based on a sophisticated critique of patriarchy and launched a series of campaigns for equal rights, equal pay, access to childcare and opportunities in education. It campaigned against all forms of discrimination and violence against women. In so doing the movement freed women to flourish in ways hitherto prevented.

TOWARDS A POST-SECULAR ETHICS

But the challenge to the moral authority of dominant groups and institutions had unintended consequences.

Before those decades citizens could at least take comfort in the certainty of unambiguous, if not always honoured, ethical guidelines. The difference between right and wrong was rarely contested, something that was psychologically reassuring. This was especially the case with relations between (and among) the sexes: premarital sex was proscribed, and a breach of the proscription brought shame and ostracism; homosexuality was condemned, and breaches were punishable with jail; it was right that women confined themselves to the home, and men knew what was expected of them.

Of course, people who were constrained by these certainties did not always find comfort in them, and their resistance provided the moral argument and social energy for the liberation movements. It was historically necessary to challenge and overthrow established authority because it had become ossified and irrelevant, a form of social control increasingly exposed as having no function other than to buttress the privileged position of particular social groups. The old regime had lost its legitimacy. In one sense, the liberation movements were the final phase of the European Enlightenment, in which everything—and especially all forms of authority—would be subject to the penetrating gaze and harsh critique of rationality.

Although few today feel the need to apologise for their lack of religiosity, it is also broadly acknowledged that the collapse of the authority of the church left most people unsure where to look for moral guidance, except to their equally confused friends. In the new autonomous moral universe individuals would be able to choose their own moral standards, subject only to the constraint that others not be injured. Yet even the

Modern moral anxiety

ethic of consent—hopelessly inadequate when confronted by predicaments that might involve third parties—cannot help us understand what is in our real interests, those moral interests lying beneath the urge to satisfy immediate desires.

Of course, in practice some of the old rules appear to have been left largely untouched. It remains wrong to cause physical harm to others. It is wrong to steal others' property or to swindle them out of it. Failure to pay taxes is treated harshly, though perhaps not harshly enough. Even in sexual relations some of the old rules continue to apply, although often with diminished force. Adultery remains wrong, although nowadays it is condemned not because it breaches God's law or social convention but because it is a betrayal of an intimate partner. And while many sexual acts that were once considered beyond the pale are now widely if not universally accepted (anal sex and bondage, for example), others (such as bestiality) are still viewed with condemnation and disgust, although even there the barriers are beginning to crumble.

Nevertheless, the liberation movements seemed to cause the ground to move, to call virtually everything into question. Moral rules became an object of criticism, the primary charge being that they served as the means by which dominant groups exercised control over subordinate ones. Straight white males and the institutions they were most closely associated with came under attack from all sides. So overwhelming were the criticisms of the old moral order that a generation, led by thinkers who challenged almost everything, rejected not just particular moral rules but the legitimacy of morality as such. If so much of the traditional ethical code could be shown to be an arbitrary instrument of oppression, perhaps the entire code was tainted and ethical rules must be socially conditioned and thus invalid. This challenge to the basis of all moral claims represented the most far-reaching cultural change. The 1960s' radicals' predilection for asserting their autonomy by publicly rejecting convention, especially mores governing sexual behaviour, caused all rules guiding personal behaviour to be contested. If moralising is the assertion of an ethical rule without the need for justification, it became uncool to do it, and even now anyone who criticises personal behaviour of almost any kind must expect to be dismissed as a 'moraliser'.

But there is a growing discomfort with the absence of rules, and nowhere is it more apparent than in the area of sexual mores. The attitude of the sexual revolution—that, apart from consent, there are no rules governing sexual behaviour—lifted the constraints on the libido. This gave permission for sex to be divorced from intimacy, a process that has reached its zenith in recent years. The perilous combination of emotional disengagement and the sexual urge is the theme of Hanif Kureishi's novel *Intimacy*. In truth, the detachment cultivated by the protagonist as he prepares to abandon his wife and children is a justification for a kind of adolescent callousness, 'a Thatcherism of the soul'. 'We must treat other people as if they were real. But are they?'[1] We are now beginning to understand that free love exacts a heavy price, one unwittingly exposed by author and libertarian Catherine Millet. The publisher describes her best-selling memoir, *The Sexual Life of Catherine M.*, as 'a manifesto of our times—when the sexual equality of women is a reality and where love and sex have gone their own separate ways'. Is this not what men, in their raw state, have always wanted, to separate copulation from intimacy? Is not every counsellor's room witness to a stream of torn relationships in which she wants more intimacy and he wants more penetration? In the world of

Catherine Millet women have entered the universe of sex constructed by men—primordial, unsocialised men driven by their ids—in which all finer feelings drown in a sea of testosterone. One begins to suspect that the sexual taboos of the past served not so much to oppress women but to protect them from the predatory urges of the unleashed male libido.

This is the new 'democracy of pleasure', in the words of Ovidie, the French porn star and author who describes herself as a feminist, artist and philosopher.[2] Ovidie starred in the mainstream film *The Pornographer*, of which one critic said, 'No film in the history of cinema had portrayed oral sex with such a superb sense of existential weariness and melancholy'. The subtext of all porn is boredom, the mechanisation of sex stripped of its excitement and mystery, reduced to what one person does to another—or, more commonly, what he does to her. Sex in porn is not the exploration of one with another; it is an act of relief, like defecation (indeed, on some internet sites the two are combined).

Perhaps we could accept this if such an attitude were confined to porn videos and sex sites on the net. But depersonalised, indiscriminate sex has crept into the cultural mainstream, so that the symbols, styles and even personnel of the pornographic genre are cropping up on television, in newspapers and in films. In Italy a porn star ran for parliament with the aim of normalising the genre, and the international media treated it as light-hearted relief from the usual dull political fare. Even respectable global corporations such as telecommunications carriers have companies that make porn videos.

The novels of Michel Houellebecq mirror the turmoil of sexual politics rippling through Western cultures. His work has been called pornographic, yet, unlike Millet, Houellebecq has a purpose with his eroticism. For his characters, sex is an antidote to the meaninglessness of modern life, but the novels are also a meditation on that lack of meaning. They are a subtle journey into the vain quest for happiness in a post-scarcity world in which the promises of plenty, and the freedoms won in the 1960s and 1970s, have left a new barrenness. If all has failed us and there is nothing left to believe in, why not fuck till we drop? Whereas Millet puts her orifices on display, Houellebecq shows us his doubts. While Millet is still playing out the fantasies of sexual freedom, Houellebecq is warning of its perils: 'The sexual revolution was to destroy the last unit separating the individual from the market'.[3]

Where is all this taking us? It seems to me that as the imperatives for self-creation and individualism reach extreme levels they are exacting a terrible price. Houellebecq's novels are suffused with a sense of the disengagement of the modern pursuit of personal freedom. For all their casual sex and post-modern nonchalance, the stories remind us of what we sacrifice. What we trade away in order to have our individualism is the most precious quality of being human—love: 'There is no love in individual freedom, in independence . . . love is only the desire for annihilation, fusion, the disappearance of the individual, in a sort of what used to be called oceanic feeling'.[4]

In *The Possibility of an Island* Houellebecq writes of a youthful generation only a few years in advance of the present, one for which sexuality is no more than a pleasant pastime, something devoid of sentiment and commitment. Despite the stylish insouciance of post-modern feminists such as Millet and, in her own way, author Kathy Lette, this form of sexuality is a triumph of the male fantasy:

> The centuries-old male project, perfectly expressed nowadays by pornographic films, that consisted of ridding sexuality of any

emotional connotation in order to bring it back into the realm of pure entertainment had finally, in this generation, been accomplished.[5]

Porn films and the sexual ennui of Millet serve the same function—to free men of the obligation for intimacy. Although Houellebecq's novels appear to adopt a marked indifference to this moral hollowing-out, in fact his work, read sympathetically, is a searing critique of post-modern moral laxity, all the more powerful because he refuses to impose any sort of judgment. He exposes the modern tragedy simply by projecting the trends forward to a world of radically isolated selves from which the prospect of intense and passionate love has been banished. He takes us to a secure, closed, affluent, technologically controlled dystopia and considers the possibility of the island John Donne said no man could be. His work expresses better than any sociological treatise the emptiness that stretches, cavernous, beneath the everyday activity of the consumer existence. Of the young generation not far into the future, he writes, 'They had reached their goal: at no moment in their lives would they ever know love. They were free'.[6] At no moment in their lives would they ever know love. They were free. In our modern pursuit of complete freedom, we deny ourselves the possibility of being truly human.

TWENTY-FIVE
Moral relativism

THE CRITIQUE OF ALL forms of moral authority that emerged from the liberation movements of the 1960s and 1970s eventually found theoretical expression in post-modernism, especially in the writings of a number of French philosophers and social critics. In the view of Bruno Latour, one of post-modernism's leaders, social constructionism, or 'critique', teaches students that 'facts are made up, that there is no such thing as natural, unmediated, unbiased access to truth, that we are always prisoners of language, [and] that we always speak from a particular standpoint'.[1] Truth is never simply 'out there'; instead, it is embodied in materials, in language, in consciousnesses. Informational materials—books, films, newspapers, television ads, and so on—should be taken not as purveyors of truth but as 'texts' that have been prepared in cultural contexts and that reflect the perspectives of author and audience. Thus, when reading texts we should be alert to the 'meaning' of what is being said, so that we do not mistake culturally specific ideas for objective truths. This process of reading with an eye to the cultural and social preconceptions of the author is one of 'deconstruction'.

Even if we are alert to lurking cultural preconceptions, though, in our deconstruction we inevitably bring our own assumptions and prejudices, so that truth is subjective, elusive and contestable. This contrasts with the positivist stance of the physical sciences—and for many years social sciences such as anthropology, psychology and economics—in which the purpose of investigation is to uncover the truth that lies within the objective world. Social scientists' predilection for adopting the methods of the physical sciences (sometimes referred to by critics of neoclassical economics as 'physics envy') made them an easy target for the social constructionists. In a sense, the process of deconstruction in the social sciences is only natural, and it has been the practice of critical readers through the ages. There is no question that it has revealed layer on layer of gendered and racial assumptions in all sorts of books and materials that had previously been presented as 'how the world is'. In retrospect, so much is self-evident. Even conservative activists who rail against post-modernism cannot help but engage in deconstruction when they read a liberal newspaper.

The next step of social constructionism is more controversial. Since every text is culturally specific and therefore has meanings embedded in it—meanings that often reflect the assumptions or opinions of dominant ideologies, such as male supremacy or racial stereotyping—there is no objective or absolute truth: all texts reflect someone's cultural preconceptions and prejudices, and all readers of texts bring their own bias to them. When applied broadly to interpreting the world, this obviously challenges the whole positivist approach, in which science is aimed at uncovering the facts. In the postmodern world all facts are inherently contingent.

If Descartes is the quintessential philosopher of scientific rationalism, and Kipling is the emblematic defender of

TOWARDS A POST-SECULAR ETHICS

colonial ideology, then, as one critic of post-modernism has asserted, 'The negation of Kipling requires the repudiation of Descartes' and 'Objective truth is to be replaced by hermeneutic truth'.[2] Although this elision of methods in the social and physical sciences might seem to be setting up a straw man, some post-modernist intellectuals have invited ridicule by taking an extreme position on 'scientific truth'. The case for an epistemological distinction between, say, the analysis of the American Civil War and the laws of mechanics is, however, not such an easy one to make. The task now is to acknowledge the need to repudiate the racism of Kipling through hermeneutics (the interpretation of texts, a relatively simple task) and to define where the scientific method should hold sway.

Kant can help here. The laws of mechanics are subject to the a priori forms of understanding all humans bring to the world. But the a priori forms are of little help if we want to understand the American Civil War: one must bring socially and culturally conditioned perceptions. There are, of course, facts—the Battle of Gettysburg occurred in 1863, not 1862—yet in themselves they have no meaning. On the other hand, there are plenty of instances of social and cultural beliefs having influenced scientific belief. Copernicus' troubles with the Catholic church are an obvious example; and even Einstein refused to accept the fundamental claim of quantum mechanics about the unpredictability of the location of particles, famously declaring that God does not play dice.

Much of the post-modernist position grew out of the tendency of the intellectuals of the liberation movements to delve ever more deeply into the meaning of culture, literature, history, anthropology and especially the popular media, and there to find entrenched but sometimes obscure oppressive beliefs. After all, the seminal texts of anti-colonialism and feminism revealed a world of prejudices in us of which we were unaware. In the context of anti-colonial liberation movements, psychoanalyst and author Frantz Fanon taught us that even activists have had to face up to and resolve forms of self-hatred inherent in oppressive structures.[3]

Among conservatives it has become fashionable to denounce post-modernism for its determination to understand texts in their cultural context and its refusal to judge moralities, but few conservatives are willing to state their own moral absolutes. When they do they typically pick the less contentious ones, but even so they are unable to say where the authority for this moral position lies. This is because, with the exception of people of faith who are willing to trust the scriptures, they have no basis other than the moral positions learnt at their father's knee.

As an intellectual force post-modernism is now in retreat. It was developed as a weapon to be used against the institutions of power at a time when the appeal of socialism was fading. Today, Latour concedes, the method of questioning the biases and prejudices lying behind facts is being turned against the progressive political positions of post-modern intellectuals by a conservative resurgence that also, oddly enough, has in its sights the modernist project of objective truth. Fundamentalism is on the march, and it pays less respect to scientific method than the most ironic social constructionist. It is not just the creationists but also the global warming sceptics who have tried to systematically undermine the credibility of a mass of scientific research.[4] Like the post-modernists in their critique of the social sciences and humanities, the sceptics have characterised climate science as a social construction of scientists motivated by career advancement and prospects of research funding. Dark forces with ulterior motives are conspiring to attack the world as we know it, they mutter.

TOWARDS A POST-SECULAR ETHICS

Environmentalists are hiding behind science to pursue their real agenda, which is to dismantle capitalism.

The neoconservatives long for a return to a pre-modern era in which faith has authority over science. Modernism elevated matters of fact over matters of belief and now finds itself under siege from both post-modernism and neoconservatism. Both reject the claim of science to objective truth. The former sees the truth of modernism as socially constructed and the real truth as always contestable; the latter refuses to accept that belief should be subject to falsification by fact.

Yet the weakness of social constructionism is now laid bare: for all its radical challenge to accepted authority, it never knew what it wanted. Latour asks, 'What were we really after when we were so intent on showing the social construction of scientific facts?'[5] and answers that, although some went too far and created 'an excessive *distrust* of good matters of fact', the aim really was 'to *emancipate* the public from prematurely naturalized objectified facts'.[6] And then what? This only displaces the answer, for how do we know when the facts have 'matured' sufficiently for us to trust them? What was the purpose of post-modernism? What was to replace the structure that critique tore down so ruthlessly? There was no vision—only the negative energy of the angry young man—and this political aimlessness stands in contrast to the purposefulness of the conservatives, who know exactly what their goal is in deploying the techniques of deconstruction to erode the standing of science.*

---

* Latour executes a magnificent *mea culpa*, going so far as to concede that constructionism took the wrong path 'because of a little mistake in the definition of its main target. The question was never to get *away* from facts but *closer* to them, not fighting empiricism but, on the contrary, renewing empiricism' ('Why has critique run out of steam?', p. 231). Although alarmed at the political use to which deconstruction has been put by conservative fundamentalists, he does not tell us why he believes it is desirable to get closer to the facts. What is the political point?

As philosophy or social theory, post-modernism no longer matters—not because it failed but because it succeeded too well. Popular culture has left the academy behind. We have already observed how popular culture, which is now largely the product of marketing, has co-opted the post-modern stance and its mood of moral relativism. The intellectuals' doubts have been voiced too late; the genie has escaped and is now living in the *Big Brother* house. Latour acknowledges it: 'It has been a long time since the intellectuals were in the vanguard'.[7] The avant-garde can now be found not in the cafes of the Left Bank, the paint-splattered garrets or the turbulent philosophy schools but in the creative department of Saatchi & Saatchi. Brand loyalty, rather than social revolution, is the order of the day.

The internet is the epitome of the post-modern attitude to truth. The internet, the text of post-modernism *par excellence*—where every user is a purveyor of truth; where no canon acts as ballast or referee as gatekeeper; where the most fantastic theories become embedded in the culture; where conspiracists can evade the ridicule they deserve; where any amateur who can compose a sentence can write an encyclopaedia, one that for university students takes on the authority of the *Britannica*; where bits of information are valued more than the wisdom of the sages; and where the restless mind can, with one click, skip from a discourse on phenomenology to hot Asian babes. There was, after all, a didactic reason for excluding pornographic magazines from university libraries.

Progressives feel reluctant to comment on these developments for fear of being branded hypocrites. Yet, as Churchill is reputed to have said when it was pointed out that he had contradicted a previous statement, it is better to be right than consistent. It goes deeper than owning up to an intellectual mistake. Among critical theorists, post-modernism is not only a set of beliefs but an attitude, and it has always been easier to discard beliefs than change attitudes. In contrast to the anger and commitment that characterised previous generations of radicals, the post-modernist intellectuals' refusal to judge is characterised by an attitude of irony and detachment. 'Whatever' is the watchword, and something that is manifestly wrong becomes simply 'weird'. When confronted by moral outrages post-modern intellectuals naturally revert to this attitude and summon up all the slippery debating points, well known to the argumentative amateur, designed to avoid having to take a stance on anything other than a stance against taking stances. Some of them also purport to be feminists, a conjunction that creates awkward moments since it is quite a feat to treat female genital mutilation ironically or, as in the case of Catherine Millet, to regard prostitution as nothing more than a lifestyle choice. These intellectuals had to accept the failure of ideologies that opposed capitalism or, in the case of the younger ones, grew up in the era of the 'death of ideology', and the view is that if one does not know what to believe why not satisfy the human need to believe in something by committing oneself, with all the energy of a zealot, to *not* believing?

The fulminations of conservative commentators against the influence of post-modernism and moral relativism have found some resonance in the wider community because of an intimation that acceptance of 'moral difference' often masks moral decline. But, for all their demands for the reassertion of decency, the conservatives are silent about the epistemological basis of the values they defend. Where is the Fukuyama of morality? Few today are willing to appeal openly to the authority of the scriptures, and those who are have little influence over the majority of the population—except perhaps the theocons in the United States. Nor can they appeal to 'tradition', or at least not directly, because tradition died in the 1960s. Even conservatives now concede that we live in an age of cultural and individual diversity, and it is an irony that these very people are often market liberals too and therefore uphold individualism and choice as the greatest good. There remains one redoubt to which conservatives feel they can still retreat, and that is the appeal to the 'family'. While characterising it, with good reason, as one of the pillars of civilised society, the conservatives have assigned to the family a highly stylised, almost mythical character.

TWENTY-SIX

Reconstructing a moral code

UNTIL THE EUROPEAN ENLIGHTENMENT the principal source of moral power had always been the commands of the deity. The fact that these commands were interpreted by the earthly representatives of the deity was immaterial as long as the people accepted the representatives' authority. The death of God—deprivation of the Christian deity of his power over the lives of men—and secularisation threatened to deprive all social rules of their authority. But entrenched moral systems are not routed overnight. God might have died in the eighteenth century, but his influence lived on. Alan Wolfe has argued that capitalism has been sustained by a moral structure that it is destroying at the same time:

> Capitalism lived its first hundred years off the pre-capitalist morality it inherited from traditional religion and social structure, just as it lived its second hundred years off the moral capital of social democracy. From pre-capitalist tradition there developed an emphasis on self-restraint, charity, and the organic unity of society that held to a minimum the damage caused by

the pursuit of self-interest. From the post-capitalist ideology of the welfare state there developed a concern with solidarity, protection of the weak, and the organic unity of society that filled in the moral gap at just about the same time that religious, family and community bonds weakened.[1]

Capitalism could flourish because the moral foundations of social cohesion continued to be provided by those who were not committed to its vision—aristocrats and the church wedded to a feudal order and socialists committed to limiting or usurping capitalism's expansion. 'Civil society has always made economic man possible.'[2] If capitalism today is doubly threatened by moral relativism and religious fundamentalism it has only itself to blame: it devoured civil society, and there was no moral capital left for it to exploit.

Attempts have been made to build moral systems based on reason—Kant's metaphysics of morals, Rousseau's social contract, neo-Kantian systems of justice, and scientific socialism. Yet in the late twentieth century the men of reason who deposed God and put forward alternatives were themselves deposed because the social order they were constructing was seen to be one that could not pass its own test of reasonableness. The rot began with the liberation movements, which held society up against its own enlightenment ideals and showed that the principles of freedom and equality that underwrote modern democracies could not consistently exclude women, non-whites, homosexuals, and so on, without making a mockery of those principles.[3] The most powerful weapon used by the liberation movements was the charge of hypocrisy: it was contradictory for societies ostensibly founded on freedom and equality to ban women from certain occupations and to pay them less than men. The

TOWARDS A POST-SECULAR ETHICS

pointing out of contradictions was used to transform subterranean feelings of grievance into public indignation, and it worked to revolutionary effect. The result was societies that were far more tolerant, open and respectful of difference—an achievement that was, along with the defeat of totalitarianism, the greatest of the twentieth century.

But what began as an extension and rationalisation of modernism soon turned into the opposite. Modernity had created its own interrogators, and once they were let off the leash every aspect of settled social life became fair game, including features of the moral structure that could not be blamed for oppression, such as respect for elders. The framework built by reason was being dismantled: so much had been shown to be false perhaps the entire rule book was corrupt. Perhaps rule making itself had no justification and if it were jettisoned 'ultimate emancipation' could be ours. Obligation, duty, responsibility and reciprocity became oppressive. The visage of the good citizen was a mask that trapped the true individual behind it. The liberation movements identified the structures and attitudes that held people back and prevented them from flourishing and being treated with dignity. The social transformation let loose, however, gave rise to an increasing preoccupation with the self; a legitimate demand for equality and liberation morphed into a demand to put one's own interests first.

Albert Camus wrote, 'Nietzsche did not form a project to kill God. He found Him dead in the soul of his contemporaries'.[4] Although it was Nietzsche who wrote the funeral notice, it was Kant who delivered the *coup de grâce*. As long as the transcendent could be confused with the mundane, there was no need to be clear about the distinction between the will of God and the laws of man. By separating the domains and

Reconstructing a moral code

declaring the noumenon unknowable, Kant unleashed a train of thought that led to the nihilism of Nietzsche, the existentialists, and ultimately the post-modernists. For Nietzsche it was nihilism of a particular sort, 'classical nihilism'; in Heidegger's words, 'that historical process whereby the dominance of the "transcendent" becomes null and void, so that all being loses its worth and meaning'.[5] The end of metaphysics was understood as marking a new age—after God, beyond faith, an age characterised by a new freedom, the freedom to construct fresh values and a new meaning for human life. If the meaning of human life cannot be grounded in the transcendent, it can be grounded only in beings themselves.[6]

Throughout the history of transformation since the Enlightenment—the death of God, the enthronement and subsequent deposing of reason, the breaking of icons and stripping away of illusions, the retreat to individualism, the sexualisation of everyday life, and the shallowness of consumerism—one fact stood firm. At their core, humans remained moral beings. We judge everything in moral terms. Every story in the newspaper is suffused with ethical meaning; we measure our leaders less by their effectiveness than by their perceived virtue; television programs (be they cop shows, soap operas, reality or current affairs) always centre on moral themes. On being sent down, the villain thinks to himself, 'But I am a good person'. The churches have retreated and ethical systems built on reason have no purchase, yet the power of moral opinion remains. Religious dogma and rationalist ethical systems have together served to conceal the true source of this power and, now that we are left with nothing but the bare fact that humans are inherently moral creatures, we can look directly at it, our gaze no longer clouded by words from the pulpit and beliefs ordained by reason or social convention.

TOWARDS A POST-SECULAR ETHICS

Ironically, the post-modernists have not blown away moral law; they have simply removed the fog of modernist ideology that obscured it. We can now discern the enduring power of the law, although its source remains to be illuminated. The question of why humans should be moral creatures also has to be answered. After three centuries of progressive demoralisation—as the layers have been stripped away to lay bare our inescapably moral natures—the possibility of the remoralisation of social life now arises. In the words of Zygmunt Bauman, 'It remains to be seen whether the time of post-modernity will go down in history as the twilight, or the renaissance, of morality'.[7]

The 1960s were a disaster for Western culture—a necessary disaster, to be sure, but a disaster nonetheless. Yet it would be a mistake to conclude that the widespread sense among the people of rich countries that they live in societies with low and declining moral standards is merely a hangover from the 1950s, a relic that will be eliminated as younger cohorts move through the population structure. For younger people often share the moral concerns of older citizens, although they tend to be more fatalistic about their situation. Despite the claims of post-modern intellectuals, all cohorts are prone to believe that, although the traditional institutions of moral authority have lost their voice, society and personal behaviour should be governed by universally applied moral norms. Unlike the post-modernists, who assert that there are no moral absolutes, and the conservatives, who believe in moral absolutes but are unable to say what they are, in subsequent sections I develop an ethical theory that will provide the grounds for a morality (that is, a source of epistemological authority) and argue for some of the moral rules that emerge from these grounds. These ideas are based not in faith but in the distinction between phenomenon and noumenon and the forms of knowledge that arise from that. An ethical theory of this kind cannot draw its legitimacy from any worldly authority, since external authorities today lack legitimacy; it must derive from an inner legislator, one, moreover, who speaks to all humankind. This means that, if morality is not to be merely relative, its primary rules must be established a priori—that is, independent of all experience—and be therefore universal and necessary.

For the discussion that follows, it is worth bearing in mind that a workable moral system entails four components, or steps.

First, it should have a grounding, a basis in principle, that is not a moral rule itself but instead provides a justification for moral rules. Before the modern era moral codes sought their justification in the divine realm or some preordained social order. Modernism found such a code in an essential quality of humanity, rationality, which provided the grounds for the good.

As the second step, the grounds for morality must be elaborated into a set of rules, a moral code, that can guide everyday behaviour and make the transition from a principle to a practical morality. Gilles Deleuze put it this way:

> If men knew what Good was, and knew how to conform to it, they would not need laws. Laws, or the law, are only a 'second resort', a representative of the Good in a world deserted by the gods ... Laws are therefore, as it were, the imitation of the Good which serves as their highest principle.[8]

If the grounding is found in the noumenon, this second task represents the leap to the phenomenal realm, where the a priori principle becomes a set of social norms.

TOWARDS A POST-SECULAR ETHICS

Third, an effective morality must include a reason for people to accept it and respect its authority. This is an intellectual process ('It is right that society, including my own actions, should be governed by these rules') or a social one ('The consequences for me of repudiating these rules are serious').

Finally, an effective moral system must give people a motive for upholding the rules. This could be the same as the reason for accepting the system, but some people might accept the rules in principle yet be insufficiently motivated to abide by them. Ideally, both the reason for accepting the rules and the motive for upholding them arise from people's explicit or implicit acceptance of the grounds for morality, from a recognition of the noumenal principle—a personal affinity with the Good.

Pre-modern Christian morality illustrates the process. The basis of the moral law was the existence of God—the epitome of Good—and our giving ourselves over to God's will. The clergy, representatives of God in the phenomenal world, elaborated this into a set of rules to guide daily behaviour, using and interpreting instructions drawn from the sacred texts. The people accepted the rules because they accepted the authority of the clergy as the interpreters of God's word or because the consequences of acting otherwise were unpleasant. For those with little faith, the motivation for behaving morally was the same as the reason for doing so; for the faithful, the motive was their love of God, their belief in his goodness, and a desire to submit to his will.

The post-secular ethical theory put forward in this book derives from, but goes beyond, the ideas of Schopenhauer. His moral theory diverged radically from the rationalist ethics of Kant, so it is worthwhile briefly considering Kant's theory, not least because Kantian ideas underpin more recent academic efforts to promote a morality for modern times.

TWENTY-SEVEN

Rationalist ethics

THERE ARE TWO DOMINANT streams of rationalist ethics. Kant's duty ethic uses pure reason to determine a universal moral imperative that defines the obligations we ought to comply with. It is sometimes known as a 'deontological ethic', from the Greek *deon*, meaning duty, that which is binding. Moral law emerges from the process of deciding the principle of how to act, rather than the consequences of the actions, and is thus known as a non-consequentialist moral theory. Utilitarianism, on the other hand, judges the morality of acts by their consequences. Actions are morally right if they maximise the good, usually understood as the social good, where the good is happiness or some wider notion of value. Utilitarianism is the philosophical basis of modern neoclassical economics. It too draws its authority from the application of reason, but it applies reason to an evaluation of outcomes rather than the principle on which decisions are made.

In previous sections I suggest that the ethical foundations of modern economics are not only flawed but are dangerous to humanity, an opinion widely held among social scientists and the general public. Some social scientists, such as Rawls, Sen and Nussbaum, have reverted to Kant for an alternative to utilitarianism, and it is to Kantian ethics I now turn. Although in some respects very different from utilitarianism, Kantian ethics shares its rationalism. My rejection of rationality as the basis for moral theory provides the springboard to the quite different approach of Schopenhauer, an approach that, with variations and elaborations, I defend in this book.

Both Kant and Schopenhauer believed that we need to use metaphysics in order to understand morality, although the metaphysics they used differed radically. In principle, the value of a theory of morality based on metaphysics—that is, beyond experience—is that the theory's results do not depend on particular forms of human behaviour or social constructions; it is therefore universally applicable. In other words, the moral rules so developed will not be specific to any particular culture, since metaphysics is by definition beyond the particularities of human experience, including social structures and religious doctrine. What emerges from my argument will provide a moral absolute in place of moral relativism, but it is an absolute that does not rely on faith in an external authority whose existence can be disputed.

The transcendental idealism of both Kant and Schopenhauer makes a fundamental distinction between noumenon and phenomenon, essence and appearances, which, I argue, correspond to distinct forms of knowledge. It is reasonable to ask in which of these realms could a source of moral authority be found. Modern secular ethical systems look to cultural and social norms—that is, to phenomenal forms—while religious systems refer to the authority of God or sacred texts that seem to have their source in the noumenon. Neither of these approaches was satisfactory for

Kant. He maintained that we can know nothing of the noumenon and, indeed, used only negative reasons to deduce its existence. The phenomenon, on the other hand, can contain no absolutes to guide moral law, nothing that is common to humanity. So Kant went to that single thing that in his philosophy joins humans together as a unique species—their capacity to reason, in particular the a priori forms humans bring to the world so as to make sense of it. This approach had the enormous benefit of making the source of moral authority autonomous (providing individual humans with their own moral guide) rather than heteronomous (determined by an outside force, social or divine). It could therefore be linked directly with the notion of freedom. As we will see, establishing that freedom means living according to moral law was an astounding philosophical breakthrough by Kant. Schopenhauer's objectives were the same, although he went searching for the source of moral authority not in the a priori forms of reason but in the noumenon itself.

Rejecting religious dogma as the basis of moral law, in his *Groundwork of the Metaphysics of Morals* Kant declared that pure moral philosophy must be 'completely cleansed of everything that may be only empirical and that belongs to anthropology'.[1] The untenability of modern moral relativism reinforces Kant's decision, but he goes much further than that. In searching for the basis of morality he insists that it cannot be found in humans as they actually are: 'the ground of [moral] obligation . . . must not be sought in the nature of the human being or in the circumstances of the world in which he is placed, but a priori simply in concepts of pure reason'.[2] Even actual human experiences that are universal, although perhaps providing practical rules, can never provide the basis for moral law. In setting out to develop 'the supreme principle of morality'—the famous categorical imperative against which all practical morality can be judged—we are already alerted to an apprehension that Kant's moral law might be so abstracted from human experience that his ethics will have little purchase in popular life.

Typically, we make judgments about morally good and bad actions not so much according to the outcomes but according to the motives. A thief might turn in his accomplice so he can keep all the loot for himself, but we do not accord moral value to his action because, although the outcome might have been socially beneficial, his intention was malicious. A woman might throw herself into the sea, without any thought for her own safety, in a vain attempt to rescue someone, but we laud her courage and attribute moral value to her action. In order to understand why such 'good-willed' actions are valued in themselves we need to separate the purely good-willed motive from other motives—that is, actions taken simply from immediate inclination or for one's own enjoyment or because they are carried out in pursuit of another end. The modern enthusiasm among big companies for corporate social responsibility is a case in point. Insofar as the corporation in question adopts social responsibility in its investment or employment practices because it will be good for the bottom line, corporate social responsibility cannot be regarded as ethical behaviour: it is just self-interested behaviour with a public relations gloss. Indeed, it is morally worse than setting out simply to maximise profits without regard to the social consequences because it adds a layer of deception to self-interested behaviour. In contrast, if the company is resigned to seeing its profits decline as a result of adopting socially responsible investment and employment practices it (or, rather, its decision makers) can be said to be operating ethically.

Kant argued that the motives for acting make an action morally good only if the action is unconditioned. This means we must know what lies behind the reason for acting in a particular way. Kant calls this the 'principle' on which someone acts. So we need to know not the immediate motive for acting but instead the principle underlying that motive. Thus, although Kant accepts that motives matter in practice, he rejects the common view that sympathy or compassion can be the reason for judging whether an act is morally praiseworthy. He argues that purely good-willed actions must be motivated not by an immediate inclination but by 'duty':

> To be beneficent where one can is a duty, and besides there are many souls so sympathetically attuned that, without any other motive or vanity or self-interest they find an inner satisfaction in spreading joy around them and can take delight in the satisfaction of others . . .[3]

In this view, the inner satisfaction a sympathetic soul derives from helping others invalidates the moral worth of the action because the principle behind the action is something like 'I help others because I want to'. On the other hand, the same beneficent action could be taken because the actor feels he or she is required by duty to act in that way. Such a person is motivated by 'respect for law', and the principle that provides the motive is something like 'I help because it is my duty'. Kant says, then, he has shown that 'neither fear nor inclination but simply respect for the law is that incentive which can give actions a moral worth'.[4] In this way Kant secularised morality.

Kant's move reverses the argument made by most other moral philosophers and reflected in our four steps to a moral system, whereby moral laws are derived from the principle of the good. For Kant, that which is morally good is deduced from the higher principle, which for him is the law of duty. Deleuze puts it this way:

> When Kant talks about the law, it is . . . as the highest instance . . . It is the Good which depends on the law, and not vice versa . . . [The law] does not tell us what we must do, but to what (subjective) rule we must conform, whatever our action. Any action is moral if its maxim can be thought without contradiction as universal, and if its motive has no other object than this maxim.[5]

In Kant's view, although it deserves encouragement, an action undertaken by someone who derives inner satisfaction from spreading joy around 'has no true moral worth' because the principle or maxim on which it is based 'lacks moral content, namely that of doing such actions not from inclination but *from duty*'.[6] The difference between a person who acts on sympathy and one who acts on duty (although both act for the benefit of others) is that, according to Kant's understanding of human psychology, the sympathetic person helps others because he or she derives pleasure from doing so, whereas the person acting according to duty acts on the principle that it is right to help others. The idea that the sympathetic person helps others *because* he or she enjoys doing so seems, however, to confuse correlation with causation.

Kant argued that moral actions are those taken out of a sense of duty, but he should also explain why anyone would feel compelled to act out of duty—the fourth step in our schema. Failure to act according to duty is a failure to act rationally, but this is not enough because reason contains no motive force, no drive to act. So Kant deifies reason, arguing that we exist to impose reason on the natural world, to create the 'noble ideal' of a universal 'kingdom of ends' populated by rational beings no longer governed by feelings and impulses. In this kingdom reason is the only organising principle; it rules not with any practical motive but solely to lend 'dignity' to its members.[7]

As critics have pointed out, this seems so far removed from how moral obligation operates in real humans it could only be a law contrived in heaven for heavenly beings. When someone acts immorally we do not criticise them for being irrational: we criticise them for being immoral. Kant would say that, whatever its motivation, we judge an act reprehensible or otherwise on the basis of whether it accords with the universal law. Schopenhauer, as we will see, accepted the common view that an immoral act is a failure of character rather than a failure of logic, a position expressed before Kant by the eloquent Rousseau: 'Although it might belong to Socrates . . . to acquire virtue by reason, the human race would long since have ceased to be, had its preservation depended only on the reasonings of the individuals composing it'.[8]

The predisposition to 'favour the head over the heart' becomes apparent to anyone who reads the works of Kant and modern Kantians: the relentless and sometimes convoluted pursuit of logic seems designed to build walls that keep living, breathing humans out. The explanation for this is the belief that reason, and nothing else, is the essence of humanity and that the rules are to be found in a priori concepts rather than the obscure corners of the human heart. In a way, this path was natural for Kant, since his 'all-crushing' insight was that the principles of reason are not to be found in the world of appearances but are imposed on that world by humans in the act of cognition. Schopenhauer argued that Kant's appeal to duty, and similar imperatives such as law, command and obligation, in fact have their origins in theology.[9] It could be otherwise only if duty—which Wordsworth called the 'Stern Daughter of the Voice of God'—can be motivated in the nature of humans or the social worlds they construct, both of which Kant denied.

Having established that acting out of respect for moral law means acting rationally, we now confront the question of what it means in practice to act rationally. Kant argued that we respond to 'imperatives', or commands to act, that can be hypothetical or categorical. Hypothetical imperatives are self-interested and are of the form 'Unless I act this way I will suffer a detriment or be punished' (by God, the law, or someone else) or 'If I act in this way I will benefit'. A categorical imperative is a reason for action in itself, not because we expect to gain or suffer; it is an unconditional imperative, a universal law to which the rules governing our own behaviour must conform if we are to act morally. There is only one categorical imperative, the famous Golden Rule, expressed roughly as 'Do unto others as you would have them do unto you'. More formally, Kant declared, '[A]ct only in accordance with that maxim through which you can at the same time will that it become a universal law'.[10] This means an action is moral only if one could consistently desire that it be applied to everyone.

In practice, this rule is applied by performing a sort of thought experiment in which we ask ourselves: Is this a law I can exempt myself from with good reason?[11] This is the kind of thought experiment that is at the core of the neo-Kantian John Rawls' famous theory of justice, and it suffers from the same problems. In Rawls' experiment, we are imagined to reach collective agreement on a set of social rules from behind a 'veil of ignorance' that prevents us from knowing how we personally will be affected by those rules. As with Kant's categorical imperative, Rawls' abstract principle can provide no reason for the people to accept his conception of social justice and no motive to act morally in the world we actually inhabit, as opposed to the celestial one in which we are imagined to decide on what is right.

Interestingly, Korsgaard compares the unconditional nature of the categorical imperative with the situation in which a person acts on the will of God.[12] It is pointless to ask why the person acted on the will of God; it is simply necessary to act according to the will of God. Obeying God is a given. This 'illustration' risks letting the cat out of the bag, because if we take away God we are left searching for the categorical, the ultimate principle. Indeed, Schopenhauer accused Kant's ethics of being 'theological morals in disguise'.[13]

Kant argues that judgments about the moral worth of our actions must be measured against a quality that is common to all humans as rational beings: '*rational nature exists as an end in itself*'.[14] This then becomes the end for everyone. Humans' rationality, which distinguishes them from animals, assigns an intrinsic value to humans, and on this basis Kant reformulates his categorical imperative. The 'supreme principle' is thus transmuted from the principle of rationality to the intrinsic value of humans, the bearers of rationality. The 'practical imperative' is that moral actions must always take humans as ends in themselves and not as means to an end: 'So act that you use humanity, whether in your own person or in the person of any other, always at the same time as an end, never merely as a means'.[15]

Compared with the conformity of one's personal maxim with universal law, this is a simple and much more compelling rule for judging moral actions. All it requires is that humans be treated as intrinsically valuable, and they can be so regarded because they are uniquely rational beings or because of some other natural quality. Thus Kant's 'practical imperative' seems to be more than a reformulation of the categorical imperative: it is a criterion based on the intrinsic value of humans, one that can be deduced in a more persuasive way, although it may require us to find a crack in the wall of unknowability that Kant constructed around the noumenon.

Conscious of the categorical imperative's difficulties, modern Kantians no longer cleave to it. Instead, they adopt a number of propositions drawn from Kant's practical imperative—the irreducibility of humans, the need for reciprocity, the importance of self-respect, and a commitment to reject exploitation of others.[16] These are all very defensible, yet for Kant the categorical imperative was deduced from his transcendental idealism, so that his ethics were grounded in his metaphysics. An example is helpful here.

Korsgaard develops one of Kant's own examples to illustrate how the categorical imperative works. How do we judge the morality of someone who borrows money, promising to pay it back next week but with no intention of honouring the promise? For Kant, our condemnation of such behaviour can provide no evidence of immorality. Before we can condemn we must first formulate the universal law against which to test the behaviour. It might be 'Everyone who needs some ready cash should make false promises'. Kant shows that, if the person willed this maxim as a universal law, this would be a contradiction 'since no one would believe what was promised him but would laugh at all such expressions as vain pretences'.[17]

Kant wanted to establish a principle by which to judge acts (the first of our four steps). The principle of non-contradiction provides the basis and allows us to decide that 'Everyone should steal' should not be willed as law. How such a principle is transformed into practical decisions (moving from the first to the second step) immediately creates difficulties. In this example, if someone decides not to steal because if everyone were free to do likewise all would suffer, the basis for the decision is self-interest. The metaphysical sublime is reduced to the money-grubbing ridiculous.

It seems that in Kant's example the moral judgment has in fact been surreptitiously inserted into the construction of the problem. It is not the contradiction between the individual action and the universal law that makes the action immoral: immorality is already contained in the construction of the universal law—that is, 'Everyone who needs some ready cash should make false promises'. We all know that in the circumstance we are imagining it is wrong to make a false promise, so we feel comfortable with Kant's 'conclusion' that it must be immoral because it is contradictory. But we have yet to answer the question of the origin of the moral condemnation that was smuggled into the example.

Rationalist moral philosophies have a characteristic that makes them incapable of providing answers to post-modern ethical questions. Kantian and utilitarian theories develop universal rules that are meant to apply equally to all agents. In each case what is morally good for the goose is good for the gander. Yet in situations where the moral decision is victimless it is common today for people to adopt the view that, although it would be wrong for them to do a particular thing, they would not condemn others for acting differently. If we were to ask a prostitute if she believed everyone should be free to sell their body for sex, she would probably say 'yes' but accept that others might not hold the same view. This cannot

TOWARDS A POST-SECULAR ETHICS

occur using Kant's approach because, for him, if it is wrong for one person it is wrong for all. The prostitute might not want to see her personal view turned into universal law—and not only for the effect that might have on the price of sex. Although on the face of it we give the law to ourselves using a priori concepts, since these concepts apply to all rational beings, in practice Kant understood moral law in the same way as civil law or Old Testament law—universal rules against which personal behaviour is to be judged for moral worthiness. In the sections that follow I put forward an alternative view, one that does not become ensnared in this way.

TWENTY-EIGHT
Genuine philanthropy

IN ADDITION TO EXPRESSING a principle that is beyond all particular forms of social behaviour, a moral system must be sufficiently compelling and intuitively powerful to motivate ordinary people to apply it to everyday life. The Kantian grounding of moral law in the most abstract principle has some intellectual appeal, but it could never move ordinary people to act on its logic. Kant understood this but insisted that the incentives that prompt people to act on duty are irrelevant to judging the moral worth of the action. In sharp contrast, Schopenhauer believed we must search for the principles of moral law in the way we actually behave:

> I assume . . . that the purpose of ethics is to indicate, explain, and trace to its ultimate ground the extremely varied behaviour of men from a moral point of view. Therefore there is no other way for discovering the foundation of ethics than the empirical, namely, to investigate whether there are generally any actions to which we must attribute *genuine moral worth*.[1]

TOWARDS A POST-SECULAR ETHICS

Kant's insistence that the way ordinary people think about morality and so shape their behaviour can teach us nothing about moral theory attracted scathing comment from Schopenhauer, directed especially at Kantian professors:

> There are difficult combinations, heuristic rules, propositions balanced on a needle point, and stilted maxims, from which it is no longer possible to look down on real life and its hurly burly. Thus they are certainly very well adapted for echoing in lecture halls and for giving practice in sagacity and subtleness, but can never produce the appeal that actually exists in everyone to act justly and do good . . .[2]

The sentiment resonates today. Take this typical passage from the neo-Kantian John Rawls, who wants to 'clarify' the definition of social disadvantage:

> In order to clarify these matters, let us recall where a theory of the good has already played a role. First of all, it is used to define the least favored members of society. The difference principle assumes that this can be done. It is true that the theory need not define a cardinal measure of welfare. We do not have to know how disadvantaged the least fortunate are, since once this group is singled out, we can take their ordinal preferences (from the appropriate point of view) as determining the proper arrangement of the basic structure.[3]

Rawls is more skilled than most at balancing propositions on a needle point, something that established his reputation as a sage, yet one can only speculate on the welcome he would have received when expanding on his views at the local soup kitchen. This is not just carping: Marx famously said,

Genuine philanthropy

'Philosophers have hitherto only interpreted the world in various ways; the point is to change it'.[4] Unless philosophers are content merely to interpret the world, a theory of morality must be persuasive beyond the academy: it must reverberate in the population. It remains the case that, although we must take our raw material from everyday life, the principle of morality must be distilled from that material and located in the essential nature of humans as they actually are. As I note, that humans have an essential nature is a contested view in the post-modern world, so it is worth giving a little more consideration to the argument that there is no absolute principle of morality, the first step in the schema I set.

The social constructionist maintains that rules can do no more than reflect the institutions and social formations in which they operate; that is, all moral rules are arbitrary and relative only to the society in which they arise. This 'moral scepticism' dates from at least the eighteenth century and has simply resurfaced in post-modern guise. It is true that in any society the majority of moral proscriptions and prescriptions are socially determined: in some countries it is extremely rude to sit with the soles of one's feet facing another person, to eat with one's left hand or, for a man, to touch a woman's clothes. And within a society rules change. In Western countries premarital sex was once met with severe sanction; now condemnation of it is widely seen as old-fashioned, even eccentric. In these cases, morally worthwhile acts are motivated by a desire to be respected or honoured by one's peers or society, and unworthy acts are avoided in order not to attract disrespect or shame. In other words, conformity is pursued for reasons of self-interest or everyday sociality, to ease one's path through the social world.

Nevertheless, the sceptical view that all morality is socially constructed must be rejected because in every society there are people who act morally while seeking no advantage for themselves. They act in such a way because they believe that to do so is right. These actions of 'disinterested philanthropy and of entirely voluntary justice'[5] are recognised for their purity and often receive special attention and admiration. The girl who finds a wallet containing a large sum of money and hands it intact to the police will probably be rewarded with praise from the authorities, gushing newspaper stories, and the gratitude of the rightful owner, perhaps taking the form of one or more of the bank notes in question. The girl does not act honestly because she expects those rewards: she does it because she believes it is the right thing to do. Indeed, if she handed in the wallet in the expectation of a reward the moral value of her act would be diminished. As Rousseau wrote, 'gratitude is a duty which ought to be paid, but not a right to be exacted'.[6] Self-interest always devalues moral worth (a position Kant took, too). The rewards demanded for 'worthy' acts need not take a monetary form. The philanthropist who gives away a large amount of money is viewed through jaundiced eyes if he expects public approbation or, as is common in the philanthropic community, requires the recipient of the gift to jump through hoops while singing the donor's praises. The gift then becomes an exchange, and philanthropy is transformed into narcissism; love of humankind is exposed as love of self.

There are, however, genuine philanthropists who give without any expectation of reward and, indeed, by giving anonymously, protect themselves from the moral pollution the bestowing of honour can impart. Every one of the anonymous charitable donations made by millions of people each year is an act of philanthropy. A newspaper reported that a passing motorist rushed into a burning house to rescue two children, risking his life for theirs, but drove away before anyone could ask him his name.

The possibility of unalloyed altruism for the benefit of strangers was confirmed by Richard Titmuss in *The Gift Relationship*, which examined why people donate blood.[7] In technologically sophisticated and individualistic societies there are few opportunities for ordinary people to practise altruism outside their immediate family and personal relationships. Giving blood is one of those few opportunities, and the beneficiary is unknown. When a large number of British donors were asked why they gave blood, half nominated purely altruistic reasons, using phrases such as 'to help others', 'because it might save somebody's life', 'a small contribution to the welfare of humanity' and 'no man is an island'.[8] Others said they were motivated by social reasons (pressure from friends or workmates, a sense of duty to the nation or community) or personal reasons (to learn one's blood group, snob appeal), including reciprocity (the donor or a family member had benefited from a transfusion).

Peter Singer illustrates his belief in the existence of disinterested philanthropy, also using the case of blood donation, by referring to studies showing that self-interested motivations become less important and philanthropic reasons more important as individuals continue to give blood.[9] People motivated by altruism are more likely to give and keep giving, while those who are selfishly motivated quickly fall away. It is not hard to see that paying donors for their blood transforms an intrinsically philanthropic act into an economic one and removes the opportunity to act altruistically. Paying for blood is an example of how putting a price on some things can actually devalue them, and it illustrates the essential ethical objection to neoliberalism.

TOWARDS A POST-SECULAR ETHICS

The fact that humans sometimes act philanthropically—without any idea of gain, often anonymously, and sometimes at personal cost—demonstrates that not all moral actions are socially determined. In *Lord of the Flies* William Golding constructed a world in which all social conventions broke down among a group of boys marooned on an island. Barbarism ensued, yet in the hearts of some boys goodness prevailed. Why? The seeds of an answer can be found in a story. An English missionary was living in India in 1984 when Mrs Gandhi was assassinated by a Sikh guard. Riots followed. A murderous Hindu mob chased a Sikh man past the home of the Englishman, who stepped out to rescue him and shield him from his pursuers. Later, the missionary's children, fearful that their father might have been set upon by the mob, challenged him for risking his life. He asked them to imagine they were the children of the Sikh man and to consider whether they would have wanted this Christian stranger to intervene to save their father. 'Of course', they said and fell silent.

What is it, then, that motivates such acts of moral virtue? It could be Kantian duty, although I argue that within the abstractions of Kant it is difficult to discern a motive for acting according to duty. A more plausible explanation would be a sense, particularly strong in the missionary, that recognition of our common humanity obliges us to act in this way. In the next section I develop this idea, drawing on the fundamental distinction between phenomenon and noumenon and leading to the fixed point of ethics, what I call 'the moral self'.

TWENTY-NINE
The moral self

IN SECTION 21 I argue that, in addition to the personal self, we exist as a universal Self. Through a form of intuition we are able to understand that the inner nature of each of us is identical with the thing-in-itself—the universal substance or subtle essence—and that all existence has a unitary nature. Returning to our metaphor, if one could pass through the 'secret passage' and enter the citadel of the noumenon, the distinction between subject and object, between self and other, would dissolve. In that world one would participate in the universe (including all other beings) rather than being a mere observer of it. So, in opposition to our everyday consciousness, in which we identify with our own bodies and egos, convinced that we are real and distinct, we are also capable of ontological identification with the being of all. The essence of the noumenon is the absence of plurality and temporality because space and time belong to the world of appearances that shapes our everyday experience and understanding. Considered metaphysically, therefore, all individuals in the world have at their core the same inner nature: the

TOWARDS A POST-SECULAR ETHICS

'subtle part' of each of us is one and the same. I call it the subtle essence, our inner nature, the universal Self.

When we identify with the universal Self the 'illusion' of our independent existence falls away and the personal self merges with the universal Self, which is shared by all. We recognise in another our own inner nature. Abolition of the distinction between subject and object and the participation of self in others give rise to what I call 'metaphysical empathy', and it is this that forms the grounds of morality and the basis of the moral self.[1] Metaphysical empathy is the awareness of participation in the being of others that arises from identification of the self with the universal essence.

If the universal Self is the subtle essence of each of us, the moral self is the most immediate expression of that universal Self in the phenomenal world. It is the innermost voice of conscience, where all personal interests, social conventions, duties and obligations are left behind. For the religiously inclined it is the aspect of themselves that communicates with their god; for the secular it is the domain of their inner judge.

In its essence the moral self, emerging from the noumenon, is universal, but it is also personal, and its elaboration into concrete moralities can take myriad forms while always grounded in the common principle. Responding to the demands of the moral self provides the reason for taking the moral path. When we have behaved in a way that falls short of our ethical standards we do not cry out, 'Oh, my God, I have violated universal law, contravened the agreement I reached behind the veil of ignorance, or breached the social contract'. No, we say, 'I have let myself down; I have gone against my better nature', and that better nature is the moral self. It is the arbiter, the inner judge, who speaks to us with an immediacy and authority no external legislation or contract can possess.

The moral self

People who lose touch with their moral self lose touch with the universal Self; the further we drift from our moral self the less 'human' we become. It is the aspect of ourselves in the phenomenal world that most directly reminds us of our origins. The birth of the moral self is at the same time the birth of the self. Lévinas is right to claim that the self is born not through differentiation from others but through union with them: 'To be human means to live as if one were not a being among beings . . .'[2] Yet the worlds constructed by Kant, Rousseau and Rawls are worlds of differentiation, of distance between one and another, where the codes governing our behaviour must be 'worked out' with the help of philosophers, theologians and legislators. In such worlds we do not trust our own moral instincts for we have none, and we must submit ourselves to a negotiated ethic, an agreed set of rules that always stands outside and above us.

From the moment of its creation the moral self is presented with an almost impossible task—to live a life honourably. Acting honourably is fraught with uncertainty because there is always doubt about what is right. Bauman writes, 'The moral self is a self always haunted by the suspicion that it is not moral enough'.[3] Not quite. In a world of ambiguity and competing ethical claims, there is a kernel of the self to which we can always retreat, where from the root point of our existence the moral self, that inner voice inaudible unless all other sounds are stilled, will soothe away the doubts.

Thus morality, as expressed in the phenomenal world of groups, societies and religions, always has its source in the noumenon: 'All genuine virtue proceeds from the immediate and *intuitive* knowledge of the metaphysical identity of all beings . . .'[4] Metaphysical empathy belongs to the noumenon but has its most direct expression in the phenomenon as the moral self. We cannot experience this form of awareness directly as phenomenon but we can feel it and be directed by it when outside the citadel, where it takes the form of the moral self. It is this form of identification that 'crosses the boundary' between noumenon and phenomenon and provides the stuff of the pure moral self, unsullied by any phenomenal idea.

I am not setting morality against humanity. Nietzsche levelled such a charge against Christianity, in which morality lies other than in us, in a 'beyond' that devalues the only world there is, consigning the good to another realm we should aspire to because real humans are fundamentally immoral and decadent and need to redeem themselves. In that morality 'God' is a 'counterconcept of life', whereas I place morality at the centre of our humanity, the universal Self: 'The morality that would un-self man is the morality of decline *par excellence* . . . fundamentally, it negates life'.[5]

Nietzsche detected a 'hostility to life' lurking beneath the Christian message, hiding behind faith in a better existence— 'a beyond invented the better to slander this life'. Christianity was more prodigal in elaborating moral themes than any other faith, 'for, confronted with morality (especially Christian, or unconditional, morality), life *must* continually and inevitably be in the wrong . . .'[6] Nietzsche contrasted the life-affirming Dionysus with the life-denying Jesus of the Gospels, and said of the latter: 'not only does he obsessively slander his enemies, he stands opposed to this world and this life, and neither takes nor teaches any joy in small pleasures and beauties'.[7] The interpretation of Christianity Nietzsche attacked arises from the idea that the noumenon stands in opposition to the phenomenon, that God inhabits a realm divorced from and superior to the life of humans and must pass down the moral law from one to another, that moral law is not something we discover within ourselves but instead is imposed on us by authorities divine.

The moral self does not set noumenon against phenomenon, God against man: it is the point at which they meet. The moral self provides a philosophical rationale for Thomas Aquinas' theological idea that conscience is the universal voice of moral law, where conscience is understood as the practical application of 'synderesis', the God-given, innate awareness of the distinction between good and evil.

Metaphysical empathy is not reserved for the sages: it is manifest in everyday life. Sometimes one's eyes meet those of a beggar in the street. You look into those eyes and the beggar looks into yours, and both of you realise that, despite the gulf in life circumstances, there is no distinction between you; you are of the same substance and thus of equal worth. Before compassion for the misfortune of the beggar can be sparked, a bond of humanity is struck, affirming equal dignity. This direct metaphysical identification should not be mistaken for pity or the guilt we might feel because we are more fortunate, something beggars can trade on by adopting supplicant poses and hangdog expressions. Confusing mutual acknowledgment of equal dignity with the pity aroused because of the inequality of the situation inspired in Nietzsche his theory of *ressentiment*, according to which reacting to pity, other than 'noble pity', is a form of weakness that must be resisted—the more so since the weak use it to enfeeble the nobility of the strong.

The idea of a direct bond with a stranger is at the heart of the story of the Good Samaritan, as told by Christ in Luke to illustrate the concept of *agape*, Christian (as opposed to erotic) love. Schopenhauer explained it this way:

TOWARDS A POST-SECULAR ETHICS

> That a man gives alms without having, even remotely, any other object than of lessening the want that oppresses another, is possible insofar as he recognizes that it is his own self which now appears before him in that doleful and dejected form, and hence that he recognizes again his own inner being-in-itself in the phenomenal appearance of another.[8]

As a principle, the recognition of self in others is widely accepted and comes to life in public debate when it is most blatantly breached. In refusing to condemn the use of 'waterboarding' to torture prisoners suspected of terrorism, President Bush's Attorney-General nominee Michael Mukasey said, 'It's a very different kind of person'.[9] We must distance ourselves from others when we want to be cruel to them. Their status as other is used to defend everything from Rwandan massacres to the decision to liquidate the populations of Hiroshima and Nagasaki instead of proving the power of atom bombs by dropping them on depopulated areas.

COMPASSION

Metaphysical empathy can take two forms in the moral self at the point where it manifests in the phenomenon—compassion and the will to justice. As an emotion, compassion, or loving kindness, can be expressed only in a human separated from the universal Self, yet it is but the shortest distance from the root point of metaphysical empathy to the moral self and the human heart, where compassion is felt. In Christian theology this idea of compassion emerging from metaphysical empathy is close to the notion of charity, which is understood as the divine form of love. In itself, compassion is pure and

The moral self

disinterested. 'Love embraces the whole of existence in each of its dimensions', wrote Pope Benedict XVI in his first encyclical, *Deus Caritas Est*.[10] The ability to feel this identification with the other is an indispensable part of being human. Indeed, people who seem to display no compassion for their fellow creatures are described as 'inhuman', and 'humanity' is often used as a synonym for compassion. The quality does not come about as a result of social conditioning, religious instruction or education, although undoubtedly these can nurture a seed planted otherwise in our hearts.

Identification of the self in others is generally experienced most intensely with those we love. When a mother stands before her sick child and wishes she could draw the illness into her own body, it is metaphysical empathy at work. In the *Upanishads* one can find familial love traced to the compassion that arises from identification with the noumenon—'It is not for the love of children that children are dear: it is for the love of the self (*atman*) that children are dear' and similarly for the love of a husband, a wife and all things.[11] Schopenhauer expressed the same thought: 'Paternal love, by virtue of which the father is ready to do, to suffer, and to take a risk more for his child than for himself ... is due to the very fact that the begetter recognizes himself once more in the begotten'.[12] In every major religion the emotion most characteristic of the gods is compassion, or loving kindness. Shakespeare saw it as the antidote to the malice that infects the human heart and in *The Merchant of Venice* wrote of the divine origins of mercy, an aspect of compassion, which 'droppeth as the gentle rain from heaven', and is

> ... *an attribute of God himself;*
> *And earthly power doth then show likest God's*
> *When mercy seasons justice* ...

TOWARDS A POST-SECULAR ETHICS

Literally, compassion means participation in another's suffering. The emphasis on the suffering of others expresses a metaphysics in which human existence represents a separation from the undisturbed serenity of the noumenon, a separation that gives rise to struggle, striving, pain, disappointment and death. It is consistent both with the Christian idea of the Fall and with the first of the Buddha's Four Noble Truths—life is suffering. Critics such as Max Scheler argue that the emphasis on compassion is one-sided, fails to account for positive values such as joy and happiness, and therefore treats pity as having a higher ethical value than rejoicing,[13] a contention that perhaps owes something to Nietzsche. Scheler also claims, however, that compassion presupposes a distinction between individuals and is thus of the phenomenal world and therefore illusory. I maintain that compassion, although of the phenomenon, is, like the moral self, separated from the noumenon by the thinnest of veils.

THE WILL TO JUSTICE

In contrast with compassion, the will to justice—the second manifestation of metaphysical empathy in the moral self—is a principle expressed more in the head than in the heart, but it is the same distance, so to speak, from the core of metaphysical empathy. Although more abstract than compassion, it is no less powerful. The sting of conscience is felt when our deeds violate the principle of justice because we have behaved badly towards someone or counter to the social interest. This is why conscience is a universal human quality. It is like a stray dog that attaches itself to you, follows you around and will not be chased away. Rationalisation can banish it from sight only temporarily, as Raskolnikov discovered after murdering the old pawnbroker.

At heart, violation of the principle of justice represents an attempt at repudiation of the Self in others and thus the inner nature of one's own being. The dull feeling of despair and regret it causes us to bear can be expiated only by a process of confession, contrition and absolution from one representing the inner self of the person we have wronged. It is at this point we give ourselves over to the unification of self with the absolute.

Without wanting to make too strong a distinction, one might say that the feeling of compassion is expressed in an ethic of care, something more in keeping with the predisposition of women, and the principle of justice is expressed in an ethic of fairness, to which men are predisposed. Each can act to forestall immoral behaviour—one considering the suffering that might be caused to particular people and the other considering the consequences for all should the immoral behaviour be permitted. David E. Cartwright observes:

> If it is true, as Carol Gilligan has argued... that a woman's morality differs from a man's morality in being more concrete and contextual than abstract, more nonprincipled than principled, more personal rather than impersonal, motivated more by care than duty, and structured more by responsibilities than rights, one could mount a strong argument that the misogynistic Schopenhauer has more of a woman's morality than a man's.[14]

In her influential book *In a Different Voice*, Gilligan argues that the ability to integrate these two approaches—an ethic of rights and an ethic of care—is a sign of moral maturity.[15] This twofold division in the phenomenon has one source in the noumenon, yet it allows us to account for both 'actions of disinterested philanthropy' (such as giving blood) and of 'entirely voluntary justice' (such as the poor man who, moved not by compassion but by justice, returns the lost wallet to the rich man). In suggesting that women are more inclined to evince compassion and men justice, I stress that the male principle is to be found in women, to a greater or lesser degree, and the female in men, in the way that in the yin–yang symbol an element of yin is seen in the yang and vice versa.

Both compassion and the will to justice are active principles. Justice is not that of the courts—cold, remote, dispassionate. It is affirmative. Nor is compassion intemperate. The two intermingle, justice seasoned by mercy, compassion fortified by reason. At their highest level emotion and judgment unite.

THIRTY

Emotions as judgments

I SAY I DO not want to draw too strong a distinction between compassion as a female principle and the will to justice as a male principle. To do so would entrench a longstanding misconception in philosophy—the belief that emotion is distinct from (and inferior to) reason. In this tradition, emotions are seen to be spontaneous irruptions from some 'natural' source that is pre-rational. They are thus seen to be outside what makes humans unique, their rational capacity. This, of course, was the hallmark of Kant's philosophy, and it frames all post-Kantian thought. John Rawls uses all the axioms of logic to construct an edifice of reason to justify his idea of justice. Like Kant's, his system is left with a gaping hole: What motivates real people, descended from the heavens he constructed and no longer blinded to their own life circumstances, to act on the principles so carefully engineered in that celestial place where no real emotion is permitted?[1] With goodness already defined as rationality, the awkward entry of human passions threatens to destabilise the entire edifice. But Rawls, like his master, is skilled at banishing the passions, or at least depriving them of any power. In this way, love of humankind is dismissed as 'supererogatory'—that is, unnecessary to motivate moral action. For Rawls, love of humankind goes beyond moral requirements because we have already convinced ourselves that adhering to moral law is for the social good. In his conception of justice, love is a luxury good, just as for the Chicago economist Gary Becker love is defined as a 'non-marketed household commodity'.[2] For Rawls there is no prior or independent self, and guilt is not spontaneous but must be constructed and emerges as a learnt dissociation between what society demands and what I want. Before my cheeks turn red from shame my brain must decide if I have transgressed. As with the neo-classical economist who imagines real humans to be no more than 'agents' engaged in an endless process of calculation in order to decide how to act, this form of philosophising idealises an emotionless domain inhabited by desiccated number-crunchers, an androcentric world in which 'wisdom' is measured by IQ. The Rawls who set out to rescue social justice ends up with a proceduralist ethic that is every bit as lacking in humanity as the world of Milton Friedman and Gary Becker.

It is an unremarked fact that the objective Rawls describes for his agents—to set and pursue a plan that would best achieve one's fundamental desires—cannot actually deliver happiness because the desires in question are all extrinsic ones. The evidence suggests that living out a life plan focused on personal freedom and increasing one's income cannot, despite Rawls, make us happy. Michael Sandal observes that Rawls' assumption is not universally shared but 'is implicated too deeply in the contingent preferences of, say, Western liberal, bourgeois life plans',[3] plans that even segments of the Western bourgeoisie are themselves now reassessing. The determination to exclude the emotional from moral judgment is an oddly Western preoccupation. In the traditional languages of Buddhism there is no word for emotions as such: all types of mental activity are associated with feelings of one kind or another.[4]

Robert Solomon has put forward a sustained case in favour of dissolution of the distinction between reason and the passions and thus the intermingling of the male and female principles. Emotions are judgments, he says, 'much more akin to thoughts than to physiological or physical commotion'.[5] If we feel indignant at an injustice, judgment and emotion are bound up together. Such a reaction is not deliberative in the way reason demands, but a spontaneous judgment is a judgment nevertheless. We move through life making moral decisions—should I open the door for that person? Should I report a litterer? Should I hand in some lost money? Should I vote for that person? Should I send my child to a private school? Should I have an abortion?—and each one, whether made spontaneously or after consideration, is stimulated and properly informed by emotions. It is untenable to maintain that deliberation using principles of reason alone, if that is at all possible, is more likely to result in better judgments than decisions made in the heat of passion. It is often true, as Shakespeare wrote, that 'a hot temper leaps over a cold decree', but the best judgments are usually warm.

People who argue that moral judgments, or any decisions, can be disentangled from emotional responses are not clarifying a messy situation but are assigning priority to one emotion over all others—the desire for emotionless activity. *Ad hominem* arguments are generally frowned on, but sometimes they help us understand positions more clearly. The philosophers and economists who are most committed to deriving theories on pure principles of reason are generally those who are most alienated from their own emotional lives. Spinoza and Nietzsche argued that such attempts are futile.[6] Perhaps the rigid division between reason and emotions would have been less pronounced had women been permitted to play a greater role in Western intellectual life.

—•—

Solomon has marshalled discursive arguments and everyday observation to establish that emotions should be considered to be judgments rather than irrational disturbances to the more normal, more desirable state of calm reasonableness. The case is even stronger for moral emotions—those that are involved in making moral judgments and that motivate moral action. More recently, a new and powerful body of evidence has confirmed and extended the idea that moral judgment springs from a complex interaction of affective and cognitive processes associated with specific neural structures in the human brain. Neuroimaging studies using modern brain-scanning techniques have given rise to the idea of a 'moral brain', defined as 'a network of closely interconnected regions that integrates the diverse functions involved in moral appraisals'.[7]

Neuroscientists have explored how the emotion-related areas of the brain contribute to moral judgment.[8] The ventromedial prefrontal cortex is the centre of the brain associated most closely with 'prosocial emotions', notably compassion, gratitude, pride, shame, regret and guilt. Rationalist philosophy's approach to understanding the formation of moral judgments in favour of conscious reasoning is contradicted by neuroimaging studies showing that when subjects are engaged in moral decision making the emotion-processing areas of the brain (as well as the cognitive areas) are activated.

In one important study neuroscientists tested subjects with damaged prefrontal cortexes that interfered with their emotional responsiveness, comparing them with subjects with unimpaired brains.[9] Individuals with lesions in the ventromedial prefrontal cortex exhibited diminished emotional responses overall and markedly reduced social emotions—including severely diminished capacity for empathy, embarrassment and guilt—although their cognitive abilities (general intelligence, logical reasoning and declared knowledge of social and moral norms) were unaffected by the damage to their brains.

If emotions play a causal role in making moral judgments, we would expect people with damage to the emotion-processing areas of the brain to reach different judgments compared with people whose emotion centres are unimpaired, especially in the case of moral judgments that are more highly charged with emotional content. This proves to be so.* In situations involving a high emotional charge—such as a decision to push someone in front of a speeding train in order to save the lives of several others—those with damaged brains are much more likely to follow a utilitarian rule, one that increases aggregate social welfare (sacrifice one to save more), even though it requires inflicting certain death on someone. In other words, people who are unable to have emotional reactions to harming others are more likely to make 'cold-blooded' utilitarian judgments. They reach their decisions by using logic and knowledge of social norms but without the leavening effect of emotions such as compassion and guilt.

---

* Other studies have shown that manipulation of affective states—making subjects feel compassion, disgust, anger, and so on—can change the moral judgments the subjects subsequently make.

TOWARDS A POST-SECULAR ETHICS

In short, brain-damaged people unable to feel prosocial emotions are much more likely to approve of pushing someone in front of a train to save others because it is the rational thing to do. The studies also show that people whose brain has been damaged later in life are able to reach decisions based on learnt social norms and attitudes, even though they are incapable of feeling the emotions that normally accompany infractions of those rules, whereas those born with brain dysfunction are unable to either feel the emotions or learn the rules and are at greater risk of becoming psychopaths.[10]

The implications of this research for the social sciences are striking. The model of the rational agent that forms the basis of neoclassical economics, around which the modern world of free markets is constructed, is one appropriate to a society of people who have been rendered incapable of feeling normal human emotions. Rational economic man is a neurological freak. The utilitarian model, in which agents calculate the best means of maximising social welfare without regard to the effects on individuals, is a sociopathic one grounded in the sort of moral calculus associated with cool intellectualising but foreign to warm-blooded humans.

The implications for moral theory are also far-reaching. The neurological studies allow us to assess how humans make moral judgments and the judgments' consistency with each of the three main moral theories of Western thought—utilitarianism, the moral principle of modern economics; the theory of duty, notably Kantian theory; and virtue ethics, emphasising the cultivation of virtues and usually associated with Aristotle.[11] Of these, virtue ethics is closest to the theory advanced in this book, although later I put forward a critique of eudaemonism, or the idea that the pursuit of happiness has moral value.

William Casebeer argues that each of these moral theories is associated with a different moral psychology that is reflected in differing patterns of cognitive activity. The utilitarian approach engages the parts of the brain that evaluate the consequences for various agents and applies the rule of maximum benefit. The motive for acting on this rule is more difficult to discern, but it could lie in self-interest or possibly cognitive areas responsible for altruism and concern for the wellbeing of others.

A Kantian moral psychology relies most heavily on our cognitive capacity to apply pure reason to decide whether our maxims could be willed as universal law—or, less formally, decide whether we are using others as ends in themselves rather than as means to our ends. What might then motivate us to act according to duty is unclear: we certainly cannot be motivated by the desire for praise or the wider social good, which are consequentialist motives and inconsistent with a duty ethic. The moral judgment itself must be based on reason alone, unaffected by emotion. The studies show that humans are quite capable of making moral judgments bypassing social emotions, but such hard-hearted decisions are not the ones normal humans make. Thus Kant's argument that actions are morally justified if they are performed in conformity with a maxim that can be willed as universal law could become the basis of a moral code only in a society where the capacity for feeling social emotions had been cauterised.

Virtue ethics requires us to combine the ability to reach a considered judgment about the outcomes that would best advance a good life with the cultivation of virtuous feelings that are consistent with reason. This moral psychology therefore activates a range of cognitive areas. Casebeer concludes that the evidence from neuroimaging studies is much more consistent with a virtue theory of morality than with a utilitarian or deontological theory.[12]

In developing a theory of morality, I have characterised compassion as an affective response, albeit with deeper roots. Neuroscientists argue, however, that compassion requires the integration of a number of neural areas—those governing emotional states such as sadness and attachment as well as those used for prospective thinking and forecasting the consequences of our actions, although the latter are perhaps activated when making the transition from feeling compassion to planning to carry out a compassionate act. As Jonathan Haidt writes, moral intuition is a kind of cognition, but it is not a kind of reasoning.[13] In making moral decisions, then, cognitive control and emotion are not, as most philosophers have maintained, competing mechanisms. Consistent with Solomon's argument, normal moral judgment requires interaction of the two, unification of the 'male' and the 'female' principles.

These studies show that moral emotions not only play a crucial role in forming moral judgments but also provide the motivating force for acting morally. Neither utilitarian nor deontological theories can provide a plausible explanation for why people would be motivated to act on the moral rules that reason arrives at. Reasoning rarely provides a motive for acting; indeed, it is more often the case that reasoning is itself motivated, a process activated by a desire to explain a judgment reached in another way. David Hume went so far as to claim that 'reason is, and ought only to be, the slave of the passions'.[14] Drawing on recent advances in moral psychology, Haidt challenges any causal role of reasoning in making moral judgments, arguing instead that in most cases reasoning comes into play only as a post hoc rationalisation of judgments that are based on sudden moral intuitions.

Where do these intuitions come from? Some neuropsychologists argue that the social emotions involved in making moral judgments are evolutionary responses to complex situations, responses that assist the survival of groups, and point out that non-human primates have an extensive repertoire of social behaviours similar to human moral behaviour.[15] The social intuitionist model argues that these behaviours are developed as a result of social learning, by absorbing from childhood and throughout life the affective correlates of moral stances from friends and family.[16] In contrast, I maintain that the core moral intuitions—compassion and the principle of justice—are not socially learnt but are innate to the moral self, as manifestations of metaphysical empathy. Haidt stresses that moral reasoning leading to moral intuitions usually occurs interpersonally and leads to a sort of Pavlovian 'emotional conditioning' of corresponding brain areas. This implies an evolutionary explanation of moral intuitions. But it fails to explain a vital fact: often the purest and most powerful moral judgments are made *against* social expectations. In a world where social conventions can serve as a substitute for natural compassion, we celebrate those few 'great cosmopolitan spirits' who, in Rousseau's words, transcend convention and embrace 'the whole human race in their benevolence'.[17] In a world of moral complexity, it is not the conformist who attracts our enduring respect: it is the one who takes an ethical stance against convention.

Neuroimaging studies show how moral judgments are in fact made, but they do not tell us how they ought to be made. To confuse one with the other is known as the naturalistic fallacy. Yet the study results suggest that if moral decisions were made in the way rationalist philosophers (including utilitarians and Kantian theorists) say they ought to be made we would be living in societies of sociopaths, societies that even rationalist

TOWARDS A POST-SECULAR ETHICS

philosophers and neoclassical economists would reject. It seems unbalanced, to say the least, to argue that we should pursue a moral philosophy based on a psychology that requires us to anaesthetise parts of the brain that are deeply implicated in making moral judgments—those parts governing the social emotions. Cultivation of reason in moral judgment is desirable but not if it requires the suppression of innate emotional responses. In both ethical theory and practical moral judgment the relationship between reason and the passions should not be one of master and slave: it should be one of enduring marriage.

THIRTY-ONE
Further thoughts

THE BASIS OF MORALITY cannot be found embedded in a categorical imperative, enshrined in principles of justice worked out behind a veil of ignorance, or inscribed in a social contract written in invisible ink. Nor can it be found in a library of laws that have evolved as a means of creating a rational social order. The basis of morality lies in identification of the Self with the universal essence, and the moral self that emanates from there. It is not necessary to be a philosopher to grasp this. Indeed, being a philosopher—especially a modern one preoccupied with narrow forms of rationality—can stand as an impermeable barrier to this insight. Carl Jung, the founder of depth psychology, was once asked which patients he found most difficult to treat. He replied, 'Habitual liars and intellectuals'. Intellectuals who insist on thinking their way to every answer are like habitual liars because they systematically deceive themselves. Even a philosopher unburdened by dogmatic rationalism might take years to grasp the idea of participation in the universal essence, whereas an ordinary person might know it merely by exchanging a glance with a beggar or being awed by a sunset. 'Whoever is morally noble reveals by his activities the deepest knowledge, the highest wisdom, however much he may be lacking in intellectual excellence.'[1]

Although an atheist might have just as strong a moral self as a person of faith, in one form or another the foundation of morality in participation is at the heart of all great religious traditions. It is central to the teachings of the East, for which leading a noble life and finding enlightenment go hand in hand. No insight is more powerful philosophically, and no teaching is more important theologically.

Philosophical systems built on this insight into the essential unity of reality are known as 'monist'. Oddly, the term is not usually applied to the systems of Kant and Schopenhauer, or even to the work of Nietzsche, who, in his earlier phase at least, wrote of our 'unity with the innermost core of the world' and our unification with all others once the veil of Maya, goddess of illusion, is lifted.[2] Among Western philosophers, Spinoza is perhaps the foremost who argued that the universe consists of one substance only, which he called Nature or God. Humans exist simultaneously in Nature as a mode of thought and as a mode of extension in space, he maintained, but these are just two attributes of the same thing. Nature is the absolute determination, and the world as we know it is simply a manifestation of the absolute. Hegel identified with this idea; he called it the absolute spirit, which reveals itself through the spatio-temporal world. This absolute is filled with the sort of 'substance' that Spinoza put forward, something that is, moreover, accessible to human intelligence.

Before Spinoza, Plotinus, the founder of Neo-Platonism, wrote, 'on account of the unity of all things, all souls are one'.
[3] In Eastern philosophy the idea is perhaps best expressed by

the Hindu sage Shankara, who used the term Brahman to describe the universal essence of all things. In Buddhism the objective of practice is to realise pure awareness, unspoilt by any thought, idea or emotion. 'Our usual understanding of life is dualistic: you and I, this and that, good and bad', writes Shunryu Suzuki. 'The true understanding is that the mind includes everything . . . This mind is called big mind . . . Big mind and small mind are one'.[4] The great Sufi sage Ibn' Arabi quotes one of his forebears, Hazreti, to the same effect:

> *You thought yourself a part, small;*
> *Whereas in you there is a universe, the greatest.*[5]

The unity of all things, the most profound realisation of metaphysics, finds expression not only in the works of transcendental philosophers and sages in Eastern and Western religious traditions but also in literature and folk wisdom. When William Blake called on us 'To see the world in a grain of sand', he was expressing this idea. And when a stranger dies those who recognise the unity of all in one will ask not for whom the bell tolls.

Yet it is the habit of theistic religions to attribute to the word of a god the moral impulses that arise naturally—unmediated by any divine personage or emanation—from our capacity for metaphysical empathy. The intercession of a divine lawgiver serves to reinforce the consequences of moral failure but robs us of our autonomy. God's retribution might act as an effective surrogate for a Christian who is insufficiently moved by recognition of the Self in others. Historically, the threat of divine justice has served social order well, but the modern preference for a mere nodding acquaintance with God makes moral law the product of a legislator lacking public confidence. It was Kant's genius to deduce the basis of morality in the anthropocentric principles of reason, thus cutting out the heavenly middleman. It was Schopenhauer's genius to replace the abstractions of reason with the more human identification with the noumenon.

Arising from metaphysic empathy (the Archimedean fixed point), compassion and the will to justice are the natural seeds of all morality. In the first instance they must be expressed in a primary moral principle for action, one from which specific moral laws can be derived and which, with the aid of self-control, can serve both as a guide to an ethical life and as the basis for social order. Kant derived the Golden Rule—'Do unto others as you would have them do unto you'—and founded it not on the idea of reciprocity but on the intrinsic worth of humans. Thus we should treat others always as ends in themselves and never as means to our ends. For Schopenhauer, the ethical principle arises from recognition of the Self in others and in its purest form is expressed as 'Injure no one; on the contrary, help everyone as much as you can'.[6]

Kant's formulation proscribes certain behaviours (those that use others as means to our ends), but Schopenhauer's includes both that command ('injure no one') and an injunction to act virtuously ('help everyone as much as you can'). These correspond to the two phenomenal manifestations of metaphysical empathy I describe: 'injure no one' is the simplest expression of the principle of justice and 'help everyone as much as you can' is the rule of compassion. The former, the male principle, is the negation of the bad; the

Further thoughts

latter, the female principle, is the affirmation of the good. Each, however, is based in the transcendence of the distinction between the self and other.

The moral rules that prevail in any society are sometimes unambiguous and universally accepted and sometimes complex, subtle and contested. Social convention, motivated by convenience or power, provides a complex overlay, and many of the rules we take to be eternal and universal are no more than convention, without any relation to the unifying principle. The post-modern failure was the inability to see through the overlay to the moral absolute beneath. In the following section I suggest how we can know the difference between social convention and moral values grounded in the noumenon.

It should not be thought that an individual's adherence to moral rules is always and everywhere a response to the unifying principle. More usually, it is the result of internalised expectations and prohibitions learnt as a child and reinforced by daily interaction. A harmonious society maintains order by widespread internalisation of the moral rules—the policeman within—and by enforcement of laws. Schopenhauer had a characteristically compelling way of making the point:

> Many a man would be astonished if he saw how his conscience, which seems to him such an imposing affair, is really made up. It probably consists of one-fifth fear of men, one-fifth fear of the gods, one-fifth prejudice, one-fifth vanity, and one-fifth habit . . .[7]

Internalisation of moral injunctions, whatever their genesis, allows us to operate by rules of thumb rather than hourly having to make decisions about how we should behave. There

TOWARDS A POST-SECULAR ETHICS

is no doubt that people who have a strong sense of metaphysical empathy—whether it is manifest more as compassion or more as the will to justice—will act in a reflex way to relieve suffering or right a wrong whenever they encounter such a situation. Principles of living drawn from this fount of morality are also the guidelines followed daily by people who lead a virtuous life. When the course of action is not clear because the mind is clouded by uncertainty and competing demands, the truly moral person will decide how best to act by excluding all self-interest and turning to the moral self for guidance. Although they can be intensified or diminished by upbringing and social environment, compassion and the will to justice are not at their core neurological or even psychological traits; they are metaphysical ones, and the proper solution to a moral dilemma always emerges from a place of tranquillity removed from both the feverish contortions of the mind and the turmoil of the heart.

This is not to say that moral dilemmas are always easily resolved. Generally, a 'moral dilemma' is not a moral dilemma at all but is instead a conflict between the right course of action and the self-interested course of action. Yet at times two moral principles do come into conflict, and a way through must be found. I met a Nepalese man who faced just such a difficulty. Joshi lived in Kathmandu, in an ancient terrace of three-storey houses enclosing a courtyard. The dozen or so families that shared the building were poor but not impoverished, although Joshi, a well-educated government official, was better off than most. One day a rabid dog entered the courtyard and bit some of the children playing there. They needed rabies injections lest they die. The old-fashioned procedure was to administer several injections over some weeks. Although the injections were relatively inexpensive, they were very painful. A new treatment for rabies required only one injection and was much less painful but much more expensive. Joshi knew that he was the only one who could afford the new treatment. Here was his dilemma: on one hand, compassion for his own children urged him to make the financial sacrifice and relieve them of considerable pain; on the other hand, using his fortunate position to buy his children freedom from the pain the other children would experience did not seem fair—quite apart from the resentment it would cause in the community. Joshi, a good man, found himself torn by the two aspects of the fundamental moral law. Compassion (help everyone as much as you can) called him to protect his children, but voluntary justice (injure no one) called him to keep solidarity with his neighbours. He had to assess the extent to which one principle would be compromised if he privileged the other. He chose justice.

The morality of capital punishment can be understood in similar terms. Although the desire for revenge can never have a moral basis—'an eye for an eye' violates every moral law—it is possible to make the case that people who support execution rather than imprisonment for murderers favour the male principle over the female, the principle of justice (including deterrence) over compassion. Opponents of capital punishment place compassion before justice. In making a judgment we must consider the extent to which one principle is compromised when the other is pursued. Showing pure mercy and releasing a murderer would violate the principle of justice since we understand that penance is essential. Thus punishment by way of a long period in confinement can satisfy the principle of justice. An execution cannot serve as penance: it can only punish, through revenge, which has no moral basis. Execution can, however, be justified if it is seen as

TOWARDS A POST-SECULAR ETHICS

a deterrent to potential murderers. Such an objective is relative—it might be more or less effective—but execution violates the will to compassion absolutely: it is a denial of the universal Self. The prohibition of torture can be understood in the same way.

We humans are flawed, and few but the saints can act solely in response to metaphysical empathy. This is why civilised societies do not allow the families of victims of crime to determine—let alone administer—the punishment that should be meted out to the perpetrator. Only the saintly can expect the compassionate impulse to be undimmed by loathing and the will to justice to be unsullied by the desire for revenge. In contrast to the will to justice, which seeks to right a wrong, formal justice as dispensed by the courts is concerned with punishment and, among the more enlightened of the bench, rehabilitation. Mercy, the companion principle, is generally in short supply. Restorative justice, in which the perpetrator is required to meet with his (or her) victims and listen to them describe the impact of the crime on the lives of others, can be understood as a process of restoring the link between one Self and another. The perpetrator is accompanied by his own family members, who are present to share in his shame and remind him of the injury he has committed against his own house—in other words, against his own Self. The effectiveness of this approach depends on reminding the perpetrator that there is no escape from the fact that the victims are not objects, instruments for his gratification, but are real human beings, ones, moreover, who in their inner nature are identical to the perpetrator. Thus one might say, at the risk of reification, that the noumenon, Brahman, sits at the table with both perpetrator and victim. This answers our question of why, in the normal courts, judges dispense more lenient sentences to those who show genuine remorse: in showing remorse these people demonstrate that they have not lost their connection with the unifying principle and are capable of being good.

THIRTY-TWO

Avatars of virtue

I ARGUE THAT THE grounds for morality lie in identification of the self with the universal essence, an intuition I call metaphysical empathy. It is this intuition that offers the possibility of moral sentiment. In the phenomenal sphere it finds expression in the moral self, the locus of ethical impulses that prefigures all social conditions and rational deliberation. A question pushes itself forward: If the moral self arises from the noumenon, how can we each turn to it as an authority by which to judge our actions?

For some, the answer lies in a particular type of introspection, in which all self-interest, all pressures and all rational consideration are cast aside and moral judgment occurs spontaneously. This opportunity is always present, but the pure voice of the moral self is usually drowned out by the confusion and chatter that fill our minds. So the noumenon needs interpreters, individuals who by common consent represent metaphysical empathy in the phenomenal world. These are individuals whose life story embodies a message that echoes powerfully in the consciousness of ordinary people. Whether these figures are secular or religious, their moral selves are closer to the surface and cause them to radiate a kind of moral greatness.

If we look at the world of recent times, three leaders stand out as models of moral clarity, akin to Rousseau's 'great cosmopolitan spirits' who include the entire human race in their benevolence. Mahatma Gandhi, Nelson Mandela and the Dalai Lama. These avatars of virtue attract admiration and reverence from ordinary people on all continents because they have lived life on a higher moral plane. They have attained their status not because of what they have said but because of the way they have conducted their lives. Each has a life story, forged in political struggle, that exemplifies the purest characteristics of the moral self. They are not gurus, experts or heroes; they are not super-human. It is their humanness that allows so many of us to imagine we could be like them. They are archetypes for us all.

What is the message of these moral exemplars that speaks so directly to people of all cultures? At the source is a goodness of heart that transcends the everyday decency of others. The presence of goodness to such a degree 'makes the heart so large that [it] embraces the world, so that everything now lies within it'.[1] From such an expanded heart spring several qualities that provide inspiration. The first is a commitment to the highest principles of justice—an unbending opposition to oppression and a commitment to equality. The second is an approach to their life's work steeped in compassion and a desire to achieve their political goals while reconciling with their enemies. Gandhi and the Dalai Lama have explicitly urged peaceful means. Mandela participated in a violent struggle but emerged as a moral exemplar through his determination to find a peaceful solution to conflict and to bring embittered communities together after the defeat of apartheid. This was seen to be all the more admirable because of the suffering he had endured at the hands of the white regime. For each of the exemplars, justice has always been seasoned with mercy, and the tolerance they have preached brings to their politics a reasonableness that is compelling. No fundamentalist, political or religious, could ever become an avatar of virtue.

Third, each of the three affirms the dignity of human life. More than dignity, for them human life has a sacred quality, no matter how mean the everyday circumstances. Indeed, material simplicity lends each life greater dignity. Because of the radical commitment to equality, these exemplary humans transcend their nationality and their culture: although they are identifiably Asian and African, their message is not ethnocentric; it is world-centred and thus all-encompassing. Their compassion is at a transpersonal level. When Ghandi went to settle in a village to serve the villagers as best he could, he was challenged by someone who asked whether his motives were purely humanitarian. He replied, 'I am here to serve no one else but myself, to find my own self-realization through the service of these village folk'.[2]

In addition to the principles that guide their political practice, these great spirits embody several personal qualities. The first is humility. They have not thrust themselves forward as leaders; they have not exploited their fame or power for personal gain; and their ability to relate directly to ordinary people has belied their exalted status. The moral self knows no ego. The second quality is moderation, even abstemiousness. None is a captive of desire. All three seem to understand that desire is the path that takes us away from the noumenon. Finally, each displays extraordinary perseverance. At an early

Avatars of virtue

age they gave over their lives to a struggle, sacrificing themselves to a higher cause. It is their determination to stay the course, no matter what the obstacles, no matter how pessimistic their colleagues might become, that wins our admiration. No young person can gain the status of exemplar because it takes a lifetime to earn it. Perseverance has a deeper quality: with their eyes set on a goal, they have followed the path wherever it led. Success or failure is not their measure; rather, it is the virtue of giving themselves over to the objective. Their love of life is also a 'love of fate'.

It is perhaps this last quality that inures these three to the barbs of their critics. No life is perfect, and the avatars are human. Gandhi slept in the same bed as his grand-niece to test his celibacy; the Dalai Lama has been criticised because he believes homosexuality is a sin; for a time Mandela had a messy and troubled married life. But they have transcended the particulars of their lives and become symbols, symbols that linger in the deepest parts of our selves.

We understand that these exemplars live out the purity of our own moral selves. They inspire us to become better people and to counter the cynicism, fatalism and selfishness that dog us. They draw us out of ourselves and stir us to commit to others in ways small and large. For many, they are more approachable than the greatest avatar of Western civilisation, Christ, who now seems distant and ethereal. He suffered and died a martyr; he lived a life none of us would want to live. Gandhi, Mandela and the Dalai Lama have lived modern lives, fending off the slings and arrows and at times being wounded, with failings that serve only to highlight their greatness. They laugh in a way Christ could not, have families to tempt them from their work but sustain them in it; they make mistakes. Above all, they have lived lives we can aspire to living. They are us as we could be. The power they radiate is not because they represent a god but because they represent us. We are drawn not to their divinity but to their integrity, their courage, their suffering, their determination, their essential human goodness.

These three avatars of virtue represent an emerging post-secular ethics, one that has broken free of dogma and sectarianism. Although he is the spiritual leader of Tibetan Buddhism and a scholar in his community, the Dalai Lama is happy to preach a 'secular Buddhism' that requires only acknowledgment of the universal values Buddhism preaches. It is perhaps no accident that Buddhism is the only one of the world's great religions that is not theistic. Gandhi was a devout Hindu but preached unity among faiths. Mandela has no church.

The churches that succeed in a world with crumbling national, ethnic and cultural barriers will be those that refuse to retreat into dogma and that retain their original links with the noumenon. The new fundamentalisms—of Christianity, Islam and Hinduism—are historically regressive and are doomed. Doctrinaire, ethnocentric, defensive–aggressive, fearful and exclusive, they are the reverse of everything the avatars of virtue represent.

THIRTY-THREE
Egoism and malice

THE METAPHYSICS OF MORALS developed thus far does not posit an outside authority whose commandments provide the grounds for judging moral worth. Instead, we have found an inner guide, the moral self, whose authority rests in the universal essence. This moral guide speaks to us directly with a voice that can be firm or weak. Virtuous behaviour depends on the clarity of the voice and our willingness to follow its advice.

On what basis do I claim that the noumenon is the origin of the good and that the closer we approach it the more it infuses our actions? I argue in section 23 that the noumenon is indifferent to our individual fate. It is mistaken to imagine that the noumenon is inherently good: it transcends good and evil. In truth, it is not that proximity to the noumenon makes us good because the noumenon radiates goodness; rather, being good gets us closer to our moral selves and thus to the noumenon. Selfishness and, even more so, malice take us away from the universal Self because they entrench us in the world of phenomena. So the journey is not from universal Self to separate self: it is the opposite, from separate self to universal

Self. Instead of wondering why the noumenon should be good, we should ask why getting closer to the universal Self makes us good. The answer is that as we strip away selfishness and disown malice we inevitably identify with others, participating in their essence. But is not this desire to get closer to the noumenon selfish? 'Wanting' to get close to the noumenon is not in fact self-interested because we can fulfil the desire only by giving up the self, by relinquishing the attachment to our ego-self and, ultimately, annihilating it. If our desire arises from the prospect of personal benefit it will simply take us further from our goal.

If our behaviour is an expression of compassion and the will to justice, it is because we are acting as philosophical idealists; we are responding to our inner essence rather than our outer form. In the words of William Law, 'People should think less about what they ought to do and more about what they ought to be. If only their being were good, their works would shine forth brightly'.[1] Otherwise, we are caught in the web of Maya, recognising others only as objects to our subjects and treating them instrumentally, as means to our ends. To live immorally means the personal self triumphs over the universal Self or, in Buddhist terms, little mind defeats big mind. There is a class of people who, through an accident of upbringing or birth, seem to have no relationship (subliminal or otherwise) to the noumenon and as a result are devoid of compassion or any idea of justice. We call these people psychopaths, and for them others are never anything more than objects.

Thus we judge actions to be morally good according to their conformity to the moral self, the point at which our separate selves dissolve into the grounds of being. Existence in the phenomenal world is always predisposed to be ego-centred, and one naturally directs one's energies towards one's own health and welfare. This is in the nature of our separate existence in the phenomenal world and 'is due ultimately to the fact that everyone is given to himself *directly*, but the rest are given to him only *indirectly* through their representation in his head; and directness asserts its right'.[2] Subjectivity is self-centredness.

Egoism and compassion do not exhaust the list of moral incentives. We characterise Schopenhauer's fundamental moral principle—'Injure no one; on the contrary, help everyone as much as you can'—as the dual emanation in the phenomenal world of metaphysical empathy. Egoism is the negation of the second part, the female principle. Malice is the negation of the first part, the male principle of justice. In its petty manifestations, malice takes the form of back-biting, envy, malicious gossip, *Schadenfreude*, bullying and spite. In its grand forms, it inspires the great wrongs of history, whether committed by a sadistic individual or by a nation caught in a collective frenzy:

> Egoism can lead to all kinds of crimes and misdeeds, but the pain and injury thus caused to others are merely the means, not the end, and therefore appear here only as an accident. On the other hand, the pains and sufferings of others are for malice and cruelty an end in itself, and their attainment is a pleasure. For this reason, malice and cruelty constitute a greater degree of moral depravity.[3]

It is sometimes said that a million people killed by a famine induced by self-interest is morally equivalent to a million killed by a human hand. But it is one thing to ignore the interests of humanity and quite another to turn against them. We acknowledge this in everyday experience. We condemn

TOWARDS A POST-SECULAR ETHICS

someone who hurries past a man dying on the street, but our condemnation is limited compared with what we feel about a man who kicks another to the point of death. If the 'uncaring stranger' were subsequently found to be hurrying home in response to a phone call from his child reporting a burglar in the house, then the charge of self-interest at neglecting the dying man would be cancelled out. We would no longer judge him to be motived by ego; instead, it would be compassion. Yet no feeling for another could ever cancel out the maliciousness of the one who kicked another to the point of death. This is how we judge our actions. When we pursue self-interest we are ignoring the interests of the noumenon; when we act maliciously we are turning against it.

THIRTY-FOUR
Eternal justice

COMPASSION AND VOLUNTARY JUSTICE are the manifestations in the world of appearances of the metaphysical empathy of the universal essence. The theological implications of this are far-reaching. Compassion and justice do not belong to the noumenon and so cannot be qualities attributed to the godhead. God does not dispense justice or compassion but instead simply provides the material from which humans take them. Thus virtue has no divine reward nor evil godly punishment, and to believe otherwise is to confuse phenomenal yearnings for noumenal intentions—an error almost impossible to avoid for those who personalise the godhead. Jesus' appeal from the cross for divine mercy was a moment of human weakness in which he forgot his own teaching. Many draw comfort from the belief that evildoers who escape justice in this world will be punished in the next. But, I argue, this renders unto God what is not his. Disconcerting as this might be, escaping both earthly and divine retribution does not mean evildoers get off scot-free, since they must face a power that follows them wherever they go until the day they die, at which point their universal Self merges with the Absolute. This is the principle Schopenhauer referred to as eternal justice.[1]

'Thou art that.' The thing-in-itself is indivisible and beyond time. The inner nature of each of us is made of the same 'subtle essence', and that is why when one person suffers we all suffer. The man who commits a crime against another commits a crime against himself. In the noumenal world retribution cannot be exacted at a later time—there is no time—and all phenomenal forms are merged into one. In his famous 'Divinity school address' in 1838, Ralph Waldo Emerson called it the 'law of laws':

> These laws execute themselves. They are out of time, out of space, and not subject to circumstance. Thus; in the soul of man there is a justice whose retributions are instant and entire. He who does a good deed is instantly ennobled. He who does a mean deed, is by the action itself contracted . . . Thefts never enrich; alms never impoverish; murder will speak out of stone walls.[2]

In dispensing eternal justice the perpetrator is the victim and the victim is the perpetrator. The suffering of the victim is felt by the perpetrator, except insofar as one is separated by an illusion. It is only here that the principle of an eye for an eye holds. In the words of Macbeth:

> *. . . this even-handed justice*
> *Commends th'ingredients of our poison'd chalice*
> *To our own lips.*

Macbeth is the archetypal fable of eternal justice, of remorse that cannot be shaken off. Lady Macbeth is unable to wash

Duncan's blood from her hands, an act of cleansing she attempts even in her sleep, whereupon she cries:

Naught's had, all's spent,
Where our desire is got without content:
'Tis safer to be that which we destroy
Than by destruction dwell in doubtful joy.

Dostoyevsky's *Crime and Punishment* is a meditation on eternal justice. Raskolnikov confesses: 'I killed myself, and not the old hag'. In 1993 a 10-year-old boy, Jon Venables, and an accomplice stood trial for the murder of toddler James Bulger, whom they had abducted from a shopping centre. At the end of each day in court Jon would take off his clothes, saying he could 'smell the baby' on them.[3]

Eternal justice needs no prosecution, judge or prison guard, no official who gouges out the eye for the eye to exact 'justice', because victim and criminal are one. The punishment does not fit the crime: it is the crime. There can be no escape from justice, no justice delayed, no guilty man freed or innocent convicted. Jesus called on us to stay the hand of retribution: 'Turn the other cheek and let vengeance be mine'.[4] For our separated selves, our phenomenal manifestations, all this seems almost impossible to accept and, if accepted, is a truth that can console the saints alone. We often see the wicked live lives of pleasure, unpunished and apparently uncaring, while the virtuous are afflicted by the tribulations of the world. Even the impartial witness to a crime feels compelled to exact retribution, which can often take a horrible form—such as the mob in a Jakarta market that chases down a petty thief and beats him to death. The mob is reacting to an unconscious recognition of eternal justice, yet misunderstands it as phenomenon; it 'demands of the phenomenon what belongs only to the thing in itself'.[5]

There are, however, some crimes so monstrous that no justice on Earth could exact sufficient retribution. Had Hitler not died in his bunker but been put on trial at Nuremburg, no scales of justice would have served, any punishment would have seemed derisory to the numberless victims, and we each would be compelled to retreat to the hope that justice would be meted out in full elsewhere. We even have an art form—tragedy—to reconcile us to the unfairness of the phenomenal world.

Yet eternal justice provides more than metaphysical consolation, since violations of transcendental law manifest themselves in the phenomenal world in the conscience of the violator, if only in the form of a worm buried deep in the unconscious but gnawing away and causing disturbance in the psyche. No matter how committed we are to the pleasures and opportunities of phenomenal life, at some level we are all aware of where we came from and where we must return.

Nevertheless, most people find it difficult to accept that we are metaphysically one with the noumenon, so the teachers of the great religious traditions have developed metaphors and myths that project onto the phenomenal world the lessons of eternal justice. In the Christian metaphor eternal justice is dispensed in heaven and hell, and Saint Peter serves as the judge. But, as is proper in the world of appearances, time separates the act from the reward. That the repayment occurs only after physical death acknowledges the apparent reality and also recognises that this form of punishment or reward belongs to the noumenon, however it is conceived. The exoteric version of Hindu teaching has reincarnation as the metaphorical form of eternal justice. This doctrine has one reborn as a creature great or small, in accord with one's actions in life. The reborn soul will suffer in the new life the same injuries he or she inflicted in the former life, so that the expiation demanded by eternal justice is seen to be done—a figurative solution more in keeping with the underlying truth than are the fires of Christian hell, which seem excessive and have lost their force as a result. Often closer to the energy of the noumenon than its Protestant counterparts, Catholicism has finessed the system by dividing sins into venial (minor) and mortal (grave and committed in full knowledge), although placing premarital sex and adultery in the mortal category along with murder does seem unjust. The decline of the churches in Western countries has meant a loss of faith in the myths and metaphors that served to remind us of divine retribution. The consequence is a breach in our belief in the fairness of life, a gap that seems to have been filled by cynicism and selfishness.

PART FOUR
Moral judge or moral adviser?

I shall drink . . . to Conscience first, and to the Pope afterwards.
Cardinal Newman

THIRTY-FIVE
Becoming good

IN THIS PART I apply the ethical theory developed in Part Three to some contemporary moral questions. Before doing so, however, I consider the notion of social and individual improvement. Can virtue be taught?

Moral rules lend themselves to inculcation, and if children were not able to internalise them as they grow, society would be impossible. We know that adults whose capacity to feel prosocial emotions is taken away by damage to the ventromedial prefrontal cortex can continue to make acceptable moral judgments if they can remember the rules and the approbation they receive when they adhere to them. Thus one's conduct can be worthy of praise or censure depending on how closely one conforms to the law and social mores, and many among the faithful receive the church's blessing and the congregation's admiration for consistently honest and upright behaviour. Yet a sermon has as much chance of producing a virtuous person as a reading of John Rawls' *A Theory of Justice*. And just as well: if the opposite were the case we could expect that for every person rendered virtuous by a righteous sermon another would be rendered malicious by a preacher of hate. And for every malicious person so created a dozen more would be converted to an unhealthy obsession with themselves by the proliferation of get-rich-quick books. Whether aimed at cultivating virtue or malice, the righteous sermon, the ethics tome and the economics text are just words, abstract knowledge conjured from social conditions and delivered by phenomenon to phenomenon.

But does this deprive us of free will, so that we are doomed to act out an inborn character? The question of the existence or otherwise of free will has profound theological implications. It was the central point of difference between Erasmus and Luther in their sixteenth-century battle for the soul of European Christianity.[1] For Luther, who denied free will, the response to this bleak fact was unswerving faith in God, a view common among conservatives of his day and one that justified their hostility towards the social reformers and revolutionaries. Our behaviour merely reflects our inherent character. The maxim, widely accepted in the nineteenth century, 'What we do follows from what we are' was based on 'the conviction that the character is unalterable and that what a man has *once* done he will inevitably do again in precisely the same circumstances'.[2] In eighteenth- and nineteenth-century Europe this belief gave rise to the notion of the 'criminal class'. It is worth noting that Luther's ghost lives on today in the United States, in the fundamentalist Christian movement known as 'Rapture', whose members believe, among other things, that catastrophic climate change resulting from human industrial activity is nothing more than God's will and no measures should be taken to prevent it.*

---

* According to the apostles of Rapture, Christians will be taken up to heaven before 'the tribulation', which will begin when the Antichrist, who will be known by the Mark of the Beast, 666, signs the seven-year peace agreement with Israel. A number of peace agreements with Israel have been signed in recent years, so the discerning believer will need to have the true one authenticated. Nevertheless, those who, having read the websites, are 'Rapture ready' will be well prepared for the ascension.

To ask whether virtue can be learnt is to ask whether we can lessen the distance that separates the phenomenal self from the universal Self. There is little doubt that some people are born with a greater predisposition to compassion and voluntary justice. And there is no doubt that children, although yet to understand its meaning, live much closer to the noumenon than adults. For them the barrier between essence and appearance is more permeable, but as they age the horizon recedes, to the point where in adulthood it can be lost in the haze. This intuition gave birth to Wordsworth's beautiful ode *Intimations of Immortality*:

> ...
> *Our birth is but a sleep and a forgetting:*
> *The Soul that rises with us, our life's Star,*
> > *Hath had elsewhere its setting,*
> > > *And cometh from afar.*
> > *Not in entire forgetfulness,*
> > *And not in utter nakedness,*
> *But trailing clouds of glory do we come*
> > *From God, who is our home:*
> *Heaven lies about us in our infancy!*
> *Shades of the prison-house begin to close*
> > *Upon the growing Boy.*
> *But he beholds the light, and whence it flows,*
> > *He sees it in his joy;*
> *The Youth, who daily farther from the east*
> > *Must travel, still is Nature's Priest,*
> > *And by the vision splendid*
> > *Is on his way attended;*
> *At length the Man perceives it die away,*
> *And fade into the light of common day.*
> ...

MORAL JUDGE OR MORAL ADVISER?

The task of the parent is to facilitate and encourage the emergence of their child's individual self and the full expression of the child's talents and character, while at the same time containing the tendency for the emerging sense of self to develop into a monster. It has often been observed that one of the greatest failings of Western society in recent decades—arising perhaps from secularisation and the impact of the baby boomers' demands for self-determination and reinforced by the later emergence of the self-esteem movement—has been the indulgence granted to children. A refusal to set boundaries has turned many suburban homes into brat camps, but without the authority figures. Every parent who is or wants to be their child's best friend should be put into a camp to be educated into proper adulthood.

The parent should permit the full flourishing of the individual in the phenomenon while always reminding the child of their origins in the noumenon. Parents can influence a child's capacity for compassion by helping the child become attuned to the emotional states, particularly the suffering, of others. Words alone are impotent for this, yet a parent's compassion, if deeply felt, can be communicated subtly to the child. This emotional transference is, however, limited in its ability to cultivate true virtue in children, and once the teenage years have arrived the opportunity has largely disappeared, since teenagers are so preoccupied with establishing a firm and comfortable identity in a world that seems to judge them at every turn that appeals to the suffering of others mostly fall on unhearing ears. Often parents are shocked by the selfishness and callousness of their teenage offspring, although such behaviour usually turns out to be temporary. The lack of compassion is reflected perhaps most alarmingly in many teenage boys' loathing of their gay peers, a disposition that loses its intensity as they move into their twenties.

So, if genuine virtue never arises from abstract knowledge communicable by words, must we resign ourselves to the conclusion that character is immutable and that one born bad will die bad—or, indeed, that Mother Teresa's work was no more than iron destiny stamped on her from the day she took her first breath and for which she therefore deserves no credit? If there are no moral choices there can be no saints. Yet we now know there is a form of knowledge other than the knowledge of the phenomenon—the 'non-sensible intuition' Kant deduced but denied we could have access to, the special knowledge Schopenhauer wanted to believe in but could not quite accept. I maintain there are times in adult life when circumstances converge in such a way as to give even the most hardboiled rationalist a glimpse of the universal essence that binds humanity. It might occur in the inhuman circumstances of war, in the delirium of illness, in a state of elation with nature, or in the depths of depression. It might arise from intense prayer or meditation. Experience shows that even the toughest carapace is liable to crack under particular pressures, revealing radical insights into the nature of being that can be found in no book.

Take the story of Nick. When he was in his twenties, Nick worked in the finance markets, earning a big salary and living a high-consumption lifestyle. He was motivated by career success, as measured by income and promotion to an office with a window. Yet Nick sensed there was something not quite right. Episodes of happiness lasted only minutes. So obsessed was he with his own advancement that others avoided him and wanted him to fail. 'Basically, I had become an arsehole', said Nick. So he decided to take a year off to travel abroad. He met people living in squalor in South

MORAL JUDGE OR MORAL ADVISER?

America, yet in the midst of the poverty he found hope and community. In Bolivia he stayed in a mining town:

> I . . . visited a mine in which children worked carrying heavy loads up and down the mine in cramped, dirty conditions. There was a boy working there who lit dynamite in a crater and scrambled out before he was blown up—all to earn money from tourists. I later found out that the materials that the children were carrying were exported to Germany to use in the manufacture of cars. Not long before that I had owned a Mercedes. At that point I realised that I was part of the problem, not part of the solution. I cried for three days.

Nick did not reason his way to this realisation: it broke through his reasoning self from a deeper place. His remorse came from the recognition that he had lost himself and that the boy who risked his life was Nick himself.

When he returned home Nick apologised to all whom he had treated badly and began to do voluntary work for non-government organisations committed to human rights and the environment. This developed into full-time, if poorly paid, work. Having previously been an intensely self-absorbed person who used others only as means to his own ends, Nick now committed himself to the interests of others, to a greater cause.

It is hard to interpret Nick's epiphany at the Bolivian mine as anything other than the noumenon breaking through into his everyday awareness. The boy who risked his life for the entertainment of tourists touched Nick's heart. No code of conduct, no law or moral system, no sermon or ethical discourse, could bring about this realisation. Although they might appeal to self-interest under the guise of helping others, moral rules can never prompt the truly virtuous act. Genuine virtue 'must spring from the intuitive knowledge that recognizes in another's individuality the same inner nature as in one's own'.[3] It arises from metaphysical identification and not from any words, laws or urgings of authority. Virtue can be learnt, but it cannot be taught.

In section 19 I describe Plato's thought experiment concerning the people living in a cave in a world of shadows. The 'philosopher' who freed himself and discovered the richer, sunlit world outside realises that he and his fellow cave dwellers have mistaken the world of shadows for the world of substance. As he stands dazzled by his vision he must make a vital decision: does he walk away and spend his life revelling in the richness and brightness of the world outside or does he return to the gloom, take up his seat and shackles, and bring knowledge of that other world to his fellow cave dwellers?

Having discovered this singular new world, Plato suggests, our philosopher will be reluctant to return to the world of shadows because 'they think they've been transported to the Isles of the Blessed even while they're still alive'.[4] This decision point is recognised as crucial in various traditions. (The Buddhists have a typically down-to-earth answer: 'Before enlightenment, chop wood, carry water; after enlightenment, chop wood, carry water'.) It is at this time we can understand the distinction between metaphysical empathy and compassion. Our philosopher has experienced the pure awareness of the noumenon, but only through the decision to re-enter the cave and participate in the everyday world can the awareness of the unity of all become the human emotion of compassion. The decision to rejoin the world transforms empathy into sympathy, 'in-feeling' into 'with-feeling'. What impels the decision one way or another remains a mystery, although in section 42 I

MORAL JUDGE OR MORAL ADVISER?

argue that, psychologically, the price of maturity is the requirement to give something back, that the glimpse of sunlight comes with a condition attached—a return to the cave.

For Plato, education should be the 'art of orientation' that allows us to cultivate the special knowledge. He sees such an education as equivalent to moral goodness and observes that the cleverest mind can be deployed for harmful ends in the absence of this special knowledge. If each cave dweller were born in the light of the sun and brought into the cave as an infant, 'trailing clouds of glory', the knowledge might be remembered rather than learnt, and a fleeting glimpse or long-buried association might be sufficient to bring the memory flooding back.

In his *Republic* Plato identifies three motives for moral behaviour; we could call them calculated, socialised and genuinely good.[5] People possessed of 'ordinary', or calculated, morality adhere to laws and norms because they have used their reason to deduce that it is in their interests to do so. Such people decide not to transgress for rational reasons and are motivated by self-interest. The second motive moves those whose upbringing saw them internalise the laws and norms of moral behaviour as the guides for their own action. They want to advance their own integrity and safeguard their communities, which means learning to moderate their self-interested desires. They cannot explain their good behaviour by reference to a metaphysical belief or an inner sense, but there is no doubt this type of person is preferable to the one who abides by the law in the interest of personal benefit or for fear of punishment. The third kind of morality is motivated not by the interests of the community, a desire to conform to moral law or calculated self-interest but by a vision of genuine goodness. This 'more perfect' morality is especially available to 'philosophers'—meaning people who have had access to the special knowledge that gives an insight into the essence of things.

The behaviour of each one of us is determined to a greater or lesser degree by all three of these motives. Plato argued that the best state would be one governed by the philosophers who have gained the special knowledge, although their modesty makes them reluctant to assume such a role. This state is akin to Kant's kingdom of ends, where noble reason rules. It can be interpreted as elitist—only the sages with that special knowledge should set the moral rules—but even Plato, who is often accused of advocating autocracy or benign dictatorship, asserts that 'the capacity for knowledge is present in everyone's mind' and that education, in the way he thought of it, should be the art of orienting the mind away from the 'world of becoming', the world of appearances, to the world of 'real being and reality at its most bright'.[6] Plato's three motives for moral behaviour provide a more flexible and optimistic account of the possibilities of human transformation and improvement in the phenomenal world than Schopenhauer's nineteenth-century belief in the immutability of character. But, like Schopenhauer, Plato believed the only source of genuine morality is the 'intelligible realm', the place of pure goodness.

THIRTY-SIX
The theory in practice

SCHOPENHAUER ARGUED THAT THERE are three fundamental incentives for human action: egoism, or the desire to advance one's own ends; malice, or the desire to harm others; and compassion, or the desire to advance another's wellbeing. He excluded a fourth—the desire to harm oneself—saying it was not essential to his argument.[1] In fact, the possibility of moral self-harm lies at the heart of the most important ethical debates of today, and failure to acknowledge it properly is the source of much moral confusion. If we include the desire to harm oneself, we can draw up a schema that will help our understanding and provide a context for the discussion that follows.

Actions can be motivated for the benefit of oneself or others and they can be aimed at improving wellbeing or causing harm. The upper left-hand portion of the schema defines morally worthy activities as they have traditionally been understood. It expresses most clearly the basic principle 'Injure no one; on the contrary, help everyone as much as you can'. Cynics often try to muddy the waters, and justify their own self-centredness, by quoting the old saw 'The road to hell is paved with good intentions'. But, to the extent that harm results from our well-intended actions, it represents a failure not of character but of comprehension. Activities that are motivated by good intentions but are persisted with when it is known they are doing harm thereby become self-interested or malicious and thus morally reprehensible. Wilful ignorance of the harmful consequences of one's actions also turns a morally worthy action into a morally reprehensible one.

	Do good	**Do harm**
Aimed at others	**Morally worthy**	**Morally reprehensible**
	Compassion and voluntary justice	*Malice*
	Donating blood	Spite
	Ending conflict etc.	Violence etc.
Aimed at self	**Morally indifferent**	**Morally uncertain**
	Self-love	*Self-hatred*
	Hedonism	Suicide?
	Eudaemonism	Prostitution?

The lower left-hand portion of the schema represents actions that are motivated by self-interest. In themselves they are morally indifferent, but obviously there are daily instances when pursuing one's own interests, with no regard for the impact of one's behaviour on others, can be morally reprehensible; such actions might not be aimed at others but can affect others. And it must be said that a life devoted solely to the interests of the self has no moral value. Self-interested behaviour can inadvertently benefit others; however, this does not render such an 'invisible hand' morally worthy since the motive remains selfish rather than compassionate, although ex-post rationalisations are adept at making selfish actions appear worthy.

The lower right-hand portion captures actions that harm oneself. Their moral status is uncertain because the question of consent is not in play, and they provide the circumstances for the most interesting and contentious moral debates of today: our inability to provide answers has given rise to moral relativism, which maintains that one answer is as good as the next. The difficulties arise because it is often uncertain whether a self-directed, voluntary activity is beneficial (and thus morally indifferent) or harmful (morally uncertain), whether it belongs in the lower left or lower right portion of the schema.

In the usual situation involving others (the upper portion of the schema) there are three parties to a moral judgment—the actor, the acted upon, and the moral judge who adjudicates between the two. When actions are aimed at oneself, actor and acted upon are one, so what is the role of the moral judge? If the judge decides the actor is violating the acted upon, the latter might simply say, 'I do not feel violated', and that is the end of the matter. When there is only one party to an activity, or when all parties are fully consenting and no others are affected, it is no longer fitting for us to approve or condemn. If another person's activities harm others, my moral judge has 'jurisdiction' over that action; if they harm no one else, my moral judge has no jurisdiction. In the latter case I have no warrant to say, 'Don't do that because it is immoral'. I might, however, be in a position to advise rather than judge—more big sister than stern father—and suggest, 'If you do that you may regret it'.

On what grounds might I advise against an activity? I deal with most of these in Part One, but in summary I might point out that the activity, although immediately attractive, is not in your long-term interests. I might remind you that your second-order, or deeper, preferences are being ignored. Or I might suggest that you are sacrificing something else in the pursuit of the goal in question. In these cases I am not claiming the action is immoral; rather, I am suggesting it is imprudent. A person who has decided on a course after due consideration, free of self-deception, moral weakness and all forms of coercion, will not need (or appreciate) this sort of advice and will not regret their decision, except perhaps in the trivial sense that their expectations about the outcomes are disappointed.

There is, however, another form of advice that goes much deeper, one that appeals not to long-term interests or second-order preferences but directly to the moral self. I might suggest that the proposed activity could be an offence against your moral self and, if so, you will regret it later. It becomes apparent in the sections that follow that the types of moral questions we are dealing with here all concern uses of the body—sex, death, mortification and self-abnegation. Many former porn stars are dogged by feelings of regret. Some men say they feel dirty after using porn. Some people succumb to mental distractions—television, the internet, shopping, gossip—and feel they are frittering their lives away. In these situations, although my moral judge has no jurisdiction, as an adviser I might suggest that your moral self may well have something to say and that your proposed action could be imprudent if you do not make an effort to listen to that moral self. Before exploring this, initially by considering the morality of suicide, a word of caution is warranted.

MORAL JUDGE OR MORAL ADVISER?

Moral decisions are often difficult. How can one distinguish between something that flows necessarily from a moral principle, and the layers of social expectation, convention and personal prejudice that enrich and bedevil every moral debate? Moreover, the moral principle—'Injure no one; on the contrary, help everyone as much as you can'—seems to set an impossibly high bar. Who but the saint does as much as they can to help others, casting aside all their own interests? If that were demanded of us as a guide to daily life, it would be seen by almost everyone as infeasible, and the injunction would in general be ignored. But everyone must start from where they are, each with a mixture of egoism, malice and compassion. Our task is to act increasingly on the last-mentioned characteristic.

Many readers will already be aware of a trap in applying ethical principles to everyday practice: even the most honest among us cannot help but compare their pre-existing moral stance with the positions the theory leads to. In other words, each of us already has ethical principles we use to make judgments about almost everything, or at least we are prone to accept as revealed moral truth the prejudices passed on to us by our parents, our peers or public opinion. The real and only test therefore resides in judging the validity of the principles first and, if they are accepted, abandoning a previously held stance if application of the principles to the question at hand goes against our opinions. Emotionally, though, it is much easier to discard a principle than it is to discard a deeply held position. On the other hand, there are philosophers and theologians who go to prodigious lengths to develop consistent and, for them, persuasive moral theories that lead them to reach strange conclusions about the acceptability of certain actions—conclusions that, although straining every moral fibre, they are unwilling to reconsider, modify or abandon. Hubris overwhelms commonsense. The ability to separate prejudice from principle is rare, even among those whose vocation it is to understand the difference.

As I note, there is a pervasive concern among citizens of Western nations that people today are more selfish and that this is what lies at the heart of the moral decline many believe blights Western society. Our ethical framework allows an explanation of this that perhaps goes beyond the usual ones. It seems reasonable to suggest that the declining influence of the churches is part of the explanation, since one of the churches' main functions has been to remind parishioners of that most important Christian injunction, 'Love thy neighbour'. This ought not to be a surprise when we recognise that, for most Christians, God took the shape of a being who resided in that mysterious space we now call the noumenon.

Trite as it might be to say, the onrush of science and rationality seemed to invalidate the authority of God. This was undoubtedly because for the ordinary believer God was characterised as the entity, rather than the grounds from which an entity might grow. In that case, the bridge between the phenomenon and the noumenon collapses under the weight of scientific thinking, and the essential source of fellow feeling, the rationale for loving thy neighbour (or at least respecting them), is no more. The widening gap between life in the phenomenal world and the noumenal ground of existence is thus at the root of the spread of selfishness. Societies have shown they can construct for a time a merely social basis for fellow feeling; this was the goal of socialism, but to the extent that such plans can succeed they must be constantly

MORAL JUDGE OR MORAL ADVISER?

recreated as society changes in response to technological, demographic and economic forces. Only the noumenon is constant. This is not to blame the churches for the increase in selfishness: they have been the victims of broader historical changes that have been responsible for the rise of secularism and the materialism and self-focus that inevitably go with it.

THIRTY-SEVEN
Suicide

THE FACT THAT, EVEN in circumstances where all hope is lost, so few people commit suicide confirms the conviction that life has a purpose, that there is something beyond existence in the phenomenon—in the words of German philosopher Karl Jaspers, 'an unfathomable transcendence calling for life . . . [that] makes men endure in the slough of despond'.[1] If the world were nothing more than that of appearances, the senselessness of life would invite suicide. I argue that the purpose can only be for life to know itself and that we need our bodily forms in order to attain this knowledge. A human life has three great metaphysical moments: conception, in which the noumenon enters into the phenomenon; death, in which the phenomenon is reabsorbed into the noumenon; and experiences of 'breakthrough', in which one's phenomenal form merges, however fleetingly, with the universal essence and thereby experiences death in the course of a life.

Only humans can choose to live or die, and we cannot consider human freedom without considering death. Choosing to end one's life can forever deny us the opportunity of fulfilling our life's purpose on Earth. Yet if this realisation be the prize it must be admitted it is one few consciously covet. For the rest, and especially the suicidal, it is a reward far from consciousness. It is therefore too harsh to judge suicide as a 'mistake' or an act of cowardice. One cannot shirk a task of which one is unaware. For Schopenhauer, in contrast, suicide is always a moral failure. It is not a denial of the will to live; rather, it is an affirmation of the will to life but one that refuses to accept life's terms.[2] Unlike the ascetic, who spurns the pleasures of life, the suicide spurns its sorrows and in doing so gives up not the will to life but life in the phenomenon. Suicide is thus a 'quite futile and foolish act' for it cannot destroy the real thing, the subtle essence; it seeks merely to escape the suffering of phenomenal life, which, whatever its travails, is the path to 'salvation'.

Unlike Schopenhauer, with his harsh and dogmatic commentary, Jaspers offers a more nuanced and compassionate analysis that is enriched by insights drawn from his work as a psychiatrist. His characterisation of a situation in which suicide becomes an expression of inner freedom is worth quoting:

> If the utterly lonely individual whose closest kin in existence have made clear to him that they live in different worlds, whose every realization is blocked, whose sense of being is no longer purely attainable, who must watch his own sinking—if he proceeds to take his own life without defiance, calmly and maturely, having put his affairs in order, it may be as if he were offering himself as a sacrifice. *Suicide becomes the last freedom left in his life.* It implies confidence, saves purity and faith, hurts no living person, breaks off no communication, commits no betrayal. It marks the limit of the capacity of realization, and no one is the loser.[3]

In such circumstances, although it is always an existential problem, suicide is no longer a moral one. Yet this situation is rare: more often, taking one's life is not the considered act of an isolated individual but involves others, and then it has moral meaning and we must understand the motives and its emotional substance.

Suicide can have at least four different motivations. If it is an act of sacrifice, to save the lives of others and for no other reason, it can indeed follow a decision based on one's own considered will, rationally decided on the basis of firm moral conviction. Such cases are infrequent, except perhaps in time of war, in which case we call it heroism. A famous act of selfless suicide was that of Captain Oates, who walked from his tent into the Antarctic blizzard because his injury jeopardised the lives of his party. Such acts of *suicide as sacrifice* are of the purest coin. Another example would be a person who is terminally ill but who can see that her continued existence is imposing an intolerable burden on the people around her. She might hasten her own death, even in defiance of her own desire to live, in order to relieve others' suffering. This form of suicide, motivated by compassion, is of the same order—done not to save lives but to spare suffering. For those left behind, the manner of the loved one's death might intensify that love or leave a heavy burden of guilt.

More typically, people who commit suicide lack the capacity to reason calmly, their judgment being clouded by anguish and confusion. They have sunk into the slough of despond, and life seems to have stopped. If they were to coolly cast their eye back over their life, with all its delights and sorrows, and then look forward to all the possibilities life could hold for them, few would follow through. But this viewpoint, which most of us can adopt when contemplating important life decisions, is foreign to the disturbed or anguished individual. They are in the grip of a depression or torment that deprives them of their freedom to choose. This form of suicide, *suicide as despair*, appears to apply in a famous recent case, that of Britain's Iraq weapons inspector David Kelly, who took his own life because, after exposing official secrets to the press, he could not live with the consequences of his actions. Had his attempt failed, there is little doubt that from the perspective afforded by the passage of five years he would conclude his suicide attempt was a personal mistake and a moral failure.

Adviser, rather than moral judge, is always the better stance to adopt in the face of threatened or actual suicide. Our task is to rescue the person from the confusion that deprives them of their freedom. If called on, we would try to persuade them that their life is not as desolate as it seems, that there are people who love them, and that the situation will improve. Moral condemnation is misplaced, selfish and futile.

While one moved by despair to suicide does so because their psychological distress becomes unbearable, *suicide as release* is a response to unremitting physical pain. If the only course confronting someone is a life of mounting pain, condemning them for considering suicide is cruel, and the person who believes his moral judge has jurisdiction must examine his motives. It is here—when a terminally ill person wishes to bring to an end their suffering—that the moral problem of euthanasia arises. If someone wants to end his life in order to relieve others of suffering, helping him do so cannot be justified, especially if one could benefit from the alleviation of the burden. But, if suicide will bring release from unendurable physical pain, the moral status of assisting the suicide in this task hinges on the motives for doing so.

Only assistance rendered purely for compassionate reasons can provide an ethical justification, and that justification would be invalidated by the presence of any form of self-interest or malice. Of course, determining someone's inner motivations is virtually impossible for an outsider, which is why the assistance is better rendered by a wholly disinterested party. (In passing, it has been shown that someone who stands to benefit from the execution of a will is much more likely than others to visit the person dying in a hospice or similar place. The cynical interpretation of this statistical fact is that the potential benefactor makes visits as a kind of insurance policy. A more charitable interpretation, and a more persuasive one, is that a loving relationship is more likely both to elicit visits and to be acknowledged in a will.)

When we consider the morality of suicide it is useful to reflect on how we as distant observers actually feel about the act. When we hear that someone has taken their life we feel it is tragic and regrettable, and we might be distressed. Our hearts are moved as we imagine the suffering the person must have experienced before being driven to the ultimate act. Perhaps we reflect on our own lives, remembering our worst episodes and trying to imagine those feelings magnified tenfold, to the point where death is greeted as a relief, the only escape. We think about the anguish of those close to the dead person, the grief, the hollowness they must feel, and in our compassion we feel with them. We do not condemn the suicide, though, nor do we accuse the person of acting immorally.

Some religious doctrines hold that suicide is contrary to the will of God and is therefore a sin. Yet this is surely a matter between the believer and their god, and in questions that are fundamentally existential no clerical intercession is warranted. What is warranted, however, is a suspicion that the

MORAL JUDGE OR MORAL ADVISER?

condemnation of 'self-murder' serves the interests of the church, or indeed of secular autocrats, because as long as the faithful live they can have power exercised over them. Jaspers wrote, 'Suicide is . . . condemned by all rulers whose rule depends upon the innermost human soul. A dominion maintained by giving men spiritual aid and comfort is lost where a free, independent individual has no need of anyone'.[4]

Things are different for those who are close to the suicide—the spouses, partners, fathers, mothers, sons, daughters and intimate friends. Another stratum of emotion—bewilderment, resentment, anger and betrayal—can overlie their grief. 'How could you do this? How could you be so selfish?' they cry. These cries may be self-interested. The question really being posed is 'How could you do this to me?' because suicide, although aimed at releasing the anguished, causes great harm to others. But can we blame someone whose own pain is so great they can no longer comprehend the pain their death might cause others? Our empathy softens our hearts.

Yet at times suicide is motivated not by despair or a fog of confusion but by malice, a form of *suicide as protest*. At times it is an action designed to punish those whom the person believes have maltreated or neglected them. To leave victims is the purpose. When it is driven by malice, suicide as revenge undoubtedly deserves moral censure. Such a radical form of protest can, however, also be a response to more noble motives. In the 1960s the Buddhist monks who self-immolated in Saigon as a protest against the war—trivialised by cynics who dubbed them '*bonze* fires'—sacrificed themselves for a higher cause. Whether they deserved praise for their sacrifice or contempt for their foolishness depends on one's belief in the justice of the cause. Unlike the suicide bomber or the kamikaze pilot, though, the monks' use of this ultimate weapon of the disempowered was aimed at the conscience of their opponents, not their own lives. Jaspers observed:

> We cannot deny that the man who thoughtfully, lucidly takes his own life strikes us as being altogether independent, as standing wholly upon himself, as defying all mundane existence that would make itself absolute or pose as the purveyor of the absolute. He strikes us as a man who leaves his victorious foe with an empty triumph. Yet all this does not ease our existential trepidation.[5]

All this would find little favour with Schopenhauer, which in a way is odd since he is famous for his disquisitions on the suffering that characterises life in the phenomenon. In one of his more striking images he observed, 'If we knocked on the graves and asked the dead whether they would like to rise again, they would shake their heads'.[6] Yet his bleak view did not suggest to him that we should renounce life: he insisted that we have a metaphysical obligation to be stoic in the face of life's vicissitudes and do what we must. In contrast to the mood of his commentary on other moral questions, which is compassionate or at least dispassionate, Schopenhauer's writings on suicide are bitter and accusatory. Perhaps he carried the anger and resentment that never leaves some who are close to a suicide: it is thought that when Schopenhauer was 17 years old his father took his own life by throwing himself into a river.

THIRTY-EIGHT

Sex

SEXUAL ETHICS

In contemporary society the most passionate moral disputes concern sexual behaviour. Despite the transformations wrought by the sexual revolution of the 1960s, debates rage about public nudity, pornography, the use of sex in advertising, the acceptability of particular sexual practices, sex and children, contraception, casual sex, group sex, and so on. What is it about sex that generates such intense moral passions? The sexual revolution was supposed to free us of our neuroses, prejudices and preoccupations so that we could enjoy sex simply for its pleasures.

One of the early signs that there is something much deeper to sex than bodily pleasure arose out of the 1960s' dalliance with 'free love', an affair that continues today in more conventional guise as 'open' relationships, 'swinging' and activities such as 'dogging', in which groups of people brought together by the internet meet at a designated public place to watch others copulate. People who began to practise free love, the uninhibited sharing of sexual partners, soon found that jealousy rose like a spectre and, no matter how much the aggrieved party worked on overcoming his or her 'hang-ups', simply would not go away. Politics and ideology, even when fervently espoused, could not overcome the primal emotion of sexual jealousy.

Before we can consider the ethics of certain forms of sexual expression, we must first pose a question: What is sex? For our purposes, sex has three aspects. The first is bodily pleasure or, more elementally, the release of an accumulating urge. The second is procreation, which is the way of extending the life of the species. (It was only with the widespread availability of reliable contraception, 40 or so years ago, that it became possible to consider intercourse as something to be pursued solely for pleasure. But, although this accident of technology might have changed behaviour, it has not changed the deeper meaning of sex.) The third aspect of sex is union, which in turn has two forms—emotional and metaphysical. Emotional union, or intimacy, belongs to humans as phenomena, as does the physical pleasure associated with sex. Metaphysical union is a direct expression of our noumenal selves; it is the aspect of sex that is least acknowledged and therefore worthy of most attention, not least because it is the one that matters most for sexual morality.

Nietzsche's epigram on sexuality—'The degree and kind of a man's sexuality reach up into the ultimate pinnacle of his spirit'—perhaps appeals more to women than to men.[1] Intercourse as an act of metaphysical union arises from its primal link with procreation, the joining of opposites and the creation of one from two. If a human being is an expression of the universal essence in the world of appearances (and it is this that makes human life intrinsically valuable) then it is conception, the receiving of the sperm by the ovum, that is the moment at which the noumenon is manifested in the phenomenon, in the form of a new life. It is this that gives sex its 'sacred' character. In the course of sexual love there is an intimation somewhere deep within that a mysterious power is at work. It is because of this metaphysical intimacy that loving sexual partners 'know' each other in a way that cannot be had by other means. It explains the incompatibility of free love and intimacy, which by its nature is exclusive. It also accounts for the peculiar awkwardness some ex-lovers feel when, having made new lives, they meet again; the special knowledge they have of each other no longer has context and expression. Experiencing an intimation of metaphysical union in the sexual act is common, although not always understood for what it is, especially by men. In the sexual act performed with devotion, time is suspended and difference is dissolved, especially at the point of orgasm. Thus the French refer to orgasm as *le petit mort*, the little death, in which time stops, the mind is silenced, and there occurs a momentary release from life in the phenomenon, a fleeting ecstatic union as self glimpses Self. Some men attest to a primal urge to disappear into the womb whence they came, the portal from which the self emerged and through which it might again be dissolved to escape the suffering of the world:

> It's where we start and where we end, and we spend the time between trying to scramble back inside . . . it's the Black Hole. It's the Singularity. It's where the laws break down. It's where, if we dare to look, the universe turns inside out. Gravity is infinite here. Space and time come to an end.[2]

The association between intercourse and conception—the new manifestation of phenomenal life out of the noumenal essence—has led many to note the peculiar feeling of sadness that often follows the act, a reflex sometimes mistaken for rejection. This was commented on even in Roman times: wrote Pliny, 'Only man feels remorse after the first copulation',[3] a sensation that arises perhaps because, being so close to our origin, we cannot help but be wistful at being reminded that we are trapped in the world of appearances, with all its trials.

An element of chance has ever been present in the link between intercourse and procreation, and humans have always tried to raise or lower the odds, using anything from the magic of spells to the magic of hormone pills. The link in practice can be broken, but the metaphysical bond cannot be separated from the act. Thus procreation and union are indivisible metaphysically even if they are separated in practice. Although intercourse might not result in the exchange of biological material it always represents the unification of the female and male principles to form a whole. It is for metaphysical reasons more than biological ones that men and women are drawn to each other; the biological imperative has a higher purpose, that of facilitating the expression of the universal essence. And it is the transcendent intimacy of coupling that, over and above the physical pleasure, gives intercourse its unique quality. With these thoughts in mind, what can we say about sexual morality?

The best known and perhaps most influential modern doctrines on sexual morality were set down by Pope Paul VI in his 1968 encyclical *Humanae Vitae*. Marriage is understood as sacred, 'the wise and provident institution of God the Creator'; its purpose is the generation of life. Husband and wife 'develop the union of two persons in which they perfect one another'.[4] Within marriage, the Catholic church understands sex as having two aspects, the procreative function and the unitive function according to which husband and wife, through their intimacy, 'become one heart and one soul'.[5] (It was only in 2006, in Pope Benedict's first encyclical, that the Catholic church acknowledged the pleasurable aspect.) The procreative function and the unitive function are indivisible—there is an 'inseparable connection, established by God . . . between the unitive significance and the procreative significance which are both inherent to the marriage act'—so that any sexual intimacy must always keep open the possibility of procreation.

The church's injunctions all flow from the assumed inseparability of the unitive and procreative functions. Such an understanding of the place of sex in marriage renders immoral all sexual acts that breach either the procreative function (including oral sex, anal sex, masturbation, homosexual sex and the use of contraceptive devices) or the unitive function (including adultery and casual sex). Raymond Belliotti points out that Pope Paul gave no reasons for this indivisibility other than scriptural ones, yet the Gospels tell us Jesus himself had little interest in social convention or legal statute. His ethical teachings always concerned inner motives, the purity or otherwise of the heart, so the Catholic church's teachings seem to have taken particular historical conventions and turned them into divine law. Despite the various encyclicals emanating from the Vatican, the view of sex as reasonable in moderation and dangerous in excess may well have received endorsement from Christ. Belliotti writes, 'Jesus nowhere stigmatizes erotic impulses as inherently evil . . . [but] castigates sex and the material world as obstacles to eternal salvation only when they become idols'.[6] There can be little doubt that in the marketing society of the modern West, the only idolatry that can compete with the sexual one is the worship of money.

My contention thus far is that the unitive function is inseparable from the reproductive function and that the noumenon-manifesting aspect of intercourse gives it its sacred character. Although in practice the connection between the two is severed, intercourse retains a quality that, as I note, other forms of sex do not possess. Of course, this does not mean other forms are immoral or of less emotional value. There is, however, a more subtle argument. Catholic doctrine has it that the sacred character of sexual intercourse is conferred by sex's procreative function because the latter leads to the preservation of the species, and life itself is sacred. The projection of the self into the future through procreation is a temporal justification of the sacredness of sex. Procreation as biology is a phenomenal aspect of sex, whereas the true value lies in the timelessness of the noumenon, in the metaphysical aspect of sexual union. The church reverts to the instrumental reproductive consequence of the act in the phenomenal world, whereas the value must surely lie in the act's transcendent nature.

I distinguish between the emotional and the metaphysical intimacies that characterise a loving sexual relationship. Emotional intimacy is created through love and companionship, as well as through sexual contact. Adultery is not immoral because, as Pope Paul maintained, it is sex outside marriage, which therefore denies the unitive and procreative functions of the institution: it is immoral because it is a betrayal of intimacy and the trust that goes with it. The sexual aspect of adultery betrays both the emotional and the metaphysical intimacy of a spouse or partner. Affairs in which there is no physical contact—such as 'coffee-cup affairs' and internet liaisons—betray emotional intimacy only. Apart from its practical and emotional benefits, marriage is above all the celebration and institutionalisation of metaphysical union. In fact, nuptials have always been seen as a declaration of intent that is realised by consummation, and behind all the bawdy jokes about the wedding night is a subliminal recognition of marriage's 'holy' purpose. It is because of this metaphysical meaning that historically the churches, traditional keepers of the metaphysical, were accorded responsibility for blessing unions. Once the churches were no longer seen to have a monopoly on the divine, it was inevitable that new agents should step in. This in itself is a loss only insofar as the metaphysical essence of the marriage union is no longer acknowledged by the celebrant.

The noumenon has a motive force. Its primary, universal energy finds expression in the libido, the sexual drive, although this of course is not its only expression. Little wonder we are so obsessed with sex, far more so than could be explained by its earthly pleasures, considerable as they are. For some, the prospect, almost exclusively unconscious, of intimate merging provides the solution to the existential tension of life because it holds promise of a rent in the veil that prevents us knowing the noumenon. As always, such glimpses can be confusing, and sexual activity can be misinterpreted and pursued for the wrong reasons. The ancient Greeks worshipped the phallus, and the lingam and yoni have featured in Hindu devotion; there is an entire sutra devoted to sex. As a means to enlightenment, the spiritual path known as tantra includes practices aimed at merging the female and male aspects of the divine energy in the sexual embrace (with or without copulation). At the same time, celibacy among some religious orders is designed to assign to devotional ends the energy that can burst through sexually. Perhaps it is for this reason that some religious traditions—notably the Catholic and evangelical churches among Christians and the more fundamentalist strands of Islam—limit sexual activity among the faithful, as if to ensure that the primal energy is released in a place of worship instead of the bedroom. Apart from the betrayal of trust and the abuse of power, it might be because paedophile priests and licentious gurus corrupt sacred energies for profane purposes that they attract special contempt.

It would be misguided to think that the phenomenon dissolves into the noumenon during intercourse only because of the possibility of conception. Sexual love itself can be one of the deepest expressions of the noumenon, in that the subtle essence of two humans can merge in the most intimate way. At its best, the ecstatic nature of sex reflects the dissolution of one manifestation of the universal essence into another, so that they become one; indeed, 'ecstasy' is derived from the Greek word *ekstasis*, meaning to stand outside of one's conscious self. Even in its latent form, this is a powerful force. Once the empathic connection has been made and consummated through sexual love, betrayal of this link through an affair with another naturally sets off a powerful reaction.

If all this is true it explains the ubiquity and influence of the sexual impulse in modern Western society. In addition to the urge to gratification, the preoccupation with Eros can be understood as a manifestation of a more elemental human urge, the need for metaphysical reconciliation. Our inability to recognise this, and the decline of institutions that might provide alternative paths to this reconciliation, explain the orgiastic character of modern sexual expression. Sexualisation fills the gap left by secularisation. If in an earlier era sex was the urge that could not speak its name, it now uses a megaphone. When the sexual revolution began to breach the wall of sexual repression it came first as a trickle then as a torrent, with no sign of surcease 40 years on, so that sex talk and erotic imagery pervade books, media, advertising, the internet and public discussion with a fascination that appears to be limitless. This unhealthy situation will continue, I suggest, until avenues are found for a more balanced and pure expression of the noumenal energy, until desecularisation permits desexualisation.

Perhaps readers are by now a little dismayed, for I may seem to have invested sex with an unwarranted esoteric significance. Sex is certainly presented as playful, pleasurable and natural in popular culture, a mood captured in books such as *The Joy of Sex*. But it is unsatisfactory, even dangerous, to refuse to acknowledge the deeper aspects of sex. We should remind ourselves of the passion it can unleash, the intensity of which is grossly disproportionate if sex is no more than good fun. Further, we should not forget the dark side of the sexual urge, which preoccupies us almost as much as the light, as we know from the public's grim appetite for the details of sexual crimes.

CASUAL SEX

Casual sex, if freely consented to, is engaged in purely for physical gratification and perhaps for the emotional pleasure of a brief social encounter. Sex without love is undoubtedly widely practised among younger adults in Western countries, and few are willing to criticise it. If both parties freely agree and are above the age of consent, what possible objection could there be?

Before attempting to answer this question, we need to think about the context in which casual sex has proliferated, since in practice casual sex is a minefield of potential consensual ambiguities. In the first instance, each party must be old enough, sober enough and sane enough to be able to take moral responsibility for their decisions. In practice, youthfulness, drunkenness and emotional distress among women are often exploited by men to sexual advantage. But it is not only girls whose emotional confusion can be exploited: the newspapers report cases of schoolboys aged 14 or 15 who are invited or seduced by their female teachers into sexual relationships. The typical reaction of men reading about these cases is to wish they had been so lucky at school, yet it is evident that few of the seduced boys escape without emotional trauma, sometimes severe and long-lasting. This reminds us that, despite the message purveyed by the media and popular culture that it is no more than good fun, sex is complex, deep and powerful.

There is also a wider set of pressures on people, especially young people, to engage in casual sex. The market is saturated with erotic imagery and content whose effect is to create and reinforce the view that engaging in sex is a natural part of social life and that those who do not participate will be ostracised. The 'cool' group at high school acquires its elevated status primarily by engaging in, or giving the impression of engaging in, premature sexual activity. Sex is associated with sophistication, non-conformity and a willingness to embrace life—in short, the Dionysian spirit before it is tamed by the Apollonian.

Perhaps the most disturbing aspect of the pervasiveness of sex is advertisers' practice of presenting children in sexually provocative clothing and poses to sell products, a marketing method sometimes referred to as 'corporate paedophilia'. This is done by even the most respectable companies. The coexistence of the social panic about paedophilia and society's apparent indifference to children being presented in the media as sexually desirable is so striking as to cause the most sanguine of us to reflect with awe on the market's power to distract us from our normal preference for non-contradiction. Corporate paedophilia is so widespread and unremarked that it stands as testimony to the power of Freudian denial on a mass scale. Signs of this disassociation are everywhere—including among the mothers of cheerleaders at football matches who insist that their daughters' routines are in no way sexual (despite the short skirts, tight tops, high kicking and bottom-thrusting), a delusion that would be crushed if said mothers spent five minutes with their ears open, listening to the lechers on the terraces as their daughters performed.

Setting aside the question of the age of consent, we must also wonder whether the consent has been extracted by subtle coercion—not by the other party but by social groups and the wider culture. We have assumed thus far that casual sex is engaged in purely for physical pleasure, but it can also be used as a means of fulfilling other needs or desires that themselves might be false, illegitimate or better met by other means. It must be admitted that a substantial portion of casual sex is sought or consented to for these other reasons. Participating can be a way of winning social approval and group acceptance. For young adults, casual sex is often seen as a means to a more permanent end, the securing of a partner, a necessary part of being 'out there'; in these cases it should not surprise us if the party that consents for social reasons feels regret.

Casual sex in which both parties consent and no third parties are affected is precisely the situation where making moral judgments is a mistake. If someone wants a one-night stand that is their moral concern alone; it is an activity outside the jurisdiction of another moral judge. A friend or family member might, however, assume the role of moral adviser. Consider the case of a young woman discussing with her friend a proposed casual encounter. The friend might question whether the proposed liaison is really in the young woman's interests. Is consent freely given or is the young woman feeling pressured? If she gets drunk will she be in a position to consent? Is the sex engaged in for its own sake or is there another objective, in which case something might be given up for nothing? Has she taken precautions against pregnancy and disease? Although the scene is presented here as an interrogation, young people engage in these sorts of conversations almost daily, often taking advice from magazines.

If the young woman can answer honestly that none of those factors presents an obstacle and all the conditions of fully informed consent apply, her friend might pose a final question. Will you regret it afterwards? In posing this question, the friend is calling into the conversation the young woman's moral self, the court of her inner judge, even though its rulings might be ignored for a time. Why might the young woman regret engaging in casual sex even though she goes into the encounter fully informed and consenting? In his defence of 'sex with love', ethicist John Hunter provides an answer. Sex in the absence of emotional intimacy is not necessarily immoral, but it can be regrettable.[7] He makes the case that impersonal sex falls short of an ideal. Loving sex goes far beyond physical gratification: it includes 'mutual trust, total mutual acceptance, and an intimacy distinguished by the sharing of one's innermost thoughts as well as one's body'.[8] Sex in the context of love and intimacy becomes part of a rich relationship marked by security and reciprocity, which nurtures the sense of value and specialness in the lovers that infuses their entire relationship and advances their health and emotional wellbeing.

Although this is a compelling case for the superior value of sex with love, it does not mean that impersonal sex is of no value. Reminding the young woman of what she might be missing out on is unlikely to evoke feelings of regret—unless one could argue that casual sex will somehow prevent her in the future from finding the much greater fulfilment to be had from sex with intimacy. Hunter's argument is that casual sex does not live up to an ideal, but for our young woman the choice is not between casual sex and ideal sex: it is between casual sex and no sex. Moreover, the ideal is open to challenge, one Belliotti spells out. People who pursue sex without love might be seeking only the inherent pleasure of sex and value a life free of emotional entanglements. Impersonal sex may be more enjoyable, he says, because it is free of oppressive expectations and obligations:

> Nonlovers experience adventure and shared risk, they sense mutual appreciation for freedom and nonpossessiveness, they entertain feelings of specialness as they exercise unique opportunities, and they perceive sex as an inherently valuable human enterprise that transcends instrumentalist concerns.[9]

This is the position taken to the extreme by Catherine Millet. It is a powerful argument with widespread appeal. Yet there is something missing because we know that feelings of regret often follow casual sexual encounters (not to mention paid ones). It is implausible to propose that it falls short of the ideal of loving sex, in the same way as it is implausible to argue that feelings of regret arise because a one-night stand does not fulfil hopes of adventure, liberation and an inherently valuable enterprise.

We regret what we have lost far more than we regret what we have not gained. If, after the event, the young woman's inner judge rules against her, the disturbance she feels will be for something she has lost, something she has sacrificed. The metaphysical intimacy she and her partner experienced has no emotional context and so might feel like a violation of her bodily integrity and a trivialisation of sexual union. For both men and women, if emotional intimacy is absent metaphysical intimacy feels hollow, for its special character seems to require care and respect. So if our young woman's friend were a philosophical idealist her advice might be, 'Girl, don't mess with the noumenon'. Perhaps this is why many people are left with a vague feeling that each time they have casual sex they give away a little of themselves, that something sacred is profaned and they are diminished as a result.

Casual sex cannot have a unitive function, yet sexual love is always invested with a deeper meaning. This deeper meaning is more available to some than to others, and it is those who have a clearer sense of the noumenal aspect of sex who find casual sex regrettable. It feels as if it is inferior sex, 'meaningless sex', in which the promise of physical gratification cannot compensate for the sense that part of the self is being lost or that one is using one's partner. The bargain is even more uneven when one party gives of his or her emotional self and receives nothing in return. In an era when premarital sex attracts no stigma and, indeed, abstinence must be defended, this seems to be at the heart of the decision by some young women, and even some young men, to go against the trend of sexual licence and 'save themselves' for their future spouses.

Some might protest that I have loaded up sexual activity with all sorts of transcendental conditions and metaphysical obligations when most people just want a good shag. Yet the various considerations just discussed, the conditions needed for proper consent and the deeper meaning of sexual intimacy, are constantly debated and negotiated by the sexually active. The test for any sexual activity must always be whether participation in it is an expression of our inner freedom, and we now understand that inner freedom goes beyond the psychological conditions laid down in Part One—absence of self-deception, akrasia and subtle coercion—and takes into account the interests of the moral self, and thus the rulings of our inner judge. The widespread but little remarked prevalence in our society of feelings of regret arising from sexual activity testifies to the fact that, no matter how much the 1960s changed our behaviour, the disruption to the moral order did not, and could not, silence the inner judge, who always speaks up for the moral self.

BESTIALITY

Acts that are considered to contravene moral norms elicit emotional responses from those who witness or contemplate them. Depending on the act's nature, they make us feel annoyed, bewildered, outraged or disgusted. These feelings are inspired both by acts that breach universal ethical principles and by acts that merely contravene social conventions or etiquette, although the intensity of the reaction is usually greater in the former case. Having noticed these strong emotional reactions, moral philosophers typically set out to understand the rules or principles that have been breached to cause such effects.

With the possible exception of necrophilia, no purely sexual act elicits in us more revulsion than bestiality. Belliotti uses a post-Kantian ethical framework in an attempt to understand why bestiality is morally wrong. With admirable philosophical honesty, he concludes that it is not at all obvious why it is wrong.[10] He notes that animals have moral status because they have interests, although they do not necessarily have a moral status equal to that of humans. The strongest argument against bestiality is the lack of consent. It is not, however, apparent that animals suffer as a result of bestiality or that their interests are greatly impaired. As a result, Belliotti says, lack of consent seems inadequate to establish the wrongfulness of bestiality. Next he asks whether it is wrong because the animal, as a sentient being, is used as a mere means to a human end. Once again, it is not apparent that the interests of the animal are affected by being used as a mere means. The animal might be exploited during the act itself but otherwise be very well treated. Despite the lack of obvious reasons, Belliotti does conclude that bestiality is immoral, although the grounds for his conclusion are weak.

Reflection on the matter does not produce any compelling explanation for why we find bestiality repugnant. This 'moral dumbfounding' is not uncommon.[11] When Rolling Stone Keith Richards told an interviewer he had snorted his father's ashes the hostile public reaction caused him to hastily announce that he was only joking, although it is not at all clear why snorting one's father's ashes should be immoral. Haidt gives the example of the brother and sister who one night in a remote cabin decide to have sex out of curiosity. They take all precautions against pregnancy and enjoy the experience but decide not to do it again and to keep it secret. It is hard to find a good reason to condemn them.[12] They were fully consenting, there was no chance of conception, and both enjoyed the experience. In cases like this we can reach strong moral judgments without a maxim in sight. Haidt argues persuasively that moral reasoning typically occurs *after* a moral judgment has been made intuitively and is used to rationalise the reaction.[13]

Yet bestiality remains a powerful taboo. So perhaps we should try a different approach and work backwards. Instead of trying to explain why we feel revulsion, let us accept revulsion as a given and ask what this fact can tell us about the ethical framework I have developed. That one feels disgust at something—as some do with homosexual sex—does not make it morally wrong, but the enduring and universal social taboo relating to bestiality makes it reasonable to accept that it is wrong. Note first that, because the interests of the animal are involved, it is legitimate to take a universalising stance: we would not just *advise* against a proposed act of bestiality; we would condemn it as immoral. Moreover, there are good grounds for believing that the person who engages in bestiality suffers from a perversion that may have an effect on other humans. Society therefore has a moral interest in bestiality.

If bestiality does not necessarily contravene a practical rule we must go to the basis of moral rules. That basis cannot be found in Kantian reason or in utilitarian calculus: it is to be found only in the notion of metaphysical empathy and the understanding of each human being as both phenomenon and noumenon. As we have seen, the reasons for the immorality of bestiality are hard to find in the phenomenon. So what is it in our moral selves that makes the practice repugnant?

Considering the functions of sex, it seems that the source of the problem must lie in the idea of metaphysical union, the joining of Selves. It is reasonable to hypothesise that there is something intrinsically different between the universal Self of each species and that the attempted merger of two differing Selves in the sexual act is an offence against what might be called 'the noumenal order'. Schopenhauer argued that each species can be considered the representation of a Platonic Idea.[14] If the world is the expression in phenomenal form of the noumenon, it is expressed in many grades or forms. Thus, while two rocks of a specific type scarcely differ, higher animals are differentiated into individual forms, yet each species of animal reflects a Platonic Idea that captures all that is universal to the species and not changed in its individual forms. These 'species ideas' are unique manifestations of the noumenon before they appear in the phenomenon. This is what lies behind Schopenhauer's conclusion that bestiality is 'really an offense against the species as such and in the abstract, not against human individuals'.[15] As a result, each of us has a moral interest in any act of bestiality.

If this argument holds it provides a basis for judging bestiality as immoral because it violates the essential integrity of both human and animal. The repugnance we feel is an inbuilt mechanism that discourages offences against the noumenal order, a metaphysical reaction that is expressed as a visceral one—perhaps analogous to the physical disgust people feel when confronted by rotten food. If there is such a thing as the noumenal order this changes the way we consider the morality of bestiality. Although the interests of an individual animal might not be harmed, the interests of each species can be. Such a view contradicts the rights-based approach of post-Kantians (such as Belliotti and Rawls) and utilitarians (such as Peter Singer), which assesses an act as right or wrong according to how it affects the interests of individuals.

It is worth noting that if there is something existentially distinct between species this fact contradicts the position of animal ethicists, notably Singer, who argue that humans and animals are in the relevant sense the same and their interests should therefore be given equal consideration. Accepting Singer's view has a number of ethical implications, including vegetarianism. The noumenal order I propose leads us to declare bestiality immoral because it violates the essence of the species, but eating meat does not have the same metaphysical implications. It might seem curious that in setting out to uncover the ethical case against bestiality we end up questioning the ethical case for vegetarianism. It seems we can eat animals but we cannot have sex with them. This is not so surprising when we remember that almost all humans feel disgust at bestiality but not many feel disgust at eating meat. Of course, this does not mean there are no other reasons for deciding to avoid meat, among them the cruelty inflicted on animals destined for human consumption and the environmental degradation associated with meat production. Nor does it mean an ethical approach to the treatment of animals should disregard their sentience and thus our obligation to respect them as manifestations of the noumenon. But if we accept our revulsion at bestiality as a given fact it does seem to make intuitive sense that animals are metaphysically distinct from humans. This deepening of our understanding of the noumenon has wider implications for humans' relationship with the natural world.

THIRTY-NINE
Nature

THE METAPHYSICS I HAVE developed provides us with a monistic view of the world, one that asserts the essential unity of reality, in which all creation is the manifestation of the 'subtle essence' of the noumenon. Although this essence takes different forms, its universality gives rise to an unbreakable connection between all things. Thus Schopenhauer coined the striking aphorism 'We must learn to understand nature from ourselves, not ourselves from nature'.[1] This truth follows directly from the profound insight he identified as his departure from Kant—recognition that we can know something of the thing-in-itself. Thus, if we want to know the essence of nature we can find it in our selves: 'a glance into the *interior of nature* is certainly granted to us, in so far as this is nothing but *our own inner being*'.[2] Wordsworth expressed the same insight:

> *One impulse from a vernal wood*
> *May teach you more of man,*
> *Of moral evil and of good,*
> *Than all the sages can.*

MORAL JUDGE OR MORAL ADVISER?

After their work had been done both Kant and Schopenhauer had crushed all outside authority and could instruct us simply: 'Obey thyself'. Yet, in seeking the basis of moral law, Kant searched for that which distinguishes humans from the world, their rationality, while Schopenhauer sought that which unites us with the world. For Schopenhauer the moral principle that governs relations between humans also governs the relationship between humans and the natural world, a truth recognised by Goethe: 'Is not the core of nature in the heart of man?'

Kant changed our understanding of the world from a theocentric to an anthropocentric view and developed moral laws that humans give to themselves rather than receive from a mysterious external force. The rational triumphed over the theological and in this way, argued Kant, humans became autonomous beings. From this he concluded that humans, as rational beings, exist as an end in themselves. But where does this leave non-human beings? By attributing the supreme ethical principle to rationality, Kant rendered all non-rational beings, all other living things, mere means to human ends. He declared, 'Man can have no duty to any beings except human'. Cruelty to animals is not intrinsically wrong, he said; it should be condemned only because inflicting cruelty on animals deadens the feeling of sympathy for their suffering, and this callousness weakens the sympathy we may feel for other human beings.[3] Finding this proposition 'revolting and abominable', Schopenhauer drew attention to the fact that, despite Kant's explicit intention to rid morals of their theological roots, in fact this view of animals reveals the Old Testament lurking in the wings.[4]

A morality that treats animals only as means to human ends 'fails to recognize the eternal essence that exists in every living thing, and shines forth with inscrutable insignificance from all eyes that see the sun!'[5] Modern Kantians, notably John Rawls, who privilege the rational above all else are caught in the same trap. It is only rational beings who assume the original position behind the veil of ignorance and from this lofty position make judgments about the best of all possible worlds based on their 'rational plan of life'—with a coherent set of preferences that can be clearly ranked, whose odds of success can be estimated and who, moreover, do not suffer from envy.[6] All other creatures, having no claim to being 'moral persons', are denied a place in the magic circle and can therefore be no more than 'resources', means to human ends. Rawls is aware that, to any real, feeling person, the exclusion of animals from his principles of justice will seem repugnant. So, in a passing reference, he lets us know he is a real human being, rather than a logic processor, by announcing that it is wrong to be cruel to animals because their sentience 'imposes duties of compassion' on us.[7] Rawls has spent the preceding 447 pages of his book constructing an elaborate theoretical structure of justice designed to obviate the need to appeal to natural human feelings, yet he now conjures from thin air the only basis for real justice, compassion, in order to clear up a technicality. His theory can tell us why a boy should not torture his sister (because his sister might one day be in a position to torture him) but it cannot tell us why the boy should not torture his cat, who has the misfortune of not being a 'moral person'. The cat will draw little comfort from Rawls' apology that its interests 'are outside the scope of the theory of justice' and will have to wait for a larger metaphysics that can accommodate Rawls' theory of justice as it applies to all rational beings.

In contrast, a moral theory grounded in the metaphysics of empathy naturally embraces all living things. Most other philosophical approaches posit a moral gulf between humans and other creatures, whether this gulf be ordained by God or traced to the exclusive rationality of humans. Yet everywhere in the face of such chauvinism nature enters her silent protest,[8] for does not every creature have a will to live equal to that of every human? Indeed, that will to live may be stronger, since humans are the only creatures that at times decide to abrogate their will to live. All creatures are manifestations in the phenomenon of the noumenon and share the same eternal essence. Although the forms in the phenomenon might be distinct, what is primary—the universal essence—is common to all creatures. The compassionate person understands this intuitively: 'Since compassion for animals is so intimately associated with goodness of character, it may be confidently asserted that whoever is cruel to animals cannot be a good man'.[9]

Although explained in evolutionary rather than metaphysical terms, E.O. Wilson's biophilia hypothesis—'the innately emotional affiliation of human beings to other living organisms'[10]—is easily recognisable in this argument. And in his essay 'Shooting an elephant' George Orwell's inexplicable remorse is nothing more than recognition of the universal Self in the elephant. 'In man, as in the animal that does not think, there prevails as a lasting state of mind the certainty, springing from innermost consciousness, that he is nature, the world itself.'[11]

I argue that morally worthy behaviour has its source in the compassion and voluntary justice that themselves arise from metaphysical empathy. It is reasonable to expect that the sense of metaphysical empathy is distinctive for one's own species (since one shares a Platonic Idea with members of one's species), but we can also identify with the will to live of other creatures, from the ant to the elephant. It is this identification that gives rise to feelings of compassion for animals—a capacity to 'participate' in their will to live and to suffer the consequences of denying it.

Such a view extends moral considerability not only to individual living things but to creation as a whole and to natural systems within it.[12] Our own identification with the universal Self naturally gives rise to a holistic viewpoint, something attested to by people who have transcended the everyday appreciation of things in experiences of participation in the natural world. Whether arrived at philosophically or experientially, such an appreciation reflects the 'expansion of the self'[13] that initiates an ethic that also expands to take in the interests of all creatures and the systems that sustain them. In place of a moral order that is handed down by some higher authority, this ethic grows from a transformation of self: what we do follows from what we are.

It is immediately apparent that the argument put here concerning identification of our selves with nature, and the understanding that follows from it, could not be further from the attitude of unrestrained resource exploitation that has characterised the history of industrial capitalism and that only in the last three decades has come under challenge. The instrumentalist approach to the natural environment—which sees the environment as no more than a catalogue of resources whose values are measured by their economic usefulness to humans, as expressed in the price they attract on the market—is a philosophical error, one with potentially catastrophic implications for humanity. It is the consequence of a philosophical and religious anthropocentrism that recognises the natural environment as essentially dead, not animated by any force, least of all one shared by humanity in our inner being.

MORAL JUDGE OR MORAL ADVISER?

It represents the ultimate contraction into the ego-self and the denial of the universal Self. The thoughtless assaults on the natural environment, which are culminating in human-induced climate change, are not first and foremost an economic, scientific or technological problem: above all, they are a metaphysical error and a moral failure. The emergence of 'environmental economics'—which recognises that there are limits to resource availability and to the capacity of the Earth's waste 'sinks' to absorb the detritus of industrial production and consumption and then acknowledges that if we fail to recognise these limits our capacity for continued economic growth will be constrained—does not represent any worthwhile philosophical shift. Being merely the application of a modicum of foresight in the pursuit of our own interests, it is equivalent to the transition a child makes from asserting the unrestrained demands of the id, which increasingly finds it cannot get its way as it confronts other ids, to the 'reality principle' that guides the ego, which seeks to get its own way by more considered means.[14] It is equivalent to the transition from pursuing the pleasant life to pursuing the good life, which differs merely in the application of prudence and is no less self-interested.

Only an approach that assigns intrinsic value to the natural world, including its systemic, species and individual components, represents a break from the 'ethic' of exploitation and offers a final chance for a reconciliation with nature.

PART FIVE
Freedom rediscovered

Freedom is the absence of choice.
Sufi saying

FORTY

The ground of inner freedom

KIERKEGAARD OBSERVED THAT PEOPLE rarely make use of the freedoms they have.[1] After centuries of hard-won struggles against various forms of tyranny and material deprivation, most people in liberal democracies today are free to make their own lives. Few take the opportunity, however, instead allowing themselves to be bought off with market freedoms and 'lifestyle' choices. We have built ourselves a grand castle of freedom but choose to live in a shack nearby.[2] It is as though we are fearful of the castle's grandeur and the trek we must make to breach its ramparts. Besides, we hear a thousand voices extolling the pleasures of the shack. We must discover for ourselves the benefits of living in the castle, yet we do not know how to go about it.

Affluence and the market promise us freedoms never before enjoyed by humanity. We can pursue our desires to wherever they take us, and we have so much choice that our rational minds have difficulty accommodating it. I can be an accountant or a plumber, a clerk or an artist. I am free to pursue my desires, for food, for leisure, for travel and for social respect. And I am free to choose between the 48 brands of breakfast cereal at my local supermarket. Yet none of these freedoms is really our own: they are all given to us by social conditions—by my conditioned preferences and life goals, by the prevailing culture, by my peers and by the market. The freedom we have been sold by the advocates of modern liberal capitalism is, in truth, the freedom to be pushed hither and thither by forces we barely acknowledge. The freedom to do as we please—the official form of freedom—is the most subtle form of unfreedom ever conceived.

The tragedy is that so many fought for so long to tear down the constraints that prevented us from flourishing, actually choosing to become what we will, yet few exercise these freedoms, preferring instead the security of social convention and the conservatism of the familiar. Freed from want, discrimination and oppression, we huddle together like sheep seeking one another's comfort after the fences have been taken down, habituated to the domesticated life and fearful of what lies beyond.

In the popular understanding, free will means being able to do whatever one wants, following one's own wishes unconstrained by rules or external authority. Yet this cannot be true freedom, inner freedom. Even if we are free to do as we will, we are not free to choose what it is that we will. If we are to exercise free will, we must be responding to no inducements, preferences, pressures or predispositions; our actions must be independent of influences. We are autonomous, and thus free, only when we act entirely volitionally, according to our *own* will. We are free only when we act according to goals and principles that we have given ourselves. In other words, we must initiate our own actions, free of attachments, yearnings, social pressures and impulses and without regard to the influ-

The ground of inner freedom

ences of peers, parents, churches or fashions. At the deepest level our very subjectivity arises in relation to other things, through the 'resistance' or effects of outside influences, and true autonomy must lie beyond all these causes of action. But how can anything be uncaused?

The answer lies in the idea put forward at the beginning of this book—inner freedom, the freedom to act according to one's own considered will. In Part One I venture some psychological reasons for the absence of inner freedom; namely, our capacity for self-deception, our moral weakness, and our openness to subtle forms of coercion. Yet there was an arbitrariness about these reasons that reflected the absence of any real grounding for the idea of inner freedom. The assumption was that if we liberated ourselves from self-deception, girded our moral loins, and repelled all forms of subtle coercion we would then be free in some deeper sense. But this is not enough: although these things constrain our freedom, their absence does not tell us what freedom is. To really answer the question we had to turn to metaphysics and the distinction between the world of phenomena and the world of the noumenon, the thing-in-itself. I argue (in section 17) that causality belongs to the phenomenal world, where everything is initiated by something else. The noumenon, in contrast, is beyond causality and is itself uncaused. As Spinoza expressed it, 'That thing is said to be free which exists solely from the necessity of its own nature, and is determined to action by itself alone'.[3] On this basis I maintained that rationality—the process by which we order and understand events using the law of causality—cannot be the source of freedom. If, as Kant told us, freedom is the ability to begin an event by oneself,[4] what is the 'self' we are referring to?

In the person who is free, the will that guides their actions must belong to the self that owes its origin to the noumenon, the realm of first causes. That self is the universal Self, the most immediate manifestation of which is the moral self. Only one who is guided by the moral self is truly free. The imperatives of the moral self are given to us not by our conditioning, nor by any outside agency, nor by the state or God or philosophy: they are given to us by our own inner nature. It is thus only by acting according to the lessons of the moral self that we can achieve autonomy. So the basis of inner freedom is our life in the noumenon, and it is only when our phenomenal self acts in accordance with the will of the universal Self that we rid ourself of all influences and coercions, all determinations and all other external laws, secular or divine.

The moral self connects our life in the phenomenon with our essence in the noumenon; it is at the heart of our existence, it is uniquely our own, yet it is everybody's. Inner freedom, then, means allowing oneself to be guided by the moral self. Our task is to find a way to express our universal Self in our everyday lives, in our rules for living. Thus freedom is always first in the being rather than in the doing. And we see that inner freedom is acting according to one's own considered will only if the will is understood as one's inner guide provided by the moral self. Only the moral self can provide the source of any lasting conviction. In this way, virtue and freedom form an inseparable pair.

Many philosophers regard the idea that 'a free will and a will under moral law are one and the same'[5] as Kant's most sublime insight, 'one of the most beautiful and profound ideas brought forth by that great mind, or indeed by men at any time'.[6] From that idea we see that 'metaphysical insights bear moral fruits',[7] because such insights allow understanding of the essence of what it is to be human, beyond our individual characteristics and the societies we live in. If freedom means living according to moral law then transcending the constraints and pressures of the phenomenal world is purchased at the cost of submitting oneself to the necessity of living in accord with the moral self. This is the antinomian quality of freedom: to be free we must submit. 'Where all being is understood as my own, I am free; where I confront all else as merely alien, I am unfree.'[8] The alternative is ersatz freedom: if we submit to no power in the noumenon we submit to all power in the phenomenon and cannot but be tossed about, anchorless, by the tides and storms of mundane life.

Living according to the moral self provides a post-secular ethics that transcends the rationalism of all modern theories of morality. In section 1 I argue that the opportunity to become autonomous individuals that was opened up by affluence and the liberation movements of the 1960s and 1970s has been hijacked by new forms of conformity—those presented to us by the market—and, instead of us writing our own biographies, our pen has been guided by an invisible hand. The moral stance that accompanied this post-modern individualism was a secular relativism, founded on nothing other than our own desires. The ethical account I put forward embraces the possibility of true individuality while avoiding the vacuous claims of relativism. My account appeals to an authority beyond the merely social and provides a metaphysical structure that allows for true agency. It gives us our moral adviser as well as our moral judge and in doing so offers a compass to guide us through the ethical confusions of the contemporary world.

The religious morality that ruled before the Enlightenment was superseded by various secular ethical systems, all based on reason. Reason's historic task was to separate science from faith, but in performing this task it deprived of its legitimacy the inner sense of what is right. It is now safe to allow the noumenon back into ethics; indeed, the failure of humanism and all Kantian ethics demands that we do. A post-secular ethics locates moral authority not in the abstractions of reason or in enslavement to faith; it places it in our own inner selves.

The idea that the individual finds liberation in the moral self represents a profound break from modern ethical systems. It repudiates all external forms of ethical authority and invests moral autonomy in the individual. If we ask why we should not lie, Aristotle would say we should not lie because lying is not part of a good character; Kant would say we should not lie because we have a duty to be truthful; Mill would say we should not lie because it reduces the social good. In truth, we should not lie because it is contrary to the moral self. Each of us must decide what is right. We must accept that we are lawgivers and only then decide to be law-followers. There is no need for God to give us laws, injunctions that must always be mediated by those who claim to represent God on Earth. Being free individuals, we do not need the statute books as our ethical guide. Nor do we need to appeal to duties derived from the principle of non-contradiction or intellectual constructions that prove the mutual benefit of social justice or contracts that we never have a chance to read. All these rob us of true autonomy as moral agents.

For three centuries Western society has lived on the moral capital accumulated first in the Christian era then in the era of social democracy. With the churches defeated by the combined armies of scientific reason and humanism, and social democracy defeated by affluence and individualism, that moral capital has been severely depleted. Fundamentalism is an atavistic cry for a return to a world of blind faith that is dead and gone. The great achievement of the Enlightenment, through all its phases of liberation, was to create the individual, and it is only a morality that honours the autonomy of the individual that can now succeed. After the death of God and the bold print of all rule books constructed by reason has faded, we can assert our own moral authority for the first time.

The market and the state have each compelled us to consent to external moral codes, systems designed by outside forces to which we accede through need, coercion or persuasion. The most enduring dictators are those who convince the subjugated that they have freely chosen their subjugation. 'All liberation depends on the consciousness of servitude.' The tricksters of post-modernism—Nietzsche's bastard children—met little resistance when they declared that we can all choose our own rules. Had we dared to inquire about the basis on which we should choose our rules, we would have simply been met with an ironic smile. They gave us an imagined agency that made us all the more vulnerable to manipulation by forces we could not see. Proud to make our own rules, in fact we became slaves to rules made by others.

Moral knowledge generated in the phenomenal world can move us only through habit, fear of punishment and the need for approval. These are flimsy threads on which to hang social order, yet forms of social control that mimic genuine ethical conduct are essential. But social order built on social convention is prone to collapse once humans find themselves beyond the reach of the institutions that embody the conventions. Classic explorations of this appear in the novel *Lord of the Flies* and post-apocalypse films such as *Mad Max* and *Waterworld* (where, it must be said, humanity is often redeemed by lone individuals who cling to moral laws drawn from a source beyond the social chaos). We do not, however, need to go to fiction for illustrations of the savagery that lies beneath the civilised exterior of many people. History fades quickly, so many Europeans were shocked at the barbarism that occurred in Srebrenica. The delusion of inherent goodness is nowhere more powerful, and dangerous, than in nations that believe they have a historic duty to liberty. The wickedness of Abu Ghraib was exposed by US Army Reserve Specialist Joe Darby, a soldier in possession of true moral goodness who acted on conviction. So enraged were his fellow soldiers that he had exposed the darkness, he feared for his life. Even in his home town in Maryland, the refusal of many of his compatriots to confront the evil in themselves led them to turn against Joe Darby and drive him from their community.

Finally—as if the litany of the perils of ethical rules based solely in the phenomenon were not already too depressing—we might dwell on the fact that many a 'fine, upstanding citizen', a pillar of the community who at every opportunity will assert our duty to adhere to moral law, frequently leads a double life in which, away from public gaze, all manner of infractions are committed. In this category we find embezzling captains of industry, priapic holy men, and tub-thumping newspaper columnists who take a break from penning their opinions to snort a line of cocaine. When Pentecostal preacher Jimmy Swaggart, who had exposed the sexual indiscretions of fellow ministers and denounced homosexuals, was caught with a prostitute in 1988, the public could not be blamed for a frisson of satisfaction at hypocrisy exposed. Social conventions are a pale shadow of genuine moral law, but they are necessary. In a civilised society, however, the institutions of law and government, as well as the more informal forms of social regulation, must codify and enforce the true if obscured emanations of the moral self.

FORTY-ONE
Finding inner freedom

DEPRESSION CHARACTERISES CONTEMPORARY CONSUMER society. Its clinical form aside, the widespread incidence of low-level and episodic depression can be explained by the promise of freedom thwarted. Depression is marked above all by a mood of powerlessness, an inability to take control of one's life, and is expressed not only in feelings of desolation but in the failure to mobilise one's rational capacities to find a way out of the morass. The fact that the incidence of depression in the United States has risen tenfold since the end of the Second World War is a most awkward one for those who laud liberal capitalism as the highest stage of history. The sense of helplessness that overwhelms the depressive mocks the claim that we live in an era of unparalleled choice. With all that freedom to choose, we are often struck by our inability to act and by a gnawing sense that we have little control over our world. In such circumstances it is quite rational to deny ourselves the power to act by sinking into melancholy and 'depriving' ourselves of our autonomy. Depression is thus an escape from freedom—or from the disappointment of the freedom promised by individualisation but denied by history. We are freed from the need to exercise our freedom. If we apprehend that in writing our own biographies the pen is indeed being moved by an invisible hand, it makes sense to stop writing.

The great irony of modern consumer life is that what prevents us from being free is the very pursuit of our own desires. If inner freedom is to prevail, the belief that freedom is the ability to choose to do as we like must be discarded. The individual in consumer society, to whom the market has given unprecedented choice, is a slave to desire even before the marketers step in. Only someone who lives according to the intuitions of the moral self is an individual in the true sense; yet, as we will see, such a life can never be individualistic, for it is always devoted to something beyond the self.

But must it be all or nothing? Must we either devote ourselves wholly to the directives of the moral self or abandon ourselves to life in the world of appearances?

There are among us saints, religious and secular, who seem to live entirely selfless lives. Imbued with fellow feeling and loving kindness, they commit themselves to the wellbeing of others without a thought to their own and rise above every slight and setback, always focused on defending the rights of the weak and dispossessed. They live every moment according to the lessons of their moral selves. I have called these modern saints, who do not necessarily have a religious inclination, avatars of virtue. We understand that, although tied for life to the causes they pursue, they are free in a way that we are not, yet could be. They act as our ethical interpreters, but they never preach to us because they do not speak for a god and know they can appeal to no higher authority. Their only authority is that which shines forth from the example of their own lives.

There are also among us some who seem to feel nothing for their fellow humans, for whom all thought and action are devoted to their own welfare, in whom every sign of consideration, even for their families, turns out to be a ruse for their own benefit. Alienated from their moral selves, they turn their faces away from the distress shown by a living thing and use their rationality as a defence for their callousness.

Most people, though, live between these two poles, and their proximity to one or the other depends on how close to their moral selves and the force of metaphysical empathy they can stay. Thus, if freedom means living according to the moral law, there are degrees of freedom depending on whether knowledge of the noumenon informs, to a greater or lesser extent, how we live our lives in the everyday phenomenal world. If inner freedom means living in close communication with the intuitions of the moral self, how can we get closer to it? Can we choose inner freedom?

If we cannot set out to live according to the intuitions of the moral self we cannot pursue our own freedom; whether we live close to it or far away is then determined by forces beyond our control. And if humans are unable to live more ethically all attempts at social reform are doomed. There is no disputing the fact that change is possible. In section 35 I recounted the story of Nick, who described how he was transformed from a self-obsessed hedonist dedicated to his own advancement into a compassionate individual who devotes himself to making the world a better place. He did not set out to change himself, at least not consciously; an inner disturbance prompted him to seek out another life path. Where this would take him he had no inkling, but it was at a mine in Bolivia that events transformed him. These events imposed themselves on a subject open to transformation.

FREEDOM REDISCOVERED

In his previous life Nick possessed the trappings of success, but he was a prisoner of his desires; when he turned over a rock in Bolivia he found the moral self and so his inner freedom.

Does this mean the moral life must be one of self-denial, of continual sacrifice? Nietzsche's attacks on Christianity were aimed at its life-denying form of moral law—a 'slave morality' that repudiates real life in preference for other-worldly values with their promise of heavenly reward. He rejected the meekness, humility and self-loathing that marked Christian teaching and urged us to take hold of life with two hands and live it to the full. Man as sinner would be superseded by those bold enough to overcome themselves. Nietzsche was writing when the Christian era was in decline. Today, nothing could stand in starker contrast to the 2000 years of Christian self-denial than the decadence and incontinence of post-modern affluence. The self-indulgence of consumerism is the antithesis of Christ's message, and we now witness the convolutions and contortions of evangelists and Pentecostals who sanction their congregation's cupidity with the prosperity gospel. Obliged to find biblical endorsement of the message that God wants us to be rich, the preachers often have recourse to the Parable of the Talents, as told by the apostle Matthew.

A master lends money (or talents) to three of his slaves and goes away for some time. When he returns, two slaves have 'put their money to work' and doubled its value. The master is well pleased and invites them to 'come and share your master's happiness'. The third slave has not put the money to work but, choosing prudence over avarice, has buried it in order to be sure he can return it in full on his master's return. When his master challenges him for his failure to double the sum, the slave replies, 'I knew that you are a hard man, harvesting where you have not sown and gathering where you have not scattered seed'. The slave feared he could not emulate his master's 'talents' for speculation and extortion and took the safe and honest course. The master announces, 'For everyone who has will be given more, and he will have abundance. Whoever does not have, even what he has will be taken away'. He demands that the prudent slave be thrown out 'into the darkness, where there will be weeping and gnashing of teeth'. It is a travesty of Christ's message to read this parable as if Jesus endorsed the slave master's view of a ruthless, unprincipled world in which the rich are rewarded with further riches and the poor are punished and cast out.

So is the path one of self-denial and asceticism or one of abandoning ourselves to excess in a world that provides opportunities for pleasure at every turn? In truth, these paths are the same: both are ruled by a single force—the lure of pleasure. One path embraces it and the other shuns it, but both are ruled by it. As with the reformed alcoholic, the addiction rules each day. Self-abasement and self-indulgence see the self as essentially weak. And, to the extent that it is engaged in the world of phenomena, the 'little self' is always beset by self-doubt.

There is, however, a third path, one that transcends both self-denial and excess. It is one of detachment. A life of detachment is not a life of disengagement from the world; rather, it is a life of engagement on one's own terms, of inner freedom. This is not the Stoic's road, where indifference is cultivated as a form of protection: instead, it is a path involving intentional participation in the world, and it is marked by purity of passion and moderation of desire. The path of inner freedom does not refuse to love: it loves purely, without emotional grasping. It loses love with sadness but without blame. It does not turn away from possessions: it owns them for what they are, not for what they promise. It insists on neither the hair shirt nor the Armani suit but is happy to wear either occasionally. It aspires without the need to aspire.

The life of detachment must be practised rather than merely theorised. Some Stoics were wont to insist on the worthlessness of all good things but decided that their commitment to the principle of renunciation, as opposed to the practice, was sufficient. Like the rich man today who casually says he could do without his wealth, the Stoics allowed themselves to indulge in pleasures because they were convinced they could give them up at will. But detachment is never proven in theory: 'between desiring and renouncing there is no mean'.[1] Without a grounding in the universal Self, rationality is no basis for equanimity and proves a feeble defence against the forces of self-deception and akrasia.

The liberation movements of the 1960s and 1970s set out to attack those structures of conservative society that were oppressive and held people back from flourishing and realising their potential. Even straight white males bore the burden of sexual repression and a plethora of attitudes that prevented them from forming mutually respectful and fulfilling relationships. In retrospect, it is now clear that the political demands for freedom, justice and autonomy also had a personal dimension, one that was intensely self-focused. At the time, it was not understood that, for all its faults, the conservatism that was being overthrown had embedded in it a sense of obligation to others, even if that obligation was often exercised in discriminatory and oppressive ways. The defeat of conservatism by the legitimate demand for self-determination thus had a shadow side—the preoccupation with self. When this new individualism became validated by the culture of the market the shadow developed into full-blown narcissism, captured in terms such as the 'me generation'. The preoccupation with self received political and social blessing and acquired a moral rationale in slogans such as 'Pamper yourself. You deserve it', 'I am my own person' and 'You can achieve anything you want'.

Despite their institutional failings, the churches were traditionally the repositories of those transcendent elements that remind us of our lives beyond the mundane, of our universal Self and its oneness with the noumenon. Although the authority of the churches as keepers of the transcendent has largely collapsed, the metaphysical ground of their former legitimacy is unchanged. Religious ceremonies such as the Mass still allow some individuals to feel a relationship with something transpersonal. But for most of us the loss of our conviction under the weight of science has closed down our access to the numinous. The modern rational mind's lack of will to believe denies it knowledge of the stream of meaning that runs beneath the surface of daily life.

God is dead, and there is no going back to the way of naive faith. As Carl Jung observed, religion is a defence against religious experience.[2] The religious path is, however, not the only one to the noumenon, to an appreciation of the unity of all things and the understanding that grows from that. There is also a metaphysical–psychological path,[3] in which the objective of the 'work' is to overcome our subjectivity—a formidable task in the modern world, which urges, compels, us to create our selves as subjects. Humility is the negation of the modern world, and we revere it in the avatars of virtue. Humility was one of the casualties of the end of the Christian

FREEDOM REDISCOVERED

era; it withered away. When Jesus said the meek shall inherit the Earth, he meant that only those who transcend their identification with the ego-self in the phenomenon will find the path to the universal Self in the noumenon.

FORTY-TWO

The individual and the collective

OF COURSE, THE AUTHENTIC self must also live a life in the phenomenon and so is always a subject too. The struggle is to prevent that self being overwhelmed by the forces of the phenomenal world, so that the individual becomes dominated again by the collective. In Hermann Hesse's novel *Siddhartha*, the eponymous hero meets the Buddha but is too proud to surrender himself. After some intellectual sparring, in which the Buddha warns against too much cleverness, Siddhartha walks on alone in search of his goal, his innermost self. He meets Kamala the courtesan and is beguiled by her, and soon he sinks into a life of gambling and indolence. Initially he treats it as a game for his amusement, but as years pass the life of pleasure comes to possess him. If, as Jung wrote, 'the experience of the Self is always a defeat for the ego',[1] the ego is always fighting back.

The authentic self must be free of the grip of social convention, yet at the same time take responsibility for the community's wellbeing. For so many today, 'freedom' means repudiating social norms for no reason other than to 'be myself', without any understanding of what 'myself' is. For the modern rebel, who loves to assert that she does not care what anyone thinks of her, independence is really no more than submitting to forces she does not see or comprehend. She is like a wild horse that breaks away from the pack but, instead of setting out for unknown places, prances in front of the pack, displaying her rebellious spirit and in doing so revealing that she remains in thrall to the herd. It is a life no more free than that of the throng—and much less honest. Successful separation means acknowledging one's debt to the collective and consciously repaying it, rather than being unwittingly bound by the forces of the collective.

It is thus possible to maintain one's individuality and integrate into the collective; indeed, for most there is no other way. Living obedient to the moral self means living according to moral rules we give ourselves. It might be thought that the autonomy and self-determination derived in this way would make one individualistic and remote from the concerns of others. In truth, the opposite is the case, because the essence of the moral self is merger with the universal Self. This resolution allows us to answer the questions posed by social theorist Ulrich Beck: 'How can the longing for self-determination be brought into harmony with the equally important longing for shared community? How can one simultaneously be individualistic and merge with the group?'[2]

Finding autonomy through the moral self is the means by which we can overcome the fragility of modern community. The true individual—as opposed to the parody represented by the modern consumer—can easily reconcile modernity with the deeper need to cultivate their social nature, to feel at home in the post-modern world. Carl Jung, who was much influenced by Kant and Schopenhauer, adds a further layer of understanding in his consideration of the process of 'individuation', the path by which a person becomes their own self and thus psychologically whole.[3] In becoming truly autonomous beings, we at the same time bind ourselves to our fellow humans.[4] When we individuate, Jung argued, we feel guilty for separating ourselves from the whole, and to expiate this guilt we must give something of value back to society: 'The individual is required by the collective demands to purchase his individuation at the cost of an equivalent work for the benefit of society. So far as this is possible, individuation is possible'.[5] On one hand, the process of individuation is one of giving up the self in order to find freedom; on the other, it entails an obligation to use that freedom to devote oneself to others.

It is apparent that individuation, although representing a separation from the collective, is the opposite of individualism, which is the dominant feature of modern Western society. The modern individual only imagines himself to be free of the collective; it is a pseudo-individuality that masks deeper conformity, and the more we try to be 'individuals' the more our lives are controlled by the social conventions we affect to discard.

But, although we might repay our debt to the collective, it is not strictly the collective that we are indebted to. Our debt is to the noumenon. In paying homage to the noumenon, one can pay homage to its various manifestations, including its expressions in the phenomenon in the form of art and the natural world. Few would argue against the proposition (put forward in section 39) that the natural world, as the phenomenal expression of the noumenon, has a sacred quality that validates a life devoted to its protection, but the idea that art can be an expression of the noumenon and that a life devoted to it can be invaluable is more contentious. It is to this that I now turn.

FORTY-THREE
Aesthetics

IF WE ARE TO believe its creators, great art is the expression in phenomenal form of noumenal insight. Francis Bacon, who saw his ability as a painter as neither skill nor gift but instead as a distinctive receptivity, spoke of trying to make his figures more real, rather than more realistic.[1] The true value of great art lies in its ability to remind us of our existence in the noumenon and to do so despite all the distractions that keep us confined to the world of everyday appearances. Differences in the degree of technical expertise aside, it is the ability to translate a vision of the world's inner nature into phenomenal representations that distinguishes the great artist from the everyday one. The great artist gives form to the noumenon, but a form 'trailing clouds of glory' whence it came. For Germain Bazin, curator-in-chief at the Louvre, the distinguishing characteristic of the great artist is the ability to see with a directness denied others.

> To see properly is the hardest thing. It requires genius. Most people see by way of their parents, their masters, or the social

> milieu in which they live. Sometimes on a youthful morning the scales fall from their eyes and the world appears, but only for a second, and for the rest of their lives they only look through that sombre curtain of images at the universe situated beyond. Only painters and poets really see.[2]

The same might be said for how some people hear music. Bazin reflects on the way concepts present an obstacle to seeing the inner nature of things: 'The act of looking tends to follow the act of thinking; only a few prophets of genius are able to look first'.[3] When they are able to gaze unflinchingly, artists see the thing as it is in its true nature, no longer defined by its relations to other things. It then takes skill to convert such a vision into a representation that can elicit in the viewer the artist's intimate insight.

Genius is the ability to see into the inner nature of the world, to contemplate it directly, undistracted by thoughts, concepts and emotional connotations. Concepts and skill can guide technique, but true insight comes from perception. It is not an intellectual power; indeed, the development of intellectual capacity can destroy genius. The artist, or at least the great artist, has both the faculty of seeing and the technical ability to translate the vision of the noumenon into a work of art—a painting, a sculpture, a piece of music or a poem, all of which attempt to reach beyond concepts—and to do so using concepts in a way that conceals as little as possible. Access to a muse, a divine inspiration that, according to myth, causes the soul to remember its higher state,[4] sets great art apart from decorative art, which merely represents phenomena.

Edward Hopper, whose paintings evoke intense feelings of interiority and the solitude and melancholy of the modern state of being, wrote, 'My aim in painting has always been the most exact transcription possible of my most intimate impressions of nature',[5] where nature could mean either a lonely lighthouse or an equally lonely New York diner. Foreshadowing Bacon's distinction between representing everyday reality and the inner reality, Wagner described the underlying subject of his great mythological work *The Ring of the Nibelung* as 'the depicting of reality'.[6] Wagner was a devoted disciple of Schopenhauer, whose main work he read repeatedly. He prefigured Jung in understanding that the function of the artist is 'to bring the unconscious part of human nature into consciousness'[7] and wrote that in Schopenhauer he discovered his own Wotan, the god who in Nordic myth was the patron of poets and visionaries.[8]

But is not the noumenon a timeless, undifferentiated oneness, without any characteristic that could be represented in art? In section 38 I argue that the existence of Platonic Ideas is the only way to explain the moral revulsion we feel at bestiality. The Ideas are the most direct manifestations of the noumenon in the phenomenon, the images that guard the threshold between the two. They are the unchanging forces of the noumenon, including the essential forms of animate and inanimate objects, and are the immediate elaboration of Kant's thing-in-itself, its 'immediate objectivity'.[9] If we are able to perceive them, the Ideas are the phenomenal forms that point most directly to the noumenon. Every particular animal is but an expression of the Idea of that animal, the general form of it. Although every individual form of the thylacine has died out, its Idea has not. Ideas are inseparable from the natural world; no manufactured item can ever express an Idea.

Jung's notion of archetypes is closely related to Plato's Ideas. As preconscious potentialities or elemental forces that manifest themselves in consciousness as images, archetypes

Aesthetics

can vary across cultures. Yet the elemental forces they reflect are independent of the creations of society; like Chomsky's universal grammar, they are imprinted on us. There are myriad possible images, but there is a limited number of archetypes. The function of the images—and the function of great art—is to provide a path for us to move from the phenomenon to the inner essence of the world. Great art has the potential to pierce the clutter of conscious life and allow us access to the nature of the world. The shadow is the most basic archetype: it represents the negative to every positive, the darkness within the light, the chaos from which order emerges; it is untamed nature, the unconscious or elemental power of the noumenon itself. Integration of the shadow was Nietzsche's task in his blasphemous *Beyond Good and Evil*, an assault on the suffocating Christian morality that hallowed the good and repudiated the bad, that elevated spirit over body.

The objective of great art is to capture the archetypal elements of life. In their raw form the archetypes are necessarily unconscious, for as soon as they take conscious form as images their essence is diluted. But the archetypal image, rendered by the master painter or composer, can take us to the archetype itself. Van Gogh was a supreme image maker of the elemental chaos of the noumenon. His style of painting natural settings, and even portraits, evokes the intrinsic instability and pulsating energy of the universe. His depiction of this energy in *The Cypresses* and *Road with Cypress and Star* is unsettling because it shatters the idea that the world is as we normally see it, fixed and stable. He confronts us with an uncontrollable force that lies just behind the veneer of everyday constancy and ordinariness. In *Road with Cypress and Star* country folk go about their evening business oblivious to the fragility, and meaning, of their existence. The trees, the clouds and the stars tremble with latent noumenal energy, yet we walk by without noticing the existential drama. As his life spiralled into the madness that would end in suicide, Van Gogh created *Self-portrait with Bandaged Ear*, which once again captured the wilful unknowingness with which we live our lives. The serenity in his eyes contradicts the turmoil of his inner life, which is caught by his brush strokes.

Myths serve the same purpose as great art: they help us recognise the elemental forces of the noumenon and integrate them into our lives. The characters in a myth represent the archetypes in a way that goes beyond the morality of fables or the emotional connection with characters in a novel. The consciousness with which we approach myth transcends the reality of daily life and takes us to a realm in which a handful of powerful forces contend. Although myths nominally occur in far-off lands, the distance in time and space from our mundane lives elevates the narrative to a new plane, one that corresponds to a level of consciousness where we are free to enter into the Platonic Ideas. The miracles and impossible turns of myths might be foreign to our rational minds, but they correspond closely to the leaps and contradictions that are natural to our unconscious lives. In this sense myths are stories about this world, whereas fictional stories conjure up alien worlds. With great art, whatever appears on canvas or immediately strikes the ear speaks to us about the nature of our existence in this world in a way that transcends everyday consciousness. Roger Scruton, who argues that art, music and poetry began to take on huge intellectual importance when the Enlightenment led to the decline in religious faith, makes a similar point:

> It is scarcely surprising, therefore, that there should attach to the products of high culture the same sense of profound mystery

> and ineffable meaning that is the daily diet of religion. Our lives are transfigured in art, and redeemed of their arbitrariness, their contingency and littleness.[10]

The ability to see into the essence of things is a gift that demands a sacrifice. Artists wittingly or otherwise enter into a bargain, sometimes exposing themselves to danger. The noumenon's raging energies are both life-affirming and life-denying and are capable of destabilising any human. William Blake identified the creative energies with both hell and eternal delight.[11] Energy is life, life is the body, and reason's role is to place boundaries on the energy. Genius is to be found in the fires of hell. The artist goes to heaven for talent and hell for inspiration, and a great work of art marries the two. Reflecting on the fact that, no matter how tame, the animal always feels the pull of the wild, Herman Melville seemed to express the same metaphysic: 'Though in many of its aspects this visible world seems formed in love, the invisible spheres were formed in fright'.[12] The rationality of the artist always threatens to deny access to the power of the noumenon, the invisible world, the fires of hell. It is for this reason that painters and composers of genius often go mad: it is the price they pay for their genius. It is as if, in a moment of abandon, they turn their eyes to the sun, the source of creative energy, sacrificing their sight for a blazing insight, while others prudently confine themselves to peeping at the source through a pin-hole.

The Idea is of the phenomenon, but only just, and can therefore be known by a subject. But we can apprehend Ideas only as subjects of a particular sort—ones that are able to cast off all concepts and learnt ways of seeing. In this way we can apprehend the thing as it is in its purest form in the phenomenon, independent of preconceptions, prejudices, likes and dislikes. Freed of all ideas of self, all desires and preferences, such a 'pure knowing subject' is able to consider the work of art as it is.[13] In this state of aesthetic contemplation we forget ourselves and release our consciousness to intuition. As a pure subject, divorced from our own particular subjectivity, from our own ideas of self, we are able to devote our entire awareness to the object before us, with a clarity untarnished by the chatter of our minds, the pull of our emotions, and awareness of our bodies. In these moments of complete disinterest, the pure knowing subject is able to perceive the representation as pure object. Time is suspended and location dissolved, so that we can see beauty as it is and experience a kind of unmediated insight into the true nature of the thing. In the same way, the baby is always beautiful to its parents, not through vanity or bias but simply because in gazing at their child the parent transcends their own self completely and can thus see the true beauty of the baby. When we look at another's baby we see it in a way that is almost always conditioned.

Art becomes great only when it pierces the barriers brought by the viewer, the phenomenal forms of receptivity we take to the gallery or the concert hall. A great painting must sidestep all concepts, all preconceptions, all expectations, all learnt ways of seeing, and go directly to the Ideas. The painting is always only a more or less imperfect rendering of the Idea it attempts to capture. Yet this ability to know the Ideas of things must be inherent not only in the great artist but in all of us, because otherwise we would be incapable of appreciating works of art. The great artist differs from ordinary mortals through a capacity to transcend the everyday self more completely and for more sustained periods and so gain a deeper intuition of the Ideas. In the artistic experience, therefore, both artist and viewer must come to the work, one as creator and the other as observer, as pure knowing subjects. The two then communicate in a way that is beyond words, beyond forms, as if sharing one pair of eyes. In a painting the great artist has created a representation of an Idea frozen in time within a frame; the viewer must stop, too, suspend time. For this reason the crowded gallery is the enemy of the aesthetic experience: the presence of others relentlessly drags us back into the present and the place. A reproduction of a great work viewed in solitude has more potential as a true aesthetic experience than the original viewed in a crowded gallery. This is why few members of the public will ever again appreciate the original *Mona Lisa*, even if they can see beyond the picture's commodification.

Art survives because both artist and audience continue to seek the deep insights great works promise. Great works are not the only guides to the noumenon, but the artist can provide a bridge from the everyday world of phenomena to the noumenal world of meaning, to the unitary reality that is the substrate of all things, to the transcendence and the immanence. Bacon's remark that he sought to make his figures more real rather than more realistic helps explain why photography struggles to attain the status of genuine art. A photograph that captures the world as the eye normally sees it can never be art; the photographer must create an image that reveals a deeper truth about the world, and for this he or she must be able to see the world in a way few can. The naive snaps of Richard Billingham come close.

If the great artist succeeds in breaking through the doors of perception and gives us an inkling of the inner meaning, the commercialisation of art stands as an absolute barrier to this insight. Great works are not possible for the artist whose consciousness is pervaded by money and the desire for success, since he degrades his muse to a whore.[14] Andy Warhol degraded his muse to something cheaper, a celebrity. He offered no apology: 'Making money is art . . . good business is the best art'. He was proud of his superficiality; there is nothing beneath the surface, he declared. The superficiality resided in his cultural boosters who wanted to find meaning in a screen print of a tin of Campbell's soup. Popular culture has no intrinsic value. Warhol spawned a generation of artists who sought fame by breaching norms and trashing sensitivities—shock with no purpose—culminating in the tragic case of Tracey Emin, who has won fame by destroying the final barriers between the public and private domains with works featuring her broken relationships, abortions, bodily secretions and vagina.

Great art has a latent appeal even to those most immune to it—that is, those most absorbed in their own selves and therefore unable to become pure knowing subjects. They unconsciously recognise the force of true art even while corrupting it in the process, as occurs when Raphael's *Alba Madonna* is put on a tea towel or Pachelbel's *Canon* is turned into muzak. Although appreciation of artistic quality can be learnt—refinement is not innate—no amount of education can open one to the possibility of aesthetic intuition as I define it here; indeed, people with little education or refinement might find themselves more open to it. The opposite is true, too; the highly educated may be denied the intuition. John Carey, professor of literature at the University of Oxford, has recently written an entire book on his own inability to experience aesthetic insight, attributing to humankind his insensibility.[15]

The view of great art I advance is sometimes seen as elitist, apparently reserving true appreciation for a cultivated few. Post-modern critics such as Roland Barthes and Jacques Derrida declared that a universal source of significance or value is an impossibility and characterised high culture as one of the methods used by the bourgeoisie to cement its own domination. 'Great art', they argued, derives its value from nothing more than the arbitrary imprimatur of a self-validating cultural elite. By kicking away the pedestal on which the great work of art stood, post-modernism wanted to bring high culture to the level of popular culture. By 'valorising' popular culture the deconstructionists at the same time devalued high culture. Historically, high culture has indeed been closely associated with political and economic power, but the correlation between the possession of financial capital and the acquisition of cultural capital has collapsed. In the neoliberal era a new moneyed class emerged, a nouveau riche thrown up by the emergent industries of entertainment, sport, IT, finance markets and speculators who profited from privatisations. Unlike stock-market fortunes, cultural capital takes time to cultivate and usually requires a number of generations within a family. The intellectuals and culture keepers who had shared a view of art with the old-money families now had to deal with culturally depauperate magnates with names such as Saatchi, Gates, Branson, Berezovsky and Trump. The type of bourgeois society that Derrida and Barthes attacked was already dying. High culture is no longer needed as a means of asserting hegemony when buying a football team will do the trick.

I think enough has been said to show that no amount of study or exposure can cultivate intuition of the noumenal core of great art. Indeed, the aesthete's training and sense of self could be obstacles to true aesthetic contemplation. Refinement might enhance the aesthete's ability to appreciate talent and to understand intellectually the nature and role of high culture; on the other hand, there are uncultivated people who have the ability to see the noumenal effortlessly.

With this in mind, a parallel can be drawn between forms of artistic appreciation and the three approaches to life set out in section 3—the pleasant life, the good life and the meaningful life. Pleasing art corresponds to the pleasant life and is enjoyed simply for the visual and aural gratification it provides, without further meaning. Good art is the product of cultivated talents and requires an advanced capacity for technique and perhaps emotional acuity. It appeals to an aesthetically refined audience that has developed the ability to appreciate more complex, abstract and sophisticated artistic forms. An appreciation of chamber music, for example, requires, for most, extended exposure to classical music and a thorough knowledge of musical forms, often including the ability to play an instrument and read music. Good art corresponds to the good life, in which talents are assiduously developed.

Great art, which corresponds to the meaningful life, goes directly to the human condition and the inner nature of the world, offering those who are able to experience it a path to the noumenal. It goes beneath the emotions to the archetypes that provide the foundation for understanding the universal Self. This is why, for some, aesthetic contemplation provides a path to inner freedom.

FORTY-FOUR
Happiness reconsidered

WE EACH MUST CHOOSE whether to pursue the pleasant life, the good life or the meaningful life, since we cannot have all three. For many, the default option is the first—a hedonic lifestyle. The pleasant life is lived always in the phenomenon. It is the life of the subject lived in the concrete and the immediate, exposed to the full force of events and with little thought of the future. In its purer form, it eschews all kinds of reflection, planning and deliberation.

The good life, devoted to cultivating one's talents, is little more than the application of rationality and self-control to overcome the impulsiveness of the pleasant life, although Aristotle took it further, asking us to find our *daemon*, our personal spirit, and to follow its path. The good life has much in common with the ideal of the Stoics, which was to use their reason and knowledge of life's pleasures and pains to maximise their happiness and to refuse to involve themselves too closely in the sources of both. Aimed unapologetically at a life of happiness, Stoicism differed fundamentally from those philosophies and religious systems that endorsed a life of virtue. In an insight that is more pertinent today than ever before, the Stoics understood that pleasure and pain are as much psychological as physical events:

> It was seen that want and suffering did not result directly and necessarily from not having, but only from desiring to have and yet not having; that this desiring to have is therefore the necessary condition under which alone not having becomes privation and engenders pain.[1]

Suffering thus becomes a function of the gap between what we have and what we want. Whereas the strategy of modern life is to try to close the gap by increasing what we have, the Stoics understood that the more we have the more we want, that everything we have can be taken away in an instant, and that a safer plan for avoiding suffering is to work at reducing our wants. This is a specific form of the good life because it means applying one's reason to develop a life plan that entails denying some immediate pleasures in order to avoid greater pain in the future. The difference is that the Stoics denied themselves the desire for pleasures so as to avoid the disappointment of not acquiring them, while those pursuing the good life deny themselves fleeting pleasures in the hope that they will in time be rewarded with more enduring ones. The Stoics cultivated equanimity; those pursuing the good life learn to apply self-discipline and defer gratification. This is the rationale behind most forms of education, especially in a world of commercial learning that trivialises the intrinsic value of knowledge and promotes its instrumental rewards.

From a pragmatic point of view, the good life may be superior to the pleasant life because it develops propensities and talents that can provide a more constant stream of pleasures during a lifetime. It is a practical strategy for minimising regret. The pleasant life borrows from the future in order to enjoy the present; the good life borrows from the present in order to augment the future.[2] It may or may not be safe to assume that the return on the investment in renunciation is sufficient to make pursuit of the good life worthwhile, although the typical resolve to 'live it up' of those who have been given only a short while to live suggests that the investment usually takes some time to mature. On the other hand, the good life can cause some people to sacrifice the wrong things in the short term. Think of fathers who work long hours while their children are growing up, having persuaded themselves that forgoing the pleasure of time with their children will free up more time for interaction later, when wealth has been secured, only to discover that in the meantime their children have moved beyond fathering. Moreover, pursuit of the good life always requires a gamble, since its promised fruits can turn rotten at any time—through a house fire, an illness, a divorce or a stock-market collapse—and, to the extent that we have invested our happiness in these fruits, we are vulnerable, perhaps more so in affluent nations than in poor ones.

Application of reason to the planning of a life distinguishes the good life from the life of an animal. But is it enough? There is nothing inherently virtuous in the good life, unless one believes that the exercise of our reason is virtuous in itself, or that we have a duty to develop our talents, a position taken by post-Kantians such as John Rawls and Amartya Sen. I think most people, even people committed to hedonism, would agree that in a perfect world a virtuous life is to be preferred to a happy one; after all, we do not revere avatars of happiness (although we do appear to be willing to pay them well if the proliferation of books and workshops on how to live a happy life is any guide). Yet to ask whether Gandhi, Mandela and the Dalai Lama have lived happy lives seems to miss the point. They have been devoted to causes much greater than their own welfare, and we revere them because their lives have meaning.

Pursuit of the pleasant life excludes pursuit of the meaningful life, and it is no surprise that the evidence of psychological studies, insofar as it can be relied on, shows that the pleasant life is often rather joyless. But it goes deeper, since the notion of wellbeing that motivates hedonistic pursuits is the enemy of purpose. I suggest that the way to achieving psychological maturity is necessarily one of abandoning the pleasant life and, perhaps via the good life, arriving at the meaningful life. Imagine the domain of our concerns to be a sphere, in which the outer layers form the conscious phenomenal world and the inner core is the noumenal world, barely accessible by awareness, except through a special form of non-sensible intuition. Schopenhauer asked:

> Why is our consciousness brighter and more distinct the farther it reaches outwards, so that its greatest clearness lies in sense perception, which already half belongs to things outside us; and, on the other hand, becomes more obscure as we go inwards, and leads, when followed to its innermost recesses, into a darkness in which all knowledge ceases?[3]

The effect of the special form of non-sensible intuition is to bring a glimmer of light to the innermost recesses, a process of personal enlightenment that is the very opposite of the European Enlightenment, which celebrates the rationality of the phenomenon. One form of enlightenment travels towards the inner core; the other moves away from it.

The attractions of the pleasant life constantly act to draw us away from the centre to the surface of the sphere. It is as though the sphere is spinning and modern consumerism acts as a centrifugal force, propelling us outwards. Never have there been so many distractions and lures; never has the superficial sparkled so brightly; never before has happiness been defined by the pursuit of emotional and physical gratification. In contrast with the frenetic striving of the conscious world on the surface of the sphere, the centre of the sphere—the noumenal world—is a place of peace. If the meaningful life is one committed to something larger than oneself—a life arising from the enlargement of the self so that it is infused with the universal Self and the ethical principles enlivening that self—then the difference between the pleasant life and the meaningful life is the distance from periphery to core. The process of individuation can be thought of as a gravitation to the core. To traverse the distance requires us to resist the centrifugal force that throws us outwards: we need to make use of the centripetal force that is sometimes characterised as the search for meaning. If this is so, the modern pursuit of the pleasant life becomes the enemy of life purpose.

Yet, in making the journey inwards, self-deception is ever present. Freud once complained that his American followers had interpreted his psychoanalytic method as a technique for making people happy. Steeped in the European philosophical tradition, he saw his work as a way to help people discover the meaning of their life. Nietzsche had made a similar observation some decades earlier: 'Man does *not* strive for happiness; only the Englishman does that'. Considered as a whole, in contrast to the continental Europeans, the citizens of Anglophone nations—and especially the United States—are particularly susceptible to the centrifugal forces of the consumer life and less subject to the countervailing forces that would propel us inwards.

Which life is to be preferred? The psychological research shows that people who pursue intrinsic goals such as self-development and deeper relationships report higher levels of life satisfaction than people who pursue external hedonistic goals and that the most satisfied are people whose lives are suffused with a sense of meaning. Some are born with a greater capacity to control their short-term desires. Some have a limited capacity to experience pleasure and can be prone to despondency. Some understand their calling at age 15, and others retire wondering what they were meant to have done. Some experience metaphysical intuitions rarely; others find their lives filled with a powerful, mysterious sense of the numinous. Some, armed with intelligence and insight and having reflected fully, decide to devote their lives to pleasure seeking. It is for each to choose in negotiation with their conscience, perhaps with the assistance of a moral adviser.

Throughout modern consumer society, however, there prevail overwhelming pressures to opt for one kind of life as opposed to the others. The official ideology endorses the pleasant life. At every turn we are urged to enjoy immediate pleasures of the material kind, to take substances to enhance our moods, to substitute instant gratification for rewards that take time to reveal themselves, to borrow from tomorrow to fund consumption today, to discount the future to the point of insignificance. We are everywhere enjoined to embrace the immediate and superficial. In such an environment the good life needs its advocates, and they can use their persuasive powers to expose the self-deception, weakness of will and subtle coercion the market exploits. The meaningful life, on the other hand, has few advocates. At best, it has those who embody its virtues and in so doing perhaps stir in the hearts of others a deeper intuition that leads them to transcend the phenomenal preoccupations of lives pleasant and good.

FORTY-FIVE
The human condition

KANT, THE EMBLEMATIC PHILOSOPHER of the European Enlightenment, took hold of reason and transformed it from a functional tool into the essence of our humanity—the basis of self, of order, of morality—and in so doing placed rationality at the centre of human progress. Although he denies it the power to see beyond the world of appearances, in that world it would be king. Modern man was born and found to be capable, in control and self-possessed. For people who sought escape from the oppressive rule of the churches and their superstitions, Kant's vision was liberating and engendered a collective optimism perhaps beyond anything humanity had previously contemplated.

Yet this was a mood that always fought deeper forces. The rule of the churches was not founded merely on ecclesiastical power, the machinations of despots or the gullibility of the masses. It was a rule that grew from something existentially profound, a sense that troubled lowly peasant and exalted lord alike.

Perhaps conscious of this, some of Kant's students, notably Schelling, rejected absolute faith in the power of reason. Schopenhauer knew the essence of humans lay in their life in the noumenon rather than in their rational capacity, but he denied that this 'second life in the noumenon' had any purpose, a position that imbued his philosophy with relentless pessimism. Although often captivated by his penetrating insights and sublime prose, his readers are left with a feeling that, in the end, life remains pointless. For Schopenhauer, our phenomenal form, as a manifestation of the universal Self, is experienced as a deviation from our original state, and the 'memory' of that state sets up a kind of existential tension, felt as a yearning to return to the peace of the noumenon. It would be senseless, though, for us to be manifest as phenomenal beings if all we did was act to return ourselves as soon as we could to the original state: that would defeat the purpose of our individual lives, of our species, and of the entire creation. So we are born with a will to live, and it is this conflict between our yearning to return to the serenity of the original condition and our will to live that leads to a life of 'suffering'.

In this context, suffering, which is also at the heart of Eastern traditions, does not mean constant pain or distress in everyday life: in our lives in the phenomenon this is generally not the case, especially for most citizens of rich countries. The idea that life in the phenomenon is always a life of suffering—in the sense of frustrated yearning—is derived a priori, before consideration of how life is actually lived. But the conflict between the yearning for a return and the will to live is expressed a posteriori in daily life, as the will to live contends with the obstacles of the body, the psyche and the social world. Philosophers, writers and artists have often been drawn to tragedy as the art form that reminds us of the suffering that befalls those who live the life of desire and turn away from their moral selves.

It was perhaps this life-denying mood that caused Nietzsche to create a philosophy infused with a wholly different feeling, one of celebration of both the dark and the light. After an early infatuation with Schopenhauer, Nietzsche broke radically from that unremittingly depressing outlook: his mentor's denial of life as it is lived was a disturbing echo of Christianity. Nietzsche's style, which is more lyrical than logical, brought to the appreciation of life and its purpose a distinctive mood that serves historically to balance the austerity of Schopenhauer and Kant. And he denounced what he called Christianity's '*hostility to life*, a furious, vindictive distaste for life itself'; its opposition to the 'world' and fear of beauty and sensuality, 'basically a yearning for non-existence', was for Nietzsche sinister and an impoverishment of life.[1] Both Christianity and Schopenhauer saw asceticism as the path to salvation; Nietzsche damned this path with his pen. The Christian distaste for life—Christianity is the only religion that adopts an instrument of torture as its symbol[2]—stands in contrast to the playfulness of the Hindu gods, the exploits of Mullah Nasrudin, and the wryness of the Buddhist sages. Perhaps Christianity would be less forbidding if the Bible had some jokes in it.

Nietzsche's figure of Dionysus stood for an energy that is chaotic, ecstatic and sexual, both life-affirming and destructive, intoxicating to the point of madness. It is the promise of ecstatic release in the company of others that Nietzsche saw in 'primitive' rituals, in Greek festivals and in the music of Wagner. Today, the lure of Dionysus draws young people to rave parties. This energy, at once creative and destructive, gives life its *rasa*, its juice. In the face of the world's essential disorder, how wonderful it is, Nietzsche exclaimed, that we should create culture with all its artistic, scientific and mythical manifestations. Such a view opposes the deification of reason and progress as the highest good. Philosophy should serve not to console but to inspire, not to help us learn how to die but to help us learn how to live.

Dionysus evolved through Nietzsche's work, taking on elements of its opposite, the Apollonian force of order, control and reason. It came to 'integrate all of one's drives and passions into a spontaneous and powerful self conceived as a well-fashioned aesthetic totality'.[3] As the principles evolved, so the Kantian distinction between noumenon and phenomenon dissolved; the transcendent was no longer needed, and life was embraced in its earthy reality. No wonder Nietzsche's vision has had its strongest influence among artists and alienated philosophers.[4]

If life in the phenomenon is arbitrary and meaningless, we can respond with disgust and resignation or with delight and pride at our ability to create order out of chaos.[5] For Schopenhauer, art is an escape from life; for Nietzsche, it is an affirmation of it. This distinction is reflected in strikingly different approaches to sexual expression: for one, intercourse is a bodily necessity resulting from biology and associated with original sin; for the other, the erotic is more aesthetic than instinctual, and the sexual energies are to be celebrated.

The mood of Kant was order and optimism, of Schopenhauer pessimism and futility, and of Nietzsche earthiness and the Dionysian, but by the middle of the twentieth century the philosophy that best reflected the popular mood was existentialism. Preoccupied with the fate of the individual, the existentialists saw the individual life as one of despair, anguish and, ultimately, absurdity. What other conclusion could be drawn from the cruelty of two world wars and the indiscriminate miseries of economic collapse? There was only one reasonable answer—a cultivated alienation.

THE FREEDOM PARADOX

So it seemed. There was another response, one rejected by the existentialists at the moment Sartre confronted the root of the chestnut tree, as he tells it in *Nausea*. Given a chance to enter the citadel, Sartre baulked and was unwilling to take the final step. He thus could not perceive a force greater than man. Recoiling from a terrible but subconsciously felt power, he instead found ... nothing. He saw a vacuum that he reified into Nothingness. He almost glimpsed the inner core of existence but instead saw only Nothingness, and it is unsurprising that he concluded life is absurd. The deaths, the slaughter and the misery were for nothing, and despair was the only sane approach to life. It was that mood that swept through the Western world after the noise of battle had subsided and the horror of war sank in.

But the 1960s and 1970s administered a forgetting potion, and the promises of wealth and liberation seemed to fill Sartre's void. Consumer culture has subsumed the individual in the grand, unifying vision of the market and has succeeded where all the despots failed; instead of forcing submission, it gilded the cage and persuaded us to enter and lock the door behind us. We fought ideologies and systems that would subjugate us to a single idea, only to succumb to the creeping colonisation of our minds by a hidden power, a power that seduced us with the promise of luxury, the vision of riches, and the opportunity to create any identity we desire.

As the despair of existentialism was swept away by the passing of time and the march to prosperity, a new mood of confidence and hope took shape. But it was not to last; in recent times, in the age of superabundance, a pervasive sense of disappointment has intruded. Once again, that disturbing feeling of meaninglessness has asserted itself. The secularisation of society meant that, as the emptiness of affluence finally had to be confronted, there was nowhere to go except to return to a gloomy nihilism.

Yet the pessimistic view can follow only from a belief that the phenomenal world is entirely without purpose and that the will is therefore blind, for then all suffering is without justification. If we have a reason to do so, we are willing to suffer. So, if we suppose that the noumenon's manifestation in the phenomenon is not without purpose but that the noumenon is intentioned, creation has a meaning. The purpose is for the noumenon to recognise itself through the phenomenon, to 'glory in its own creation', and to do so through human consciousness or, rather, the transcendence of it. If this is so, the will to live in humans has a purpose beyond biological survival and reproduction. Such a view gives value to the phenomenon: it is not merely a pale and otiose shadow of the noumenon; it is a partner in its own being, and this lends intrinsic value to the phenomenal existence of each human. Daily life is then not a heavy stone carried in the knapsack of the eternal Self. Within each day lies dormant the possibility of attaining inner freedom, of finding our purpose.

Notes

PREFACE

Harry Frankfurt, 'On the necessity of ideals', in Gil Noam and Thomas Wren (eds), *The Moral Self*, MIT Press, Cambridge, Mass., 1993.

SECTION 1 *The disappointment of liberalism*

1. This is now well established: see, for example, Bruno Frey and Alois Stutzer, *Happiness and Economics*, Princeton University Press, Princeton, 2002; Richard Layard, *Happiness: lessons from a new science*, Penguin, New York, 2005; and Tim Kasser, *The High Price of Materialism*, MIT Press, Cambridge, Mass., 2002.
2. Martin Seligman, 'Why is there so much depression today? The waxing of the individual and the waning of the commons', in Rick Ingram (ed.), *Contemporary Psychological Approaches to Depression*, Plenum Press, New York, 1990.
3. C. Murray and A. Lopez (eds), *The Global Burden of Disease: summary*, report prepared by Harvard School of Public Health for WHO and the World Bank, Geneva, 1996, p. 21.
4. Friedrich von Hayek, *The Road to Serfdom*, George Routledge & Sons Ltd, London, 1944, p. 13.
5. See Ulrich Beck and Elisabeth Beck-Gernsheim, *Individualization*, Sage Publications, London, 2002.

6 Although, as Zygmunt Bauman says (*The Individualized Society*, Polity Press, Cambridge, 2001, p. 7), echoing Marx, 'People make their own lives but not under conditions of their choice'.

7 David Rowan, 'The bodyshapers', *The Times* 'Body and soul' supplement, 6 September 2003, p. 4.

SECTION 2   *Rationale*

1 John Stuart Mill, 'On liberty', in *On Liberty and Other Essays*, Oxford University Press, Oxford, 1991, p. 67.

2 Friedrich von Hayek, *The Constitution of Liberty*, Routledge & Kegan Paul, London, 1960.

3 Hayek, *Road to Serfdom*, p. 18.

4 Francis Fukuyama, *The End of History and The Last Man*, The Free Press, New York, 1992, p. xii.

5 Milton Friedman is perhaps the best known advocate of Hayekian liberalism, especially in his book *Capitalism and Freedom*. But, whereas Hayek is subtle, Friedman is crude: Hayek reads like a philosopher; Friedman reads like a propagandist. Friedman might have taken more careful note of Hayek's observation, 'Probably nothing has done so much harm to the liberal cause as the wooden insistence of some liberals on certain rough rules of thumb, above all the principle of *laissez-faire*' (*Road to Serfdom*, p. 13). Had Friedman observed this Hayekian subtlety, the libertarians might have been less successful.

SECTION 3   *Types of happiness*

1 Mill, 'On liberty', p. 63.

2 ibid.

3 ibid., pp. 65, 78.

4 Alain de Botton, *Status Anxiety*, Penguin, London, 2004.

5 Seligman has written extensively on the subject; his writings are summarised in popular form (maybe too popular) on the website www.authentichappiness.org.

6 Arthur Schopenhauer, *The World as Will and Representation*, vol. I, Dover Publications, New York, 1969, p. 235.

7 See especially his *Nicomachean Ethics*, Penguin, Harmondsworth, 1976.
8 See, for example, Carol Ryff's MIDUS study and her contributions to Burton H. Singer and Carol D. Ryff (eds), *New Horizons in Health*, National Academy Press, Washington, DC, 2003.
9 Martha Nussbaum, 'In defense of universal values', in Martha Nussbaum, *Women and Human Development: the capabilities approach*, Cambridge University Press, Cambridge, 2000.
10 See in particular the important book by Tim Kasser, *The High Price of Materialism*, MIT Press, Cambridge, Mass., 2002.
11 A point made by Carol Ryff in the MIDUS study.

SECTION 4 *Freedom and happiness*
1 See, for example, Frey and Stutzer, *Happiness and Economics*.
2 These are not the terms she uses. Nussbaum, 'In defense of universal values'.
3 Germaine Greer, *The Whole Woman*, Doubleday, London, 1999, pp. 1–2, 309.
4 Hayek, *The Road to Serfdom*, p. 105.

SECTION 5 *Types of liberty*
1 Hayek, *The Constitution of Liberty*, p. 13.
2 Isaiah Berlin, *Liberty*, Oxford University Press, Oxford, 2002. 'Two concepts of liberty' was first published in 1957.
3 ibid., p. 171.
4 Quoted in Berlin, ibid., p. 173.
5 ibid., p. 175.
6 Or Anglophone ones at least. Survey evidence shows they account for about one-fifth to one-quarter of adults in the United States, the United Kingdom and Australia. See Clive Hamilton and Richard Denniss, *Affluenza*, Allen & Unwin, Sydney, 2005.
7 ibid.
8 Hayek, *The Constitution of Liberty*, p. 15.
9 Neoliberalism is not the only political philosophy to feel

uncomfortable with the idea of inner freedom. Amartya Sen asks whether, if we do not have the courage to choose to live in a particular way even though we could, we can be said to have the freedom (that is, the capability) to live that way. 'This is a difficult question', he notes, and immediately moves on to easier ones ('Capability and wellbeing', in Martha Nussbaum and Amartya Sen (eds), *The Quality of Life*, Clarendon Press, Oxford, 1993, p. 33). It is a difficult question if one does not want to introduce a fissure in one's entire argument by confronting it.

SECTION 6 *Inner freedom*

1   I later take the argument further and define inner freedom in terms of the ground that underlies those processes.
2   Berlin, 'Two concepts of liberty', p. 180. The same criticism can be made of neoliberal economic ideology, which asserts that, because choice in the marketplace is good for us, it is legitimate to coerce us into being private consumers by denying us the opportunity to act differently, as citizens who own things collectively. We are not really coerced, it is suggested, because no one could object to having more choice.
3   Juliet Schor, *The Overspent American*, HarperCollins, New York, 1999, p. 6; Clive Hamilton, *Overconsumption in Britain: a culture of middle-class complaint?*, Discussion paper no. 57, Australia Institute, Canberra, 2003; Clive Hamilton, *Overconsumption in Australia: the rise of the middle-class battler*, Discussion paper no. 49, Australia Institute, Canberra, 2002.
4   The phrase is used by Graham Smith and Corinne Wales in 'Citizens' juries and deliberative democracy', *Political Studies*, vol. 48, 2000, p. 53.
5   ibid.
6   'It is clear that there is a marked difference between the pre-deliberative preferences of citizens which would have been aggregated within existing social choice mechanisms and their preferences and judgements after the process of deliberation'—ibid., p. 60.

THE FREEDOM PARADOX

SECTION 7 *Do we prefer what we choose?*

1. See especially David George, *Preference Pollution*, University of Michigan Press, Ann Arbor, 2001. See also Lanse Minkler, 'Preference pollution, reasons, and other murky motivations: on some hidden costs of the market', *Review of Social Economy*, vol. LXII, no. 2, June 2004.
2. David George, *Preference Pollution*, p. 16.
3. Minkler, 'Preference pollution, reasons, and other murky motivations', p. 269.
4. David George makes this point in *Preference Pollution*.
5. Mary Winter of Grey Worldwide.

SECTION 8 *Self-deception and akrasia*

1. For example, Alfred Mele, *Irrationality: an essay on akrasia, self-deception and self-control*, Oxford University Press, New York, 1987; Herbert Fingarette, *Self-deception*, University of California Press, Berkeley, 2000. Mele provides a helpful overview in the *Routledge Encyclopedia of Philosophy*, Routledge, London, 1998.
2. Mele, in *Routledge Encyclopedia of Philosophy*, p. 630.
3. ibid. This doubles as a definition of political spin.
4. 'Part of the problem—a large part of it, I believe—is that philosophical models for the explanation of action and belief are typically designed specifically for rational behaviour'—Mele, *Irrationality*, p. 169. The word 'philosophical' in this sentence could be replaced by the word 'economic' and the statement would be just as valid.
5. Fingarette, *Self-deception*.
6. *The Kilroy Show*, broadcast on BBC Television in November 2003.
7. Mele, *Routledge Encyclopedia of Philosophy*, p. 629.
8. See Justin Gosling, *Weakness of the Will*, Routledge, London, 1990, p. 101.
9. Mele, *Routledge Encyclopedia of Philosophy*, p. 141. In response to the claim that one cannot act contrary to one's better judgment, Mele writes: 'Odysseus's having himself lashed to the mast in

order that he may safely hear the Sirens' song shows what a little foresight can do'—*Irrationality*, p. 3.
10 Mele, *Routledge Encyclopedia of Philosophy*, p. 142.

SECTION 9 *A digression on the ethic of consent*
1 Mick Brown, 'Erotic review', *The Telegraph Magazine*, London, 16 June 2007. The words quoted are those of Mick Brown.
2 Catherine Millet, *The Sexual Life of Catherine M.*, Serpent's Tail, London, 2002. Millet has declared that the decision to become a prostitute is a free choice no different from deciding to become a truck driver, a waiter or a school teacher. Yet few truck drivers, waiters or school teachers are driven to those professions by the need to supply a drug habit.

SECTION 10 *Exercising inner freedom*
1 John Rawls, *Theory of Justice*, Oxford University Press, Oxford, 1972, section 64.
2 ibid., p. 417.
3 It might be observed here that it is because he does not start from real conditions that John Rawls' theory of justice—while creating a sensation among philosophers and political theorists—has had little impact beyond the walls of the universities. His theory is based on an act of imagination, a pure thought experiment more abstract than the contractarians' social contract and divorced from what exercises the popular mind. It is an intellectual's political philosophy without popular intuitive appeal, one that Rawls himself says he had to 'work out'.
4 ibid., p. 423.
5 ibid., pp. 426, 428–9. Rawls acknowledges that there are risks associated with pursuing training and that effort might in the end be wasted, but without the risks life would be dull, stripped of its 'vitality and zest' (p. 429).
6 ibid., pp. 433, 550.

SECTION 11 *Subtle coercion*

1 Hayek, *The Constitution of Liberty*, p. 133. Hayek goes on to make the following peculiar statement: 'Coercion is bad because it prevents a person from using his mental powers to the full and consequently from making the greatest contribution that he is capable of to the community' (p. 134). This suggests that Hayek condemns coercion not because it reduces the wellbeing of the coerced but because restricting one's mental powers means one cannot maximise one's contribution to the community, a view alien to latter-day libertarians.
2 Hayek, *The Constitution of Liberty*, p. 139.
3 ibid., p. 142. 'We must not think of this sphere as consisting exclusively, or even chiefly, of material things', although property rights receive heavy emphasis, along with the right to freely use publicly provided facilities such as sanitation and roads (pp. 140–1).
4 Clifford Cobb, Ted Halstead and Jonathan Rowe, 'If the GDP is up, why is America down?', *Atlantic Monthly*, October 1995.
5 Mill, 'On liberty', p. 16.
6 ibid., pp. 16–17.
7 Hayek, *The Constitution of Liberty*, pp. 143–4.
8 ibid., p. 144.
9 Quoted, approvingly, by Hayek, *The Road to Serfdom*, p. 66.

SECTION 12 *The decline of free will*

1 Avner Offer, *The Challenge of Affluence*, Oxford University Press, Oxford, 2006.
2 See, for example, Clive Hamilton, *Overconsumption in Britain*.
3 See the thoroughgoing review of 138 studies by Jean Twenge, Liqing Zhand and Charles Im, 'It's beyond my control: a cross-temporal meta-analysis of increasing externality in locus of control, 1960–2002', *Personality and Social Psychology Review*, vol. 8, no. 3, 2004. See also the interesting commentary on this question by Richard Eckersley, *Well and Good*, Text Publishing, Melbourne, 2004, especially ch. 5.

4 Zygmunt Bauman, *The Individualized Society*, Polity Press, Cambridge, 2001, pp. 155–6.
5 ibid., p. 157.
6 See Clive Hamilton, *Growth Fetish*, Allen & Unwin, Sydney, 2003. For other accounts see Naomi Klein, *No Logo*, Flamingo, London, 2001; David Boyle, *Authenticity: brands, fakes, spin and the lust for real life*, Flamingo, London, 2003; and Alissa Quart, *Branded: the buying and selling of teenagers*, Arrow, London, 2003.
7 Hayek, *The Constitution of Liberty*, p. 408.
8 ibid., p. 13.

SECTION 13 *From political philosophy to metaphysics*
1 Mill, 'Utilitarianism', in *On Liberty and Other Essays*, p. 134.
2 Carl von Clausewitz, *On War*, Princeton University Press, Princeton, 1976 [1832], p. 84.
3 Arthur Schopenhauer, *On the Basis of Morality*, E.F.J. Payne (trans.), Hackett Publishing Company, Indianapolis, 1995, p. 83.

SECTION 14 *The need for metaphysics*
1 Plato, *Republic*, Robin Waterfield (trans.), Oxford University Press, Oxford, 1993, p. 246.
2 Immanuel Kant, *Prolegomena to Any Future Metaphysics*, Gary Hatfield (ed.), Cambridge University Press, Cambridge, 1997, pp. 43, 45.
3 ibid., p. 82.
4 Kant wrote that the widespread misinterpretation of the term 'transcendental idealism', which many took to mean that he denied the existence of the corporeal world, might require a different term and proposed 'critical idealism'—ibid., p. 45.
5 Arthur Schopenhauer, *The World as Will and Representation*, vol. II, Dover Publications, New York, 1969, p. 164.
6 ibid.

THE FREEDOM PARADOX

SECTION 15 *Consciousness and the subject*

1. Schopenhauer, *The World as Will and Representation*, vol. II, p. 5. Our own consciousness alone is immediate and 'everything else, be it what it may, is first mediated and conditioned by consciousness, and therefore dependent on it' (p. 4).
2. Existence in the everyday world is inseparable from consciousness, and 'to analyze existence is to analyze consciousness'—Karl Jaspers, *Philosophy*, E.B. Ashton (trans.), vol. 1, University of Chicago Press, Chicago, 1969, p. 49.
3. Schopenhauer, *The World as Will and Representation*, vol. II, p. 3.
4. ibid., vol. I, p. 3.
5. ibid, vol. II, p. 5.
6. ibid., vol. I, p. 30.
7. The argument comes from Schopenhauer, ibid., vol. II, p. 6.
8. ibid.
9. ibid., vol. I, p. 420.

SECTION 16 *Phenomenon and noumenon*

1. For a discussion of Kant's differing uses of the term and their importance—whether it is a different thing or a different way of considering a thing—see Henry Allison, *Kant's Transcendental Idealism: an interpretation and defense*, rev. ed., Yale University Press, New Haven, 2004, pp. 52ff.
2. Schopenhauer, *The World as Will and Representation*, vol. II, p. 7.
3. ibid., vol. I, pp. 29–30.
4. ibid., vol. II, p. 13.
5. Allison, *Kant's Transcendental Idealism*, p. xvi.
6. There is some debate in the Kantian literature about the equivalence of the two pairs of terms—appearances and thing-in-itself on one hand and phenomenon and noumenon on the other (see Allison, *Kant's Transcendental Idealism*, pp. 57–9). But this seems to confuse Kant's speculations about what might lie in the noumenal world that does not correspond to an appearance with his clear statements that the two modes of expression

are interchangeable (see especially his *Critique of Pure Reason*, pp. 211–14).
7. See Kant's seminal chapter 'The ground of the distinction of all objects in general into phenomena and noumena' in *The Critique of Pure Reason*, pp. 204–15.
8. ibid., p. 211.
9. ibid., p. 213.
10. ibid., p. 214.
11. *Cambridge Dictionary of Philosophy*, Cambridge University Press, Cambridge, 1999, p. 460.

SECTION 17 *The 'legislation for nature'*
1. Allison, *Kant's Transcendental Idealism*, p. 27.
2. On what follows, see Kant, *Critique of Pure Reason*, pp. 48–60.
3. ibid. p. 32.
4. Schopenhauer, *The World as Will and Representation*, vol. I, p. 25.
5. Kant, *Critique of Pure Reason*, p. 15. To avoid misrepresenting Kant, I should qualify this. Kant makes this claim in the context of making metaphysical arguments rather than in relation to physical objects. So it applies when considering the conditions that are necessary for experience.
6. Allison, *Kant's Transcendental Idealism*, p. 37.
7. Much of what follows is based on Kant, *Prolegomena to Any Future Metaphysics*, pp. 32ff.
8. ibid, p. 39.
9. Rupert Sheldrake, *A New Science of Life: the hypothesis of formative causation*, Paladin/Grafton Books, London, 1987.
10. See Robin Waterfield's introduction to Plato's *Republic* (Oxford University Press, Oxford, 1994, p. xlvi); Schopenhauer, *The World as Will and Representation*, vol. I, pp. 172–3.
11. This argument is based on Brian Magee, *The Philosophy of Schopenhauer*, Oxford University Press, Oxford, p. 63.
12. Schopenhauer, *The World as Will and Representation*, vol. I, p. 16.
13. Kant, *Prolegomena to Any Future Metaphysics*, p. 54.

14 ibid., p. 98 n.
15 See ibid., pp. 97–8.
16 Quoted in Aldous Huxley, *The Perennial Philosophy*, Triad Grafton Books, London, 1985, p. 238.
17 ibid., p. 240.
18 Schopenhauer, *The World as Will and Representation*, vol. I, p. 419.
19 The *Upaniṣads*, Valerie J. Roebuck (trans.), Penguin, London, 2003, p. 203.
20 Arthur Schopenhauer, *On the Basis of Morality*, Hackett Publishing, Indianapolis, 1995, p. 207.
21 Sen T'sen, quoted by Huxley, *The Perennial Philosophy*, p. 31.
22 Huxley, *The Perennial Philosophy*, p. 54.

SECTION 18 *Scientific thinking*
1 Stephen Hawking, *A Brief History of Time*, Bantam Books, 1989, p. 22; see also Fritjof Capra, *The Tao of Physics*, Flamingo, London, 1983.
2 Quoted by Capra, *The Tao of Physics*, p. 183.
3 Schopenhauer, *The World as Will and Representation*, vol. II, p. 5.
4 ibid., vol. I, p. 28.
5 Carter first proposed the principle at a seminar in Krakow, Poland, in 1973.
6 David Bohm, *Wholeness and the Implicate Order*, Routledge, London, 1980.

SECTION 19 *Knowing and being*
1 Plato, *Republic*, p. 240.
2 ibid., p. 245.

SECTION 20 *Instances of non-sensible intuition*
1 Kant, *Prolegomena to Any Future Metaphysics*, pp. 67–8.
2 Kant, *Groundwork of the Metaphysics of Morals*, Cambridge University Press, Cambridge, 1997, p. 57.
3 Schopenhauer, *The World as Will and Representation*, vol. II, p. 372.

4   The 'ground of consciousness' in Tibetan Dzogchen teaching.
5   Quoted in Bob Brown, *Tasmania's Recherche Bay*, Green Institute, Hobart, 2005, p. 53.
6   Jean-Paul Sartre, *Nausea*, Lloyd Alexander (trans.), New Directions Publishing, New York, 1969 [1938]. I am quoting from p. 126 and elsewhere.
7   Personal communication with the author. The book in question was written by Christmas Humphries.
8   Max Scheler, 'Idealism and realism', in *Selected Philosophical Essays*, Northwestern University Press, Evanston, 1973, p. 295.
9   ibid., p. 294.

SECTION 21   *The noumenon and the Self*
1   Magee, *The Philosophy of Schopenhauer*, p. 107.
2   Schopenhauer, *The World as Will and Representation*, vol. I, p. 99.
3   ibid., vol. I, p. 173.
4   ibid., vol. II, p. 191; vol. I, p. 285. Schopenhauer gave conflicting accounts of this crucial insight. At times he wrote that the thing-in-itself can be known directly, and at other times (and more often) he argued that we can approach very close to the thing-in-itself but that direct knowledge of it is always separated by 'the lightest of veils'. Perhaps Schopenhauer's definitive statement is to be found in chapter XVIII of volume II of *The World as Will and Representation*, which, under the title 'On the possibility of knowing the thing-in-itself', addresses the question directly. Initially he describes a form of direct unmediated knowledge of the thing-in-itself, but then he swerves away, claiming that, since the will that knows exists in phenomenal form, true knowledge is always concealed by the 'lightest of veils'. In fact, I think Schopenhauer confuses knowledge of the thing-in-itself with the memory of that knowledge. The possibility of direct knowledge of the thing-in-itself is the central insight of the Eastern philosophies Schopenhauer so admired. Whatever his position, I adopt the view that direct knowledge is possible.

5 Magee strongly disagrees, arguing that the self-knowledge Schopenhauer spoke of is still a manifestation of the phenomenal world (Magee, *The Philosophy of Schopenhauer*, pp. 444ff)—see the previous note. One cannot help thinking that some commentators feel a sense of outrage that anyone could assert that Schopenhauer believed in some form of 'non-sensible intuition' that allows direct knowledge of the thing-in-itself because it is beyond their own experience and seems akin to mysticism, the sworn enemy of academic philosophers.

6 The argument is set out in section 18 of volume I of *The World as Will and Representation* and elaborated in chapter XVIII of the second volume.

7 Schopenhauer, *The World as Will and Representation*, vol. I, p. 370.

8 ibid., vol. II, p. 484.

9 'In no way, however, are there given to me directly, in some general feeling of the body or in inner self-consciousness, any extension, shape, and activity that would coincide with my inner being itself, and that inner being accordingly requires no other being in whose knowledge it would manifest itself, in order so to exist . . . The existence of my person or my body as an extended and acting thing always presupposes a knowing being different from it . . .' (Schopenhauer, *The World as Will and Representation*, vol. II, p. 6). A handful of statements like this allows Magee to mount a strong case that it is fundamentally erroneous to suggest that Schopenhauer believed we can have direct knowledge of the noumenon and that what we directly apprehend as the noumenon is the Will (Magee, *The Philosophy of Schopenhauer*, ch. 21). But Nicholls argues more persuasively that Schopenhauer changed his position over the course of his life and became less willing to acknowledge the possibility of direct knowledge of the noumenon in later writings. See Moira Nicholls, 'The influences of Eastern thought on Schopenhauer's doctrine of the thing-in-itself', in Christopher Janaway (ed.), *The Cambridge Companion to Schopenhauer*, Cambridge University Press, Cambridge, 1999.

10 Schopenhauer, *The World as Will and Representation*, vol. I, p. 428. See also vol. II, p. 494.
11 ibid, vol. II, p. 136.
12 See, for example, John M. Koller, *Asian Philosophies*, 5th edn, Pearson Prentice Hall, New Jersey, 2007, pp. 18–28.
13 *Upaniṣads*, p. 198.
14 Quoted by Huxley, *The Perennial Philosophy*, p. 21.
15 Koller, *Asian Philosophies*, pp. 96–102.
16 Shunryu Suzuki, *Zen Mind, Beginner's Mind*, Trudy Dixon (ed.), Weatherhill, New York, 1970, pp. 34–5.
17 Sogyal Rinpoche, *The Tibetan Book of Living and Dying*, Rider, London, 1992, p. 47.
18 Muhyiddin Ibn' Arabi, *Kernel of the Kernel*, Beshara Publications, Sherborne, England, n.d., p. 7. I have used translations, provided in the original, of some difficult words.
19 Quoted by Huxley, *The Perennial Philosophy*, p. 17.
20 ibid., p. 29.
21 ibid., p. 9.

SECTION 22 *A digression on the existence of God*

1 Kant, *The Critique of Pure Reason*, pp. 407–12.
2 Schopenhauer, *The World as Will and Representation*, vol. I, p. 510.
3 Kant, *The Critique of Pure Reason*, p. 403.
4 In this discussion I draw on S. Morris Engel, 'Kant's "refutation" of the ontological argument', in Robert Paul Wolff (ed.), *Kant: a collection of critical essays*, Macmillan, London, 1968.
5 Richard Dawkins, *The God Delusion*, Bantam Press, London, 2006, p. 48.
6 ibid., p. 60.
7 ibid., p. 59.
8 Spinoza, 'Ethics', in *The Essential Spinoza*, Michael Morgan (ed.), Hackett Publishing Co., Indianapolis, 2006, pp. 3–8.
9 Friedrich Nietzsche, 'The genealogy of morals', in *Basic Writings of Nietzsche*, The Modern Library, New York, 2000. See, for example, pp. 526ff, 566–9, 580ff.

THE FREEDOM PARADOX

SECTION 23 *On death*

1 Schopenhauer, *The World as Will and Representation*, vol. II, p. 463. Parts of this section are based on Schopenhauer's remarkable chapter XLI of *The World as Will and Representation*, 'On death and its relation to the indestructibility of our inner nature', in volume II, along with section 54 of volume I.
2 ibid., vol. II, p. 496.
3 ibid., vol. I, p. 283.
4 ibid., vol. II, p. 601.
5 *Upaniṣads*, p. 53 (slightly edited).
6 Nicholls, 'The influences of Eastern thought', p. 191.
7 Quoted in Huxley, *The Perennial Philosophy*, p. 267.
8 Schopenhauer, *The World as Will and Representation*, vol. II, p. 488.
9 ibid., vol. II, p. 495.
10 'The end of the person is just as real as was its beginning, and in just that sense in which we did not exist before birth, shall we no longer exist after death. But no more can be abolished through death than was produced through birth; and so that cannot be abolished by which birth first of all became possible.'—Schopenhauer, *The World as Will and Representation*, vol. II, p. 495.
11 Quoted by Schopenhauer, ibid., p. 481 n.
12 Schopenhauer, *The World as Will and Representation*, vol. II, p. 474.

SECTION 24 *Modern moral anxiety*

1 Hanif Kureishi, *Intimacy*, Faber and Faber, London, 1999, p. 68.
2 Andrew Hussey, 'The pornographer's manifesto', *New Statesman*, 19 August 2002.
3 Michel Houellebecq, *Atomised*, Vintage Books, London, 2001, p. 136.
4 Michel Houellebecq, *The Possibility of an Island*, Weidenfeld & Nicolson, London, 2005, p. 300.
5 ibid., p. 241.
6 ibid.

SECTION 25 *Moral relativism*

1. Bruno Latour, 'Why has critique run out of steam? From matters of fact to matters of concern', *Critical Inquiry*, vol. 30, no. 2, 2004, p. 227.
2. Ernest Gellner, *Postmodernism, Reason and Religion*, Routledge, London, 1992, pp. 30, 35.
3. Frantz Fanon, *The Wretched of the Earth*, Grove Press, New York, 1963.
4. Latour's reconsideration was motivated by the arguments of the anti-greenhouse sceptics ('Why has critique run out of steam?', p. 226).
5. ibid., p. 227.
6. ibid.
7. ibid., p. 226.

SECTION 26 *Reconstructing a moral code*

1. Alan Wolfe, *Whose Keeper? Social Science and Moral Obligation*, University of California Press, Berkeley, 1989, p. 30.
2. ibid.
3. I am indebted to a reader for sharpening this point.
4. Albert Camus, 'The rebel', reproduced in Walter Kaufmann (trans. & ed.), *Basic Writings of Nietzsche*, The Modern Library, New York, 2000, p. 856.
5. Martin Heidegger, 'Nihilism', reproduced in *Basic Writings of Nietzsche*, p. 849.
6. ibid., p. 851.
7. Zygmunt Bauman, *Postmodern Ethics*, Blackwell, Oxford, 1993, p. 3.
8. Gilles Deleuze, *Kant's Critical Philosophy: the doctrine of the faculties*, Hugh Tomlinson and Barbara Habberjam (trans.), University of Minnesota Press, Minneapolis, 1990, p. x.

SECTION 27 *Rationalist ethics*

1. Immanuel Kant, *Groundwork of the Metaphysics of Morals*, Cambridge, University Press, Cambridge, 1997, p. 2.

> The account that follows draws primarily on this work by Kant and the very useful explication of it in the introduction by Christine Korsgaard.

2 ibid., p. 3.
3 ibid., p. 11.
4 ibid., p. 46.
5 Deleuze, *Kant's Critical Philosophy*, p. x.
6 Kant, *Groundwork*, p. 11.
7 ibid., pp. 41–2.
8 Jean-Jacques Rousseau, *The Social Contract and Discourses*, J.M. Dent & Sons, London, 1913, p. 185.
9 Schopenhauer, *On the Basis of Morality*, p. 54.
10 Kant, *Groundwork*, p. 31.
11 Korsgaard, introduction to Kant, *Groundwork*, p. xviii.
12 ibid.
13 Schopenhauer, *On the Basis of Morality*, p. 120.
14 Kant, *Groundwork*, p. 37.
15 ibid., p. 38.
16 Raymond Belliotti, *Good Sex: perspectives on sexual ethics*, University of Kansas Press, Lawrence, 1993, p. 87.
17 Kant, *Groundwork*, p. 32.

SECTION 28 *Genuine philanthropy*

1 Schopenhauer, *On the Basis of Morality*, p. 130.
2 ibid., p. 120.
3 Rawls, *A Theory of Justice*, p. 348.
4 Karl Marx, 'Theses on Feuerbach' [1845], Friedrich Engels and Karl Marx, *Ludwig Feuerback and the End of Classical German Philosophy*, Foreign Languages Publishing House, Moscow, 1950, appendix.
5 Schopenhauer, *On the Basis of Morality*, p. 126.
6 Jean-Jacques Rousseau, 'Discourse on the origin of inequality', in *The Social Contract and Discourses*, p. 209.
7 Richard Titmuss, *The Gift Relationship: from human blood to social policy*, Vintage Books, New York, 1972.

8   ibid., p. 227.
9   Peter Singer, *How Should We Live?*, Text Publishing, Melbourne, 1993, pp. 168–9.

SECTION 29 *The moral self*

1   Bauman's notion of the moral self, derived from Emmanuel Lévinas, has parallels with the one described here, except that Bauman, who recognises no notion similar to the noumenon, must postulate that the moral self has no origin but is 'self-creating': '[T]here is no other place for morality but *before being* . . . in that realm-not-realm which is *better* than being'—*Postmodern Ethics*, p. 75. In truth, before being is the ground of being or, put another way, before being-in-particular is being-as-such.
2   Emmanuel Lévinas, *Ethics and Infinity*, Duquesne University Press, Pittsburgh, 1985, pp. 100–1.
3   Bauman, *Postmodern Ethics*, p. 80.
4   Schopenhauer, *The World as Will and Representation*, vol. II, pp. 600–1.
5   Nietzsche, 'Ecce homo', in *Basic Writings of Nietzsche*, pp. 789, 790.
6   Nietzsche, 'Attempt at self-criticism', prefacing 'The birth of tragedy', in *Basic Writings of Nietzsche*, p. 23.
7   Peter Gay's introduction to Nietzsche, 'Ecce homo', in *Basic Writings of Nietzsche*, pp. 663–5.
8   Schopenhauer, *On the Basis of Morality*, p. 212.
9   Quoted in 'Voting for torture', *The Nation*, editorial, 26 November 2007, p. 3.
10 Benedict XVI, *Deus Caritas Est*, Libreria Editrice Vaticana, Rome, January 2006.
11 *Upaniṣads*, p. 34.
12 Schopenhauer, *The World as Will and Representation*, vol. II, p. 569.
13 Max Scheler, *The Nature of Sympathy*, Routledge & Kegan Paul, London, 1954. Scheler's translator chose 'pity' instead of

'compassion', thus losing sight of Schopenhauer's meaning. 'Pity' and 'mercy' presuppose an imbalance of power.
14 David E. Cartwright, introduction to Schopenhauer, *On the Basis of Morality*, p. xxviii, n. 27.
15 Carol Gilligan, *In a Different Voice*, Harvard University Press, Cambridge, Mass., 1993, ch. 6. 'The morality of rights is predicated on equality and centered on the understanding of fairness, while the ethic of responsibility relies on the concept of equity, the recognition of difference in need. While the ethic of rights is a manifestation of equal respect, balancing the claims of other and self, the ethic of responsibility rests on an understanding that gives rise to compassion and care' (pp. 164–5). See also Belliotti, *Good Sex: perspectives on sexual ethics*, pp. 134–6, for a brief exposition and critique of Gilligan's approach. Some feminist critics use an instrumental criterion to judge the truth or otherwise of Gilligan's argument, asking how useful the truth is for social purposes, an approach that has little to recommend it.

SECTION 30 *Emotions as judgments*
1 Rawls, *A Theory of Justice*, p. 417.
2 Gary Becker, *The Economic Approach to Human Behavior*, University of Chicago Press, Chicago, 1976.
3 Michael Sandal, *Liberalism and the Limits of Justice*, 2nd edn, Cambridge University Press, Cambridge, 1998, p. 27.
4 Mathieu Ricard, *Happiness: a guide to developing life's most important skill*, Atlantic Books, London, 2007, p. 109.
5 Robert Solomon, *Not Passion's Slave: emotions and choice*, Oxford University Press, Oxford, 2003, p. 94. See especially his famous 1988 essay, reproduced there, entitled 'On emotions as judgments'.
6 'Like Spinoza, Nietzsche always maintained that there is the deepest relationship between concept and affect.'—Gilles Deleuze, 'Nietzsche and philosophy', reproduced in *Basic Writings of Nietzsche*, p. 860.

7 Jorge Moll and Ricardo de Oliveira-Souza, 'Moral judgments, emotions and the utilitarian brain', *Trends in Cognitive Sciences*, vol. 11, no. 8, June 2007, pp. 319–21.

8 The following paragraphs draw mainly on the studies and commentaries of Michael Koenigs, Liane Young, Ralph Adolphs, Daniel Tranel, Fiery Cushman, March Hauser et al., 'Damage to the prefrontal cortex increases utilitarian moral judgements', *Nature*, vol. 446, no. 19, April 2007, pp. 908–11; Jorge Moll and Ricardo de Oliveira-Souza, 'Moral judgments, emotions and the utilitarian brain', pp. 319–21; Joshua D. Greene, 'Why are VMPFC patients more utilitarian? A dual-process theory of moral judgment explains', *Trends in Cognitive Sciences*, vol. 11, no. 8, July 2007, pp. 322–3; Jorge Moll and Ricardo de Oliveira-Souza, 'Response to Greene: moral sentiments and reason—friends or foes?', *Trends in Cognitive Sciences*, vol. 11, no. 8, July 2007, pp. 323–4; Jorge Moll, Roland Zahn, Ricardo de Oliveira-Souza, Frank Krueger and Jordan Grafman, 'The neural basis of human moral cognition', *Nature Reviews Neuroscience*, vol. 6, October 2005, pp. 799–809.

9 Koenigs et al., 'Damage to the prefrontal cortex increases utilitarian moral judgements'.

10 Moll et al., 'The neural basis of human moral cognition', p. 807.

11 See William D. Casebeer, 'Moral cognition and its neural constituents', *Nature Reviews Neuroscience*, vol. 4, October 2003, pp. 841–6.

12 ibid.

13 Jonathan Haidt, 'The emotional dog and its rational tail: a social intuitionist approach to moral judgment', *Psychology Review*, vol. 108, no. 4, October 2001, pp. 814–34.

14 David Hume, *A Treatise of Human Nature*, books Two and Three, Fontana/Collins, London, 1972, p. 156.

15 Moll et al., 'The neural basis of human moral cognition'.

16 Haidt, 'The emotional dog and its rational tail'.

17 Jean-Jacques Rousseau, 'A discourse on the origins of inequality', p. 206.

THE FREEDOM PARADOX

SECTION 31 *Further thoughts*
1. Schopenhauer, *On the Basis of Morality*, p. 210.
2. Friedrich Nietzsche, *The Birth of Tragedy*, Penguin, London, 1993, pp. 17, 18.
3. Quoted by Schopenhauer, *On the Basis of Morality*, p. 208.
4. Shunryu Suzuki, *Zen Mind, Beginner's Mind*, pp. 29, 34–5. '[T]o realize the nature of mind is to realize the nature of all things'— Sogyal Rinpoche, *The Tibetan Book of Living and Dying*, p. 47.
5. Ibn' Arabi, *Kernel of the Kernel*, p. 14.
6. Schopenhauer, *On the Basis of Morality*, p. 69.
7. ibid., p. 127.

SECTION 32 *Avatars of virtue*
1. Schopenhauer, *The World as Will and Representation*, vol. II, p. 232.
2. See Warwick Fox, *Towards a Transpersonal Ecology*, Green Books, Totnes, Devon, 1995, p. 112.

SECTION 33 *Egoism and malice*
1. Quoted by Huxley, *The Perennial Philosophy*, p. 226.
2. Schopenhauer, *On the Basis of Morality*, p. 132.
3. ibid., pp. 135–6.

SECTION 34 *Eternal justice*
1. The following discussion is based on Schopenhauer, *The World as Will and Representation*, vol. I, sections 63, 64.
2. Ralph Waldo Emerson, 'Divinity school address', 15 July 1838.
3. In David James Smith, 'Without a trace', *Sunday Times Magazine*, 23 July 2006.
4. Romans 12:19.
5. Schopenhauer, *The World as Will and Representation*, vol. I, p. 357.

SECTION 35 *Becoming good*
1. See John Carroll, *The Wreck of Western Culture: humanism revisited*, Scribe Publications, Melbourne, 2004, ch. 4.

2   Schopenhauer, *On the Basis of Morality*, pp. 122–3. Schopenhauer held that the 'empirical character' in the phenomenon is the temporal unfolding of one's 'intelligible character' in the noumenon, which is given and fixed, so that our ethical conduct is determined (*The World as Will and Representation*, vol. I, p. 301). Yet he goes on to outline a third type of character, acquired character, which is the character we acquire as we become fully conscious of our own inner natures through life; it is 'nothing but the most complete possible knowledge of our own individuality' (pp. 303–5). It is not at all clear how this third form helps the argument and, in particular, whether it vitiates the claim that our degree of virtuousness is inborn and unchangeable.

3   Schopenhauer, *The World as Will and Representation*, vol. I, p. 368.
4   Plato, *Republic*, p. 247.
5   See also Waterfield's introduction to Plato, *Republic*, pp. xli–xlii.
6   Plato, *Republic*, p. 245.

SECTION 36   *The theory in practice*

1   Cartwright discusses the reason for this exclusion in his introduction to Schopenhauer, *On the Basis of Morality*, p. xxiv, 23 n.

SECTION 37   *Suicide*

1   Karl Jaspers, *Philosophy*, E.B. Ashton (trans.), vol. 2, University of Chicago Press, Chicago, 1970, p. 269.
2   See especially Schopenhauer, *The World as Will and Representation*, vol. I, section 69.
3   Karl Jaspers, *Philosophy*, vol. 2, p. 269 [emphasis added].
4   Jaspers, *Philosophy*, vol. 2, p. 273.
5   ibid.
6   Schopenhauer, *The World as Will and Representation*, vol. II, p. 465.

SECTION 38   *Sex*

1   Nietzsche, 'Beyond good and evil', in *Basic Writings of Nietzsche*, p. 271.

2   Lindsay Clarke, *The Chymical Wedding*, Picador, London, 1990, p. 455.

3   Quoted by Schopenhauer (*The World as Will and Representation*, vol. II, p. 569, 2 n.), who himself observed, 'A peculiar sadness and remorse follows close on it; yet these are felt most after the consummation of the act for the first time, and generally they are the more distinct, the nobler the character'.

4   *Humanae Vitae*, Encyclical of Pope Paul VI on the Regulation of Birth, 1968.

5   See the excellent discussion in Belliotti, *Good Sex*, p. 44.

6   ibid., p. 28.

7   John Hunter, *Thinking About Sex and Love*, Macmillan, New York, 1980. Here I am relying on the discussion of Hunter's work in Belliotti, *Good Sex*.

8   Belliotti, *Good Sex*, p. 71.

9   ibid., pp. 74–5.

10 ibid., pp. 228–33.

11 See Haidt, 'The emotional dog and its rational tail'.

12 ibid.

13 ibid. Haidt advances a 'social intuitionist' model of moral judgment, in which children learn the emotional responses to culturally determined moral propositions. Haidt stresses that moral reasoning is usually carried out interpersonally, that moral judgments are *social* intuitions, whereas I maintain that the core moral judgments emerge from the moral self. The social intuitionist model has difficulty explaining why the strongest and purest moral judgments are often made contrary to social expectations and ethical conventions.

14 Schopenhauer, *The World as Will and Representation*, vol. I, p. 169. See especially G.E. Varner, 'The Schopenhauerian challenge in environmental ethics', *Environmental Ethics*, vol. 7, 1985, p. 215.

15 Schopenhauer, *On the Basis of Morality*, p. 60.

SECTION 39 *Nature*
1. Schopenhauer, *The World as Will and Representation*, vol. II, p. 196.
2. ibid., p. 352.
3. Immanuel Kant, *The Metaphysics of Morals*, Cambridge University Press, Cambridge, 1991.
4. Schopenhauer, *On the Basis of Morality*, p. 96.
5. ibid.
6. Rawls, *A Theory of Justice*, pp. 123–4.
7. ibid., p. 448.
8. Schopenhauer, *On the Basis of Morality*, p. 176.
9. ibid., p. 179.
10. E.O. Wilson, *Biophilia*, Harvard University Press, Cambridge, Mass., 1984, p. 31.
11. Schopenhauer, *The World as Will and Representation*, vol. I, p. 281. 'Everything is entirely in nature, and she is entirely in everything.'
12. Some of what follows is prompted by Varner, 'The Schopenhauerian challenge in environmental ethics'.
13. The term is from Warwick Fox, *Towards a Transpersonal Ecology*, p. 204.
14. Fox, ibid., pp. 204–6, suggests something similar to this.

SECTION 40 *The ground of inner freedom*
1. In Robert C. Solomon, *Existentialism*, The Modern Library, New York, 1974, p. 8.
2. The metaphor is borrowed from Kierkegaard, ibid.
3. Spinoza, *Ethics*, definition 7, p. 4.
4. Kant, *Prolegomena to Any Future Metaphysics*, p. 98 note.
5. Kant, *Groundwork of the Metaphysics of Morals*, p. 53.
6. Schopenhauer, *Essay on the Freedom of the Will*, Dover Publications, Mineola, New York, 2005, p. 96.
7. Konstantin Kolenda, introduction to Schopenhauer, *Essay on the Freedom of the Will*, p. xi.
8. Jaspers, *Philosophy*, vol. 1, p. 2 (slightly modified).

SECTION 41 *Finding inner freedom*

1 Schopenhauer, *The World as Will and Representation*, vol. II, p. 156.
2 Attributed to Jung by Joseph Campbell in *The Power of Myth*, Anchor Books, New York, 1991.
3 Jung, quoted by Edward Edinger, *Ego and Archetype*, Shambhala, Boston, 1992, p. 131.

SECTION 42 *The individual and the collective*

1 ibid., p. 49.
2 Ulrich Beck and Elisabeth Beck-Gernsheim, *Individualization*, p. 158.
3 See, for example, Carl Jung, *Memories, Dreams, Reflections*, Flamingo, London, 1983, p. 414.
4 This is the answer to critics who might claim that a theory such as mine dissolves individuality by subordinating the 'other' to 'the same', thereby depriving each part of its place in the whole. Such an argument is made by Emmanuel Lévinas in *Ethics and Infinity* (Duquesne University Press, Pittsburgh, 1985). See also Gary Gutting, *French Philosophy in the Twentieth Century*, Cambridge University Press, Cambridge, 2001, pp. 354–5.
5 Carl Jung, *Collected Works*, vol. 18, Routledge & Kegan Paul, London, 1953–79, p. 452. See also Carl Jung, *Psychological Reflections*, Ark Paperbacks, London, 1971, pp. 163, 172.

SECTION 43 *Aesthetics*

1 Wilfried Seipel, Barbara Steffen and Christoph Vitali (eds), *Francis Bacon and the Tradition of Art*, published in association with an exhibition of the Kunsthistorisches Museum, Vienna, Skira Editore S.p.A., Milano, 2003, p. 35.
2 Germain Bazin, *French Impressionist Paintings in The Louvre*, Harry N. Abrams Inc., New York, n.d.
3 ibid.
4 Joseph Campbell, *The Masks of God: creative mythology*, The Viking Press, New York, 1968, p. 104.

5 Edward Hopper, in *Edward Hopper: exhibition catalogue*, National Gallery of Art, Washington, 2007, from Museum of Modern Art exhibition catalogue, New York, 1933, p. 17. He also said, 'Great art is the outward expression of an inner life in the artist'.
6 Robert Donington, *Wagner's 'Ring' and its Symbols*, 3rd edn, Faber and Faber, London, 1974, p. 31.
7 ibid., p. 32.
8 ibid., p. 69.
9 The following draws in part on Schopenhauer, *The World as Will and Representation*, vol. I, sections 30–2, and vol. II, chs XXIX–XXX. See also Arthur Schopenhauer, *Parerga and Paralipomena*, Clarendon Press, Oxford, 1974, ch. XIX.
10 Roger Scruton, *Modern Culture*, Continuum, London, 2005, p. 40.
11 William Blake, *The Marriage of Heaven and Hell*, originally published in 1825–27 and reproduced in facsimile from the original by J.M. Dent and Sons Ltd, London, 1927.
12 Herman Melville, *Moby Dick*, Oxford University Press, Oxford, 1998, p. 175.
13 Perhaps the best of Schopenhauer's writing on the idea of the pure knowing subject is his essay 'On the metaphysics of the beautiful and aesthetics', *Parerga and Paralipomena*, vol. 2, pp. 414–52.
14 The expression is due to Schopenhauer, *Parerga and Paralipomena*, vol. 2, p. 428.
15 John Carey, *What Good Are the Arts?*, Faber and Faber, London, 2005.

SECTION 44 *Happiness reconsidered*
1 Schopenhauer, *The World as Will and Representation*, vol. I, p. 87.
2 ibid., vol. II, p. 150.
3 ibid., p. 325.

THE FREEDOM PARADOX

SECTION 45 *The human condition*

1 Nietzsche, *The Birth of Tragedy*, p. 9. This is from Nietzsche's 'Attempt at self-criticism', which opens the book. See also the introduction by the editor, Michael Tanner.
2 Schopenhauer, *The World as Will and Representation*, vol. II, p. 584.
3 Lee Spinks, *Friedrich Nietzsche*, Routledge, London, 2003, p. 22.
4 And in perverted form, it must be said, over German fascists—see Peter Gay, introduction to *Basic Writings of Nietzsche*, pp. xi–xii.
5 Martha Nussbaum, 'Nietzsche, Schopenhauer, and Dionysus', in Christopher Janaway (ed.), *The Cambridge Companion to Schopenhauer*, Cambridge University Press, Cambridge, 1999, p. 364, describing the responses of Schopenhauer and Nietzsche respectively.

Index

Abbott, Dianne, 52–3
Abu Ghraib, 304
Acton, Lord, 24
adultery, 163, 243, 274–5
advertising, 43, 69–71, 78
    see also marketing
aesthetics, 87, 129, 316ff
    see also art
affluence, 3–5, 38, 73, 74–5,
    161, 297, 301, 302, 308,
    329, 339
agape, 205
    see also love
akrasia, 37, 45, 51–4, 56, 58, 59,
    60, 65, 80, 81, 85, 259,
    284, 310, 332–3
Alba Madonna, 324
altruism, 40, 199–200, 217
    see also philanthropy
animals, 284–8, 290–3, 318, 321
anthropic principle, 117–8

apartheid, 232
Apollonian spirit, 279, 337
appearances *see* phenomenon
Aquinas, Thomas, 101, 205
archetypes, 318–20, 326
Archimedes, xvi, 224
Aristotle, 16, 54, 64, 216, 302,
    327
art, 315, 316ff
    and archetypes, 318–20
    commercialisation of, 323–4
    genius and, 234–5, 316–7
    good, 326
    great, 316–26
    and myths, 320
    and noumenon, 316–8,
        320–1, 323, 325
    pleasant, 326
    see also aesthetics
asceticism, 154, 264, 309, 336
assured free sphere, 69–72

atheism, 143, 147–8
Atman, 139–40, 151, 152, 207
authentic life, 48–9, 78, 313
avatars of virtue, 230–4, 306, 311, 329
awareness, considered and superficial, 35–7

Bacon, Francis, 316, 318, 323
Baggins, Bilbo, 105
Barthes, Roland, 323
Bauman, Zygmunt, 76–7, 180, 203
Bazin, Germain, 316–7
Beck, Ulrich, 314
Becker, Gary, 212
being, nature of *see* existence, nature of
Belliotti, Raymond, 274, 282, 285, 288
Belloc, Hilaire, 73
Benedict XVI, Pope, 207, 274
Berlin, Isaiah, 27–8, 35
bestiality, 163, 284–8, 318
Beyond Good and Evil, 319
Bible, 146, 194, 290, 336
  biblical literalism, 146
Big Brother, 173
Billingham, Richard, 236
biophilia, 292
Blake, William, 223, 321
blood donation, 199
body dysmorphia, 56
Bohm, David, 118
Botton, Alain de, 15

Brahman, 110–2, 139–40, 153–4, 223, 228
  see also essence (universal or subtle)
Buddhism, 112, 139–40, 208, 213, 223, 234, 236, 253, 268, 313, 336
Bulger, James, 241
Bush, George, 206

Camus, Albert, 178
capitalism, 10, 172, 174, 176–7, 293, 298, 305
  consumer, 15, 18, 28–9, 30–1, 40, 66, 73, 78, 332
capital punishment, 227
Carey, John, 324
Carter, Brandon, 117
Cartwright, David E., 209
Casebeer, William, 217
categorical imperative, 186, 190–2, 221
Catholic Church, 101, 170, 243, 274–7
  see also Christianity
causality, 87, 90, 95, 104, 107, 108–10, 122, 134
  and inner freedom, 299
celibacy, 233, 277
  see also sex, casual
character, 247–51, 255
charity, 206
Chomsky, Noam, 319
Christianity

on death, 150, 153, 154
decline of, 155, 162, 176, 182, 261–2, 302–3, 311
and free will, 248
fundamentalism in, 234, 248
and judgment, 158, 242–3
as keeper of the transcendent, 311, 334
and knowledge of God, 110, 141, 153
and morals, 180, 204–5, 207–8, 224, 319
Nietzsche's attack on, 148, 204, 308, 319, 336
and sex, 275–7
and suicide, 267–8
see also Catholic church
Churchill, Winston, 173
citizens' juries, 36–7
Clausewitz, Carl von, 81
climate change, 171, 248, 294
coercion, subtle, 56, 58, 60, 68–73, 80, 81, 85, 259, 280, 284, 299, 332–3
compassion
for animals, 290–2
in children, 250–1
as expression of metaphysical empathy, 206–8, 237, 239, 253
Kant's view of, 187
as motive for moral action, 187, 205, 249, 256–60
as prosocial emotion, 214–5, 218–20
see also metaphysical empathy
conception, 156–7, 263, 271–4
see also sexual intercourse
conceptualism, 101
conscience, 202, 205, 208, 269, 332
consciousness
and knowledge, 92–7, 98–100, 321
participating, 118, 120, 127–30, 137–8, 168, 221, 292–3
as philosophical starting point, 92, 106
pure, 93, 125, 131, 136–7, 140, 222, 252 (*see also* Atman)
role in universe, 117–8, 148, 339
and subject-object distinction, 92–3, 140
see also knowledge; unconscious, the
Constant, Benjamin, 27
consumer choice, 23, 38–9, 42, 63, 73, 74, 78, 175
consumerism, 6, 15, 18, 54, 72–3, 156, 167, 179, 305–6, 308, 331
see also capitalism; consumer choice
Copernicus, Nicolas, 105, 106, 170

corporate social responsibility, 186
creationism, 146, 147, 171
Crime and Punishment, 241
cultural capital, 325
culture, 78, 170
   high, 320, 325–6, 337
   popular, 71, 173, 278, 279, 324, 325, 337
The Cypresses, 319

Dalai Lama, 231–4, 330
Darby, Joe, 304
Da Vinci Code, 124
Dawkins, Richard, 142, 147–8
death, 150–8
   in the course of life, 263
   little, 272
deconstruction *see* social constructionism
defence mechanisms (psychological), 46–7, 280
Deleuze, Gilles, 181, 188
deliberative democracy, 36–7
deontological (duty) ethic, 183, 218
   see also Kant, Immanuel, moral theory of
depression, 3, 4, 251, 305
Derrida, Jacques, 325
Descartes, René, 96, 98, 114, 169–70
Deus Caritas Est, 207
Diderot, Denis, 157
Dionysian spirit, 204, 279, 336–7

Donne, John, 167
Dostoyevsky, Fyodor, 241
downshifting, 29
dualism, 96, 115, 121, 140, 223

Eastern philosophy, xvi, 91, 96, 108, 110–2, 131, 137, 138–40, 144, 148, 153, 221–3, 335
   see also Buddhism; Hinduism
Eckhart, Meister, 110, 141, 154
economic growth, 3, 5, 78, 156, 294
economics (neoclassical), 5, 11, 34, 39, 41–3, 62, 65–6, 122–3, 183, 212, 216, 220, 293–4
   see also neoliberalism
egoism, 138, 155, 235–8, 260, 294, 306
Einstein, Albert, 113, 114, 148, 170
Emerson, Ralph Waldo, 240
Emin, Tracey, 324
emotions, 213
   as judgments, 211–20
   prosocial, 214–20
Enlightenment, European, 101, 103, 162, 176, 177, 179, 301, 303, 320, 330, 334
environmentalism, 8, 171–2
   see also climate change; nature
Epicureans, 16
epistemology, 87, 115, 147, 170
   see also knowledge

Erasmus, 248
essence (universal or subtle)
   and death, 157, 263
   defined, 110–2
   in Eastern philosophy, xvi, 91, 132, 223
   identity with universal Self, 139, 150–2, 201–3, 230, 251
   and morality, 221, 235–6, 239–40
   and nature, 289–94
   and noumenon, xvi, 91, 111, 137
   and sex, 270*ff*
   see also Brahman; Self (universal or noumenal)
eternal justice, 158, 239–43
ethic of care, 209
ethic of consent, 4, 55–60, 163
ethic of rights, 152
ethics, post-secular, xvii, 182, 234, 301
   rationalist, 179, 182, 183–94, 214*ff*
   utilitarian, 216–9, 286, 288
   virtue, 216–8
   see also Kant, Immanuel, moral theory of; morality; Schopenhauer, Arthur, and morality
eudaemonism, 16, 18, 64, 216, 257
   see also good life, the
euthanasia *see* suicide, as release
existence, nature of, 96–7, 121–2, 126–7, 129, 131, 139
existentialism, 79, 179, 337–8

Fall, the, 208
false consciousness, 34–5
Fanon, Frantz, 171
female genital mutilation, 174
feminism, 35, 165, 166, 171, 174
   see also women, liberation of
Fingarette, Herbert, 48
Four Noble Truths, 208
Frankfurt, Harry, xv, 39
freedom, 4, 8–9
   and happiness, 20–4
   and moral law, 185
   see also free will; inner freedom; liberty
free will, 29–30, 40, 74–9, 248, 298
Freud, Anna, 46
Freud, Sigmund, 138, 331
Friedman, Milton, 8, 9, 15, 212
Fukuyama, Francis, 9, 79, 174
fundamentalism, 10, 147, 148, 171, 172n, 177, 232, 234, 248, 277, 302

Gandhi, Indira, 200
Gandhi, Mahatma, 231–4, 330
geometry, 105, 113

George, David, 38–41
The Gift Relationship, 199
Gilligan, Carol, 209
God, 103, 117–8, 267
   Christian conception of, 150–1, 152–3, 158, 176, 248, 261
   existence of, 91, 142–9
   and morality, 163, 181–2, 190, 202, 204, 222, 273–4, 302–3
   nature of, 101, 110, 140–1, 222, 311
Golden Rule, 190, 224
Golding, William, 200
good life, the, 15–9, 20, 38, 43–4, 64, 77, 86, 217, 294, 326, 327–32
   see also meaningful life, the; pleasant life, the
Good Samaritan, 205
Greer, Germaine, 24
Groundwork of the Metaphysics of Morals, 185
guilt, 212, 214–5, 265
   see also conscience

Haidt, Jonathan, 218–9, 286
happiness, types of, 14–9, 64, 77, 81, 85–6, 212
   versus meaning, 327–33
   as reward for virtue, 158
   see also good life, the; meaningful life, the; pleasant life, the

Hawking, Stephen, 113
Hayek, Friedrich von, 5–9, 15, 24, 25–30, 33, 45, 61, 68–72, 78–9
Hazreti, 223
Heart (pyramid scheme), 49
heaven, 154, 189, 242
Hegel, Georg W.F., 79, 222
Heidegger, Martin, 179
Hesse, Hermann, 313
Hinduism, xvi, xvii, 110, 139, 151, 152, 223, 234, 242, 276, 336
Hitchens, Christopher, 147
Hitler, Adolf, 10, 26, 242
Homo economicus, 29, 46, 65–6, 216
homosexuality, 162, 233, 250, 274, 286, 304
Hopper, Edward, 317
Houellebecq, Michel, 165–7
Humanae Vitae, 273
humanism, 101, 302
Hume, David, 108, 134, 218
Hunter, John, 282
Huxley, Aldous, 112

Ibn' Arabi, 140, 223
idealism (transcendental or German), 88, 95–7, 99–101, 105, 108, 109, 110, 113–7, 131, 142, 148, 192, 236, 283
identity, formation of, xv, 6, 19, 41, 72–3

immortality, 151, 154
implicate order, 118
impulsiveness, 42, 51, 60, 62, 63, 68–9, 74–7, 86, 327
  see also self-control
In a Different Voice, 209
incest, 286
individualisation, 6, 11, 14, 76, 162, 250, 301–3, 311, 314
individualism, 5, 19, 28, 75, 77, 166, 175, 179, 301–2, 311, 314
individuality, 6, 14, 28, 301
individuation, 315, 331
inner freedom, xiv, 11, 33–7, 58, 80–2, 85–6
  and art, 326
  and death, 265
  defined, 30–2, 33
  enemies of, 45–54 *passim*, 68, 77
  exercise of, 61–7
  finding, 305–12, 339
  grounds for, 81–2, 85–6, 131, 297*ff*
  and sex, 284
inner judge, 202, 281–4
  see also moral judge
internet, 173
Intimacy, 164
Intimations of Immortality, 249
intuition, 87, 107, 124–5, 135–6, 230, 306
  aesthetic, 325

non-sensible, 88, 91, 102–3, 124–32, 133, 136, 146, 201, 251, 330
  see also moral intuition
Islam, 234, 277
  see also Sufism

Jaspers, Karl, 263, 264, 268, 269
jealousy, 271
Jesus Christ, 125, 157, 204, 205, 233, 239, 241, 274, 309, 312
The Joy of Sex, 278
Jung, Carl, 221, 311, 313, 314, 315, 318
justice, 61, 158, 177, 190, 211, 228, 231
  restorative, 228
  social, 65, 191, 212, 302
  see also eternal justice; will to justice

Kant, Immanuel, 114, 255, 314, 336
  as Christian, 103
  and existence of God, 142–8, 178–9
  on forms of knowledge, 95–7, 119–21, 133–9 *passim*
  on freedom, xiv, 300
  as idealist, xv, 88, 95–7
  metaphysics of, xv–xvi, 81–2, 95–108, 111, 116, 119–21, 222

moral theory of, 177, 182,
183–94, 195–6, 200,
203, 211, 217–20, 224,
286, 302
on nature, 289–90
on non-sensible intuition,
102–3, 107, 120, 133,
251
and rationality, 40, 81, 86–7,
170, 334
Kantians, 43, 65, 81, 156, 177,
189, 192, 195–6, 211,
285–6, 288, 291, 329, 337
Kelly, David, 266
Kierkegaard, Søren, 297
kingdom of ends, 189, 255
Kipling, Rudyard, 169–70
knowledge
forms of, 92–4, 115–6,
119–23, 130, 134–41,
142–6, 184, 254–5,
263, 272, 322
of noumenon, 91, 102–3,
105, 119–21, 125,
131–2, 138–9, 180–1,
253
see also consciousness; epistemology; intuition,
non-sensible
Koran, 146
Korsgaard, Christine, 191, 192
Kristel, Sylvie, 57
Kureishi, Hanif, 164

Labillardière, Jacques-Julien, 126

Latour, Bruno, 83, 168, 171–3
Law, William, 140, 236
legislation for nature, 104–6
Leibniz, Gottfried, 141
Lévinas, Emmanuel, 203
liberalism, 5, 20, 80
liberation movements, 4, 10–1,
13, 55, 161–4, 168,
170–1, 177–8, 180–1,
284–5, 301, 310
see also women, liberation of
libertarianism, 5, 8, 9, 10, 14,
20, 25, 55, 68, 80
liberty
metaphysical (*see* inner
freedom)
types, of, 25–32
Lord of the Flies, 200
The Lord of the Rings, 146
love, 165–7, 206–7, 275–6
of fate, 233
as non-marketed household
commodity, 212
see also agape
Luther, Martin, 248

Macbeth, 240–1
Mad Max, 303
Magee, Brian, 134
malice, 235–8, 256–7, 260,
267–8
Mandela, Nelson, 231–4, 330
market, the, 11, 18–9, 29,
39–43, 69, 78, 297–8,
303, 338

see also marketing; neoliberalism
marketing, 66, 68–73, 77–8
  see also advertising; market, the
marriage, 273–6
Marx, Karl, 34, 196
Maslow, Abraham, 23
Maya, doctrine of, 111, 236
meaningful life, the, 15, 17–9, 20, 86, 326, 327, 331, 333
  see also good life, the; pleasant life, the
meaninglessness, 10, 49, 86, 166, 337, 339
meditation, 128, 251
Mele, Alfred, 46, 47
Melville, Herman, 321
mental illness, 66
  see also depression
The Merchant of Venice, 207
metaphysical empathy, 201–9, 219, 223–6, 228, 230, 237, 253, 287, 291–2, 307
metaphysics, xii, 82, 87–8, 89, 179, 184–5, 208, 223
metempsychosis, 152
Mill, John Stuart, 7, 13–4, 27–9, 51, 70, 81, 86, 302
Millet, Catherine, 57–8, 164–7, 283
Minkler, Lanse, 41
modernism, 172, 178, 181
Mona Lisa, 323
monism, 222, 289

moral adviser, 257–9, 266, 281–2, 301, 332
moral dilemmas, 226–7
moral dumbfounding, 285
moral emotions *see* emotions, prosocial
moral intuition, 218–9
morality, 181–2, 214
  authority for, 161–2, 168, 171, 176, 180, 183–5, 235
  grounds for, 181, 230
  male and female orientation of, 209–13, 218, 224–5, 227, 237
  motivation for, 182, 187, 195, 197–200, 217–20, 254–5
  and universal Self, 138
  see also ethic of consent; ethics, post-secular; moral judgment; moral relativism
moral judge, 257–8, 266, 281, 301
moral judgment, 214–20, 230, 247, 257, 281
moral relativism, xv–xvi, 167, 168–75, 184, 185, 226–7, 257
  see also post-modernism
moral scepticism, 197–8
moral self, xvii, 200
  defined, 201–10

as a guide to action, 224,
232–6 *passim,* 258–9,
281–2
and inner freedom, 298–308
passim, 314
and metaphysical empathy,
201–2, 204, 219
relation to the universal Self,
202–3, 204, 221, 230
moral weakness *see* akrasia
morphic fields, 108
Mother Teresa, 251
Mukasey, Michael, 206
multiverse, 117–8
muse, 317, 324
music, 317, 320, 326
see also art
mysticism, 89, 111, 140–1, 153
myths, 320

Nasrudin, Mullah, 336
naturalistic fallacy, 219
nature, 157, 222, 230, 251,
289–94
Nausea, 126, 338
necrophilia, 285
neoconservatism, 172, 174
neoliberalism, 4n, 12, 13, 16,
25, 26n, 71–2, 199
see also libertarianism
neuroimaging studies, 214–20
Newman, Cardinal, 245
Newton, Isaac, 113
Nietzsche, Friedrich, 178–9,
204–5, 222

on Christianity, 148, 204–5,
308, 319, 336
and post-modernism, 303
on sexuality, 271
nihilism, 179, 339
nominalism, 101
noumenal order, 287–8
noumenon
and animals, 285–8
and causality, 108–10
and children, 249–51
and death, 150–4, 156–7
defined, 98–101
as distinct from phenomenon, xvi, 91, 98–103,
109, 111, 119, 121,
124, 143, 180–1,
184–5, 204, 261
as domain of God, 141,
142–4, 148, 234, 311
and inner freedom, 131,
299–301, 314
knowledge of, 101–2, 105,
119–20, 125, 138–40,
178, 253
life in the, 328–39 *passim*
and nature, 289–94
reasons for existence of,
98–103, 115–7, 120–3,
130
and science, 115–6
and the Self, 133–41
and sex, 270–2, 275, 276–7,
283

as source of moral authority, xvi, 109, 132, 181, 184–5, 191, 200, 202, 204, 209–10, 225, 228, 230–3, 238, 239
numinous experience, 125–9, 311, 316, 332
Nussbaum, Martha, 17, 23, 184

Oates, Captain Lawrence, 265
obesity, 39, 75
object, 92–3, 105, 133–4, 138–9, 145, 322
see also subject-object distinction
Offer, Avner, 75
Onfray, Michael, 147
ontology, 87, 102, 119, 122, 142
Orwell, George, 292
Ovidie, 165

Pachelbel, Johann, 324
Parable of the Talents, 308
passions, 30, 31, 52, 211–3, 218–20, 270, 337
see also emotions
Paul VI, Pope, 273–5
perennial philosophy, 141
phenomenon (most references are listed under noumenon)
and conditions of sensibility, 104–12, 131–2, 298
as distinct from noumenon (*see* noumenon)
life in the, 230, 248, 250, 263–4, 286, 300, 313, 327, 330, 335, 337
as manifestation of noumenon, 287, 339
and scientific thinking, 137
see also noumenon
philanthropy, 198
genuine or disinterested, 195–6, 197–9, 205–6, 209–10
see also altruism
philosophy (modern), 66, 87, 88, 124, 156, 221, 260
photography, 323
see also art
physics, Newtonian *versus* quantum, 113–8
Plato, 86, 108, 111, 122–3, 253–5
Platonic Ideas, 287, 292, 318–23
Plato's cave, 122, 132, 253–4
pleasant life, the, 15–9, 20, 38, 86, 294, 326, 327–32
see also good life, the; meaningful life, the
Plotinus, 222
The Pornographer, 165
pornography, 57–8, 165–6, 259
positivism, 169
The Possibility of an Island, 166
post-modernism, 55–6, 166–7, 168–75, 179, 193, 197, 225, 303, 325

see also moral relativism; social constructionism
prayer, 128, 251
preferences, 62
  first and second-order, 38–44, 259
  moral considerations in, 41
principle of justice *see* will to justice
prostitution, 174, 193–4, 283–4
psychopaths, 216, 236
purpose of life, 16, 19, 81, 139, 263–4, 330–1

Raphael Santi, 324
Rapture, 248
Raskolnikov, Rodion Romanovic, 209, 241
rational economic man *see Homo economicus*
rationality, 62–6, 81, 86–9, 90, 109, 147–8, 183, 191, 299, 310–1
  and art, 320–1
  Kantian, 40, 192–3, 290–1
rational theology, 142–3, 146–7
Rawls, John
  mistakes the metaphysical for the intellectual, 156
  on rationality, 61–2, 63, 65–6, 86, 211–2, 291, 329
  on theory of justice, 61–5, 183, 190–1, 196–7, 203, 247, 288, 291
  and veil of ignorance, 63, 65, 191, 202, 221, 291
realism, 94–6, 100–1, 106, 107, 110, 113–7, 131
reality, nature of, 93–7, 113
  see also noumenon; phenomenon
reality principle, 294
reason, 52–4, 61, 80–1, 143–6
  and morality, 178, 187, 211*ff*
  see also rationality
regret, 60, 258–9, 281–4, 329
reincarnation, 152–3, 242
Republic, 254
ressentiment, 205
Richards, Keith, 285
The Ring of the Nibelung, 318
Road with Cypress and Star, 319
Rousseau, Jean-Jaques, xv, 177, 189, 198, 203, 219, 231
Ryff, Carol, 17

Saatchi & Saatchi, 173
Sachs, Mendel, 113
Sandal, Michael, 212
Sartre, Jean-Paul, 126–7, 338
Scheler, Max, 130, 208
Schelling, Friedrich, 335
Schopenhauer, Arthur
  on art, 245, 318
  on consciousness, 92–3, 98, 115, 330
  on death, 150–3
  and Eastern philosophies, xvi, 80, 110–1

Index

on eternal justice, 240
on forms of knowledge, 102, 115, 125, 130, 134–7, 138–9, 156
on happiness, 1, 16, 334–6
his concept of the Will, 94, 135–6, 151, 153
as idealist, xv, 88, 156
on incentives for action, 255, 256*ff*
metaphysics of, xv–xvi, 81, 88–9, 97, 98–103, 115, 134–8, 145, 184, 222
and morality, 182, 184–5, 189, 191, 196, 205–6, 207, 224, 237
on nature, 157, 289–90
and rationality, 88, 89, 334–5
on sex, 287
on suicide, 264, 269
Scruton, Roger, 320
The Secret, 125
secularism, 250, 262, 278, 339
self, xv, 17, 91, 133, 154, 249
    authentic, 35, 54, 313 (*see also* authentic life)
    dissolution of, 125, 127, 128–31, 202, 236
    metaphysical, 134
    see also identity, formation of; moral self; Self
Self (universal or noumenal)
    argument for existence of, 133–41
    and death, 151–4, 155–6
    as inner nature of the subject, 133–5, 331, 334–5
    and morality, 202–4, 230, 292
    and moral self, 235–6, 249, 300, 309–10, 314
    and sex, 271*ff*
    see also Brahman; self, dissolution of; subject-object distinction
self-control, 63, 72, 74–5, 224
self-deception, 37, 45–51, 56, 58, 60, 81, 85, 259, 284, 299, 310, 331, 332
self-esteem, 250
self-harm, 256–7
self-immolation, 268
self-interest, 197, 217, 226, 230, 254, 257, 266, 294
    see also egoism
Self Portrait with Bandaged Ear, 320
Seligman, Martin, 15, 18, 19, 64
Sen, Amartya, 17, 23, 184, 329
sex, 162, 337
    casual, 270, 274, 278–84
    ethics of, 270*ff*
    and intimacy, 57, 164, 271–6
    as pleasure, 271–3, 278–80
    premarital, 162, 197, 243, 273–4, 284
    as procreation, 271*ff*
    as union (emotional and metaphysical), 271ff, 283, 287

see also adultery; bestiality; homosexuality; pornography
sexual intercourse, 156, 271*ff*, 337
sexualisation, 179, 278
The Sexual Life of Catherine M, 57, 164
sexual love, 275, 277, 282, 283
  see also sexual intercourse
sexual morality, 57, 156, 161–7
sexual revolution, 161, 164, 166, 270, 278
shadow (as archetype), 319
Shakespeare, William, 65, 150, 207, 213
Shankara, 140, 223
Sheldrake, Rupert, 108
Siddhartha, 313
Singer, Peter, 199, 288
social constructionism, 168–72, 197, 325
  see also moral relativism; post-modernism
social contract, 221
social democracy, 11, 176
socialism, 8, 73, 78, 177, 261
Socrates, 150, 189
solidarity, 12, 177, 227
Solomon, Robert, 213, 214, 218
soul, the, 151, 154
space, 88, 89, 90, 95, 97, 104–34 *passim,* 201

Spinoza, Benedict de, 111, 148–9, 222, 299
Srebrenica, 304
Stoics, 12, 310, 327–8
subject, 110–1, 115, 133–5, 138–40, 149
  pure knowing, 321–2
subject-object distinction, 91, 99, 107, 115, 119–20, 130, 131, 133, 135, 139, 201–2
  see also self, dissolution of
suffering, 328, 335, 339
Sufism, 110, 111, 140, 223
suicide, 259, 263–9
  as despair, 266
  as protest, 268
  as release, 266
  as sacrifice, 264
Suzuki, Shunryu, 223
Swaggart, Jimmy, 304
synderesis, 205
synesthesia, 93

Talmud, 101
tantra, 276
Thatcher, Margaret, 11
theory of everything, 97
A Theory of Justice, 247
thing-in-itself *see* noumenon
time, 88, 90, 95, 97, 104–34 *passim,* 151, 201
Titmuss, Richard, 199
torture, 206, 228
tragedy, 242, 335

transcendental idealism *see* idealism (transcendental or German)

unconscious, the, 126, 138, 318–20
universe, nature of, 116–8
 see also multiverse
Upanishads, 111, 139, 153, 207
utilitarianism, 183
 see also ethics, post-secular, utilitarian

Van Gogh, Vincent, 319
vegetarianism, 288
veil of ignorance *see* Rawls, John
Venables, Jon, 241
virtue ethics *see* ethics, post-secular, virtue
voluntary justice *see* will to justice

Wagner, Richard, 318, 336

Warhol, Andy, 324
Waterworld, 303
Wheeler, John, 118
Will, Schopenhauer's concept of, 129, 134–6, 151, 153
will to justice
 as expression of metaphysical empathy, 206, 208, 224–9, 239, 292
 as motive for moral action, 199, 211, 218, 236–8, 248
 see also justice
Wilson, E. O., 292
Wolfe, Alan, 176
women, liberation of, 13, 24, 76, 161
 see also liberation movements
Wordsworth, William, 128–9, 141, 190, 249
Wotan, 318